The Danzig Church:
Its Origin and History from 1569-1919

The Danzig Mennonite Church:
Its Origin and History from 1569-1919

by H. G. Mannhardt

Translated by Victor G. Doerksen
Edited and annotated by Mark Jantzen and John D. Thiesen
Epilogue by Tomasz Ropiejko

Bethel College
North Newton, Kansas
2007

Co-published with
Pandora Press
Kitchener, Ontario

Library of Congress Cataloging-in-Publication Data

Mannhardt, H. G. (Hermann Gottlieb), 1855-1927.
[Danziger Mennonitengemeinde. English]
The Danzig Mennonite Church : its origin and history from 1569-1919 / by H.G.
Mannhardt ; translated by Victor G. Doerksen ; edited and annotated by Mark Jantzen and
John D. Thiesen.
    p. cm. -- (Cornelius H. Wedel historical series)
    Includes bibliographical references and index.
    ISBN 978-1-889239-04-0
    1. Mennonites--Poland--Gdansk. 2. Gdansk (Poland)--Church history. I. Jantzen, Mark,
1963- II. Thiesen, John D. III. Title.
    BX8119.P7M3613 2007
    289.7'43822--dc22
                                                                        2007003737

Photos on the front cover: center: the Gdańsk church building in 1998. Bottom, left to right:
Dirk Philips, congregational records rescued after World War II, Mennonite marriage
proposal (by Chodowiecki), H. G. Mannhardt.

Wedel Series logo by Angela Goering Miller

ISBN 1-889239-04-6

Copies available at www.pandorapress.com

Cornelius H. Wedel Historical Series

Series editor: vols. 1-4, David A. Haury
            vols. 5-14, John D. Thiesen

Contents

Illustrations

Maps

Series Preface

The Cornelius H. Wedel Historical Series was initiated by the Mennonite Library and Archives at Bethel College as part of the college centennial celebration in 1987. Cornelius H. Wedel, the first president of Bethel College from the beginning of classes in 1893 until his death in 1910, was an early scholar of Mennonite studies. His four volume survey of Mennonite history, published from 1900 to 1904, helped to rescue Anabaptism and Mennonitism from their marginal and denigrated portrayal in standard works of church history. Wedel saw Anabaptism and Mennonitism as part of a tradition of biblical faithfulness going back to the early church.

Wedel also believed in the cultivation of the intellect in all fields of knowledge. The current college mission statement continues the commitment to intellectual, cultural, and spiritual leadership for the church and society. The Wedel Series furthers these goals by publishing research in Mennonite studies with a special emphasis on works with a connection to Bethel College, such as campus lecture series and projects based on the holdings of the Mennonite Library and Archives.

Of the thirteen volumes published in the series prior to this time, eleven have originated in campus lecture series or symposia, four arose out of library or archival holdings at Bethel College, and two had both ties. One volume has been reprinted since its original publication. Topics in the series have included Mennonite identity, biography and autobiography, Bethel College history, nonviolent interpretations of United States history, Menno Simons, Mennonite literature, and theology.

The volume you have before you opens up new ground for English-language readers with the story of Mennonites in the Vistula Delta.

John D. Thiesen
Series Editor

Introduction

Historical anniversaries are commemorated on a schedule that past events prescribe for the present generation. Thus in 1919, in spite of particularly inauspicious circumstances, the Mennonite congregation in Danzig/Gdańsk observed the 350-year anniversary of its founding and the 100-year anniversary of the dedication of its church building. The press report on the event began with the comment "This is no time to be celebrating."[1] The reasons for such reluctance were at least two-fold. A terrible war had ended just the year before. A report from September 1918, just two months before the end of World War I, noted that 248 members of the congregation, almost half of the male members, had served or were serving in the German armed forces. In November 1919 the congregation dedicated two memorial plaques hung inside the church that listed the twenty-eight fallen soldiers from the congregation, including the Mennonite flying ace Hans Janzen who had thirteen "kills."[2] Along with the death caused by the war, the economic misery and hunger of the last war years weighed heavily on the congregation as well.

The results of the war were perhaps even more difficult for the congregation to accept than the deaths it caused. Germany lost, a fact that transformed the geopolitical situation of the Danzig Mennonites and the broader Vistula delta region. Two new states emerged on territory that had been part of Prussia and Germany for over a hundred years, the large, recreated state of Poland and a small semi-independent state, the Free State of Danzig (see map on page 242). The latter emerged as a compromise between the irreconcilable claims of both Germany and Poland to the city and port of Danzig. For the Mennonites of Danzig it meant starting over after a lost war in a new and onerous political system. More importantly, it also meant separation from the political nation in which they had found a

---

[1] "Jahrhundertfeier in Danzig am 14. September," *Mennonitische Blätter*, 66, no. 10 (Oct. 1919), 74.

[2] H. G. Mannhardt, "Die Danziger Gem. an ihre Männer im Felde," *Mennonitische Blätter*, 65, no. 9 (September 1918), 66-8; *Zwei Gedenktage der Danziger Mennonitengemeinde im Herbst 1919* (Danzig, 1919), 10.

home over the course of the previous hundred years, as this book documents.

Nonetheless, on September 14, 1919, the congregation celebrated their anniversary with a special church service and the publication of this congregational history. A prime reason to celebrate, according to the press release, was gratitude for the faithfulness and witness of earlier generations, especially those who had given money to erect the current church building in 1819 after another war that had rocked the area, the Napoleonic wars of the early nineteenth century.[3]

Unlike the original publication of this book, this translation is not tied to any particular anniversary, begging the question of why it was translated now and more importantly, why it might be of interest to an English-language reader. This congregational history offers important new perspectives on religious minorities in early modern and modern Germany for those interested either in German or in Mennonite history as well as evidence for the early roots of Europe's multi-confessional present.

Contributions to German History

German historians have long noted the special importance of historical sources that come from further down the social scale as well as from the margins of society.[4] The drama of confrontations that triangulated Mennonite artisans and merchants outside the city walls, guild masters, and the ruling patrician families illuminate how religious and economic interests fed off each other in early modern Danzig, perhaps complicating older narratives of progressive or economic determinism. One graphic way to capture the freshness of the lens a Mennonite historical imagination provides is to examine the maps in this volume of Danzig and the Vistula delta. These only reproduce the locales that figure in this history of the congregation. This particular ordering of their own geographical

---

[3]"Jahrhundertfeier in Danzig," 74-5.

[4]For a discussion of how sources impact the development of historical narratives see, for example, Dieter Langewiesche, *Nation, Nationalismus, Nationalstaat in Deutschland und Europa* (Munich: Verlag C. H. Beck, 2000), 14-79.

space, while familiar, is nonetheless distinctive from the maps of the area drawn either by scholars or by Mennonites' contemporaries.

Studying the history of Mennonites in Danzig also suggests that the religious history of Europe, certainly of Danzig, was more complex than that of simply Catholic versus Protestant. Chapter eight provides a rich description of Mennonite rituals and practices, providing evidence of the ability of a community to regulate its own affairs, both secular and sacred, without the support of the state, indeed in some cases in opposition to it. At the same time the gaps in this account are equally revealing. Although Jews lived in the same villages as Mennonites outside the city walls and faced many of the same challenges, this history ignores their presence and common struggles despite the fact that we know relationships existed between the two communities; the local synagogue sent "friendly greetings" to the 1919 celebration that were publicly and gratefully acknowledged.[5]

This history also demonstrates at two levels the transformation of European society in the eighteenth and nineteenth century from one that derived status from birth and tradition (*Standesgesellschaft*) to one that based status on merit as well as equal rights and equal duties (*Staatsbürgergesellschaft*). The narrative that follows starts with Mennonites as courageous outsiders and ends with them as valued, if still slightly eccentric, insiders, fitting the liberal expectation that the price of admission to modern, democratic society is checking one's religious commitments at the door of the public sphere. The impact of the Mennonites' acceptance of these social arrangements for their own beliefs and practices becomes apparent when one notes, for example, the increase in reverence for the state by comparing the opening pages of chapter ten with those of chapter twelve, that is, the time period of 1800 with 1870. At a second level, of course, this process is exemplified by the interpretations offered by Mannhardt, who

---

[5]"Jahrhundertfeier in Danzig," 75. The Jewish historiography on Danzig reciprocates by ignoring the Mennonites, Samuel Echt, *Die Geschichte der Juden in Danzig* (Leer: Verlag Gerhard Rautenberg, 1972).

xvi   The Danzig Mennonite Church

himself as author was obviously a product of this development. One prominent example of this is his careful noting of the causes of Mennonite emigration from Danzig and the Vistula delta while not commenting on its scope or meaning for those who remained behind. His narrative only follows those who chose to stay and adapt to German society even though the emigrants created much larger communities in Russia than the one they left behind in Prussia. Additional examples of Mannhardt's internalization of German social norms are highlighted throughout in the footnotes.

Contributions to Mennonite History

Readers more interested in the specifics of Mennonite history might observe with some surprise that this volume presents a continuous history of urban Mennonites. American Mennonites are well along in their own urbanization process, but American urban Mennonites often feel like they are charting completely new territory. European Mennonite history, in fact, offers five hundred years of urban history and the Danzig Mennonites constituted one of Germany's leading examples of that.[6] Menno Simons, the sixteenth-century Dutch Catholic priest who became the group's namesake, visited here and one of his closest co-workers, Dirk Philips, was the founding leader, or elder, of one of the two original Danzig Mennonite congregations.

A related question for Mennonite readers and scholars of religious minorities would be how this urban, Polish, Prussian, and German context shaped Mennonites' understandings of

---

[6]On American Mennonite urbanization see J. Howard Kauffman and Leo Driedger, *Mennonite Mosaic: Identity and Modernization* (Scottdale, PA: Herald Press, 1991). Other nineteenth-century examples of German Mennonite urban congregational histories are Berend Carl Roosen, *Geschichte der Mennoniten-Gemeinde zu Hamburg und Altona* (Hamburg: H.O. Versiehl, 1886-1887) and Carl Harder, *Kurzgefaßte Geschichte der Elbinger Mennonitengemeinde* (Elbing: Vorstand der Elbinger Mennonitengemeinde, 1883). Contemporary histories of urban German Mennonite congregations include Michael D. Driedger, *Obedient Heretics: Mennonite Identities in Lutheran Hamburg and Altona during the Confessional Age* (Burlington, VT: Ashgate, 2002) and Wolfgang Froese, editor, *Sie kamen als Fremde: Die Mennoniten in Krefeld von den Anfängen bis zur Gegenwart* (Krefeld: Stadt Krefeld, 1995).

themselves, their world, and the relationship between the two. Having this source in English allows the reader to reach his or her own conclusion and there is much to ponder. Before 1808, when two distinct congregations existed in Danzig, Mennonite identity was shaped by internal differentiation as well as external ostracism and discrimination. In the seventeenth and eighteenth centuries the literal price of buying the freedom to live, work, and worship was a predominant theme while in the nineteenth century, and under Prussian rule, the rejection of military service became the main marker of Mennonite identity. By the beginning of the twentieth century the avoidance of oaths and especially independence from the state and the state church system came to the fore. One common thread throughout seems to have been the determination to form a voluntary community on the basis of adult, or young adult, commitments to join or leave the church. Thus Mennonite identity as described here changed over time even as a strong claim to continuity persisted.

One particular interesting example of continuity amidst change is the use of Mennonite and Anabaptist history in the latter half of the nineteenth century as a rallying point for increasingly educated and acculturated Mennonites. The first two chapters, which recount the history of the Anabaptist movement, were heavily influenced by attempts to revitalize late nineteenth-century German Mennonite churches around carefully selected sixteenth-century Anabaptist ideals, a process repeated in the mid-twentieth century in the United States.[7] This revival even led to a new form of national organization for the Mennonites, the creation of the Alliance of Mennonite Churches in the German Empire in 1886 as described in chapter thirteen.

Also striking in the nineteenth-century portion of this book is the clear rejection of separation from and ostracism by the broader society that resulted in a critical engagement with German culture. In that century modern German nationalism

---

[7]For an introduction on Harold S. Bender's use of *The Anabaptist Vision* to rallying American Mennonites, see Albert N. Keim, *Harold S. Bender, 1897-1962* (Scottdale, PA: Herald Press, 1998).

xviii The Danzig Mennonite Church

was created and its impact on Mennonites was profound. Mannhardt's account thus provides the reader a front-row seat for the Mennonites' changing relationship to their world. What they counted as gains are evident in Mannhardt's careful notation of the titles of successful businessmen and local politicians that the church leadership appended to their names as well as their relocation into more respectable quarters of the city. The pitfalls are marked by contentious debates, the occasional lament for the passing of honored traditions, and emigration. When, however, we read in chapter ten that for Mennonites in 1814 "the hour of salvation" appeared as the French garrison was driven out of the city or in chapter twelve that the unification and creation of the German Empire in 1871 was an object of long-standing desire, then clearly some wrenching reordering of Mennonite priorities since the sixteenth century had taken place. This book repays a careful reading with ample material for reflection on how European history both impacted and was shaped by ordinary people.

H. G. Mannhardt and His Intellectual Interests

The process of increasing self-identification with Germany is clearly reflected in the life of Hermann Gottlieb Mannhardt. He was born into a prominent and wealthy Mennonite family on January 14, 1855, on the family's estate of Hanerau in Schleswig-Holstein. His father, also named Hermann Gottlieb, was the forester for the estate; his mother, Bertha Weihe, was the daughter of a Protestant pastor. The family often visited his uncle, Jacob Mannhardt, who was the preacher and elder of the Danzig Mennonite Church. Mannhardt lived with his uncle's family from 1871 to 1875 while he attended Danzig's classical high school (*Gymnasium*). Here he shared a study with and was heavily influenced by his cousin, Wilhelm Mannhardt, a prominent scholar of both German folklore and Mennonite history who was also the first German Mennonite to earn a doctorate. Years of his own study followed in the fields of Protestant theology and history at the universities of Strasbourg, Berlin, and Kiel. He interrupted his education during the academic year 1876-1877 to serve a one-year term as a volunteer in the Prussian army. The regular term for draftees was three years, but educated young men who volunteered had long been allowed much shorter terms as a way to make military service more palatable to the upper middle class. Although his education and apparent formal membership in the state Protestant church would have entitled him to a career as pastor, his theological opposition to a state church drove him to take another path.

Mannhardt returned to Danzig in 1878 where he took a number of teaching jobs in schools for girls to support himself, working mostly in the school owned and operated by his cousin, Luise Mannhardt. He also began to preach in the Mennonite congregation to relieve the workload of his aging uncle. In 1879 his preaching position was made official. In June 1880 he passed the state teacher exams in German and history, in September he was ordained as co-elder of the Danzig Mennonite Church and in October he married Else Dyck, a young Mennonite woman from the nearby village of Einlage/Przegalina. The couple moved into the parsonage built for them in 1884. Soon afterwards Else took a fall, causing the stillbirth of twins. She was not able to conceive after this accident, but the couple later adopted and raised her brother Elias' daughter Margot. Mannhardt taught part-time until 1900; after that he was able to devote himself entirely to his congregation. Much of his career as a pastor is documented in chapters twelve and thirteen.[8]

Comparing Mannhardt's prolific writings during his career with his narrative here of Danzig Mennonite history documents how his own interests both mirrored and shaped his congregation. As one would expect from a highly educated nineteenth-century German pastor, Mannhardt was vitally interested in German culture and wanted Mennonites to participate in and benefit from it. Befitting the mixed religious background of his family and education, he was an active proponent of close ecumenical ties with the state Protestant

[8]Biographical information has been taken from Christian Neff, "H. G. Mannhardt," *Mennonitische Blätter* 74, no. 9 (Sept. 1927), 75-80; Erich Göttner, "Hermann Gottlieb Mannhardt," *Christlicher Gemeinde-Kalender* 38 (1929), 36-47; and Heinz-Jürgen Mannhardt, ed., *Die Mennonitenfamilie van der Smissen und Ihre Nachkommenschaft*, 2nd ed. (Darmstadt: Mannhardt, 1999), 62-65, 269, 274-5.

church while still working hard to maintain an independent
Mennonite church. The same influences made him an ardent
German nationalist who nonetheless remained publicly critical
of German nationalism's worst excesses.

Mannhardt was broadly engaged in literary endeavors well
beyond the parochial boundaries of his congregation and
denomination. For years he was a member and leader of a local
literary society, "Literatia." He lectured at the local community
college and technical university on the early history of
Christianity and for community groups on the German authors
Goethe and Schiller. Widely admired as a public speaker, he was
invited to address the crowds at public ceremonies that marked
the eightieth birthday of the first Imperial Chancellor, Otto von
Bismarck, and the one-hundredth anniversary of the birth of the
first German emperor, William I.[9]

His main activities nonetheless were clearly directed toward
serving and strengthening the Mennonite church, activities that
were defensive when necessary and creative where possible. A
literary controversy early in his career threw Mannhardt and
Mennonites on the defensive. One of the era's most prominent
playwrights, Ernst von Wildenbruch, wrote a drama entitled *Der
Menonit* (The Mennonite) that portrayed Mennonites as
dangerous and cowardly traitors of the German fatherland
because they had refused to fight against Napoleon. Mannhardt
wrote extensively on the play and was a leader in the
unsuccessful efforts to keep the play off the stage of the Royal
Theater in Berlin.[10]

More commonly, however, Mannhardt strove to present
attractive literary models for Mennonites to emulate. For
example, at about the same time as the controversy over

---

[9]Göttner, "Mannhardt," 46; H. G. Mannhardt, *Predigten und Reden* (Danzig:
John & Rosenberg, 1905), 362-382.

[10]The longest piece he wrote on the play is "Die Mennoniten in der
dramatischen Literatur," in H. G. Mannhardt, ed. *Jahrbuch der Mennoniten-
Gemeinden in West- und Ostpreußen*, 2nd ed. (Danzig: Self-published, 1883), 23-
53. On his role in this controversy see Mark Jantzen, "At Home in Germany?
The Mennonites of the Vistula Delta and the Construction of a German
National Identity, 1772-1880" (Ph. D. diss., University of Notre Dame,
2002), 391-5.

Wildenbruch's *Menonit*, the archivist and historian Ludwig Keller began publishing monographs based on archival sources that were highly favorable to the sixteenth-century Anabaptists. As described in chapter thirteen, Mannhardt promoted his works in his congregation and adopted Keller's findings in his own historical writing, evidenced here in the first chapter. Mannhardt edited yearbooks in 1883 and 1888 that brought together a great deal of statistical information on Mennonites for the first time in decades.[11] He used the commemoration of the four-hundredth anniversary of Menno Simons' birth to publish and to educate Mennonites on their own history.[12] He contributed regularly to the Mennonite newspaper of his day, the *Mennonite Journal (Mennonitische Blätter)*, on a wide range of topics. He even tried his own hand at writing fiction, publishing a short story entitled "Behold, although dying we live" under the pseudonym Gerhard Mondberg in the South German Mennonites' *Christian Calendar for Congregations (Christlicher Gemeindekalender)* in 1894.[13] Thanks to the work of two student assistants, Eric Stucky and Braden Hiebner, a comprehensive listing of his writings is available in the appendix.

Strengthening church life was also a prime motivation for Mannhardt's interest in closer cooperation with the state Protestant church. He was clearly worried about a decline in the number of Mennonites, one made even more dramatic since it contrasted sharply with the rapid increase of the German population in the second half of the nineteenth century.[14] His own congregation more than doubled its membership during the forty-eight years of his pastorate, going from 448 members in 1879 to 1,150 members in 1927. He concluded in one of his last articles that the two main causes of this growth were the increasing urbanization that brought rural Mennonites to live in

---

[11]*Jahrbuch der Mennoniten-Gemeinden in West- und Ostpreussen* (Danzig, 1883); *Jahrbuch der altevangelischen Taufgesinnten oder Mennonitengemeinden* (Danzig, 1888).
[12]*Festschrift zu Menno Simons' 400jähriger Geburtstagsfeier den 6. November 1892* (Danzig: Selbstverlag der westpreussischen Mennoniten-Gemeinden, 1892).
[13]Neff, "Mannhardt," 80.
[14]In addition to several articles dealing with statistics he published in *Mennonitische Blätter*, see especially his "Statistik der Menn.-Gem. in West- und Ostpreußen" in his 1883 *Jahrbuch*, 15-22.

Danzig and join the congregation and the way in which his congregation, in contrast to more traditional rural congregations, accepted non-Mennonite marriage partners as members or even allowed couples to retain the separate church memberships they had before marriage.[15]

Where possible, Mannhardt was a strong advocate of cooperation with Protestants, promoting Mennonite contributions to Protestant foreign and domestic mission work. When Mennonites complained about the clear discrimination they felt from some corners of the Protestant church, Mannhardt cautioned against a rush to judgment and initiated personal conversations with the offending Protestant parties.[16] He even went so far as to speculate that in the future Mennonites together with Lutherans and the Reformed would leave narrow denominational concerns behind and join together in a great Christian all-German church (*christliche deutsche Volkskirche*).[17]

At the same time, Mannhardt throughout his life articulated firm commitments that ruled out Mennonites joining the state Protestant church as it existed at that time. He laid out this relationship succinctly in his 1892 booklet on Menno Simons. He noted that Mennonites had joined in the celebration of Luther's four hundredth birthday in 1883 because Luther belonged to all German Protestants, Mennonites included. The fact that Lutherans were not joining in the celebration of Menno was, according to Mannhardt, a reflection of Menno's lesser status and his lack of any dramatic deeds.[18] After reviewing Mennonite history and the changes in Mennonite theology since the sixteenth century, Mannhardt listed repentance, new birth, free will, the symbolic nature of baptism

---

[15]"Wo bleiben unsere Täuflinge?" *Mennonitische Blätter* 74, no. 6 (June 1927): 44-5 and "Innere Mission II," *Mennonitische Blätter* 49, no. 8 (August 1902), 67-9.

[16]See, for example, his article "Mennoniten-Gemeinden und Diakonissenhäuser," *Mennonitische Blätter* 40, no. 8 (August 1894), 60-1.

[17]"Zur Abwehr," *Mennonitische Blätter* 35, no. 14 (July 2, 1888), 83.

[18]H. G. Mannhardt, *Menno Simons*, 48. See also Abraham Friesen, *History and Renewal in the Anabaptist/Mennonite Tradition* (North Newton, KS: Bethel College, 1994), 42.

and communion, the church as the community gathered by the Holy Spirit, and the avoidance of swearing oaths as the ongoing marks of the Mennonite church. He made particularly clear that unlike sixteenth-century Mennonites who sought to build a church separate from the world, contemporary Mennonites were interested in building a church that permeated the world.[19] The intersection of human free will, a voluntary church, and the permeation, not coercion, of society was the crux of the theology that kept Mannhardt out of the state church.

Despite his disagreements with Protestants over theological principles, Mannhardt was open-minded enough to borrow ideas from the state church that he thought had merit. As his own career demonstrated, he found great value in an educated, professional Mennonite clergy, a clear departure from tradition for German Mennonites. Providing a Mennonite supplement to or replacement for Protestant theological study for Mennonite pastors was the first reason he gave for his active role in founding the Alliance of Mennonite Congregations in the German Empire.[20] He agreed that regional and national level church organizations were essential for the church to fulfill its tasks and he talked of the Alliance as the Mennonite version of a Protestant home mission board.[21] In short, while rejecting the theology behind the state church, Mannhardt promoted its structural solutions to the challenges facing the Mennonite church in his day.

The biggest shift in Mennonite identity and theology in Mannhardt's lifetime was the acceptance of military service in the Prussian army. It may come as a surprise to Mennonite readers to hear that there were many Mennonite soldiers in the German armies of both World War I and II and no conscientious objectors. One key element that made this shift possible was the internalization of German nationalism. In

---

[19]Ibid., 52-5.

[20]*Bericht über die in Berlin am 2. und 3. October 1884 stattgehabte Conferenz deutscher Mennoniten erstattet in einer Ansprache an die Brüder-Versammlung der Danziger Mennoniten-Gemeinde am 19. October 1884* (Danzig: Mannhardt, 1884), 4-9.

[21]"Innere Mission," *Mennonitische Blätter*, 49, no. 7 (July 1902), 54; "Innere Mission III," *Mennonitische Blätter*, 49, no. 9 (September 1902), 74-5.

Mannhardt's writings this is perhaps easiest to find during the ·
opening days of World War I, a time when all the European
countries involved in the war were gripped by hypernationalism.
His initial reaction differed not at all from other nationalistic
liberals. England was Germany's "worst enemy." Mannhardt
was grateful to God for the way in which the German people,
previously bickering over matters of class and religion, pulled
together now in a sense of "unity, sacrifice and growing
power."[22]
   As the war ground on, Mannhardt's writing became more
pastoral. He published several articles on preaching during
wartime. While applauding the limited success the German navy
had in 1915, he also lambasted the empty-headed and one-sided
propaganda of the German press, reminding his readers that
God was judging the Germans, too.[23] By 1918 he saw the
"human irrationality" of war and expressed the hope that people
would realize that "real peace between the nations can never be
the work of violence and cleverly negotiated formal treaties, but
rather it is a fruit of Christian inclination and morality."[24]
   As we noted at the outset, the German defeat in World War
I meant that H. G. Mannhardt and the Danzig Mennonite
congregation had to deal with the failure of a worldview –
commitment to the German nation and culture as an important
source of meaning – in addition to the loss of life. He lamented
the partition of Germany and a peace after the war that had not
created a sense of peacefulness. At the same time, he noted with
satisfaction that Mennonite efforts to have constitutional
recognition of their right not to swear oaths had been achieved
in the new Free State of Danzig even as similar efforts failed in
Germany and Poland.[25]

---

[22]"Der Krieg und wir," *Mennonitische Blätter* 61, no. 11 (November 1914),
82-3. For the background to the response of the educated in Germany to the
outbreak of war, see Klaus von See, *Die Ideen von 1789 und die Ideen von 1914:
völkisch Denken in Deutschland zwischen Französischer Revolution und Erstem
Weltkrieg* (Frankfurt a. M.: Athenaion, 1975).
[23]"Was predigen wir in der Kriegszeit?" *Mennonitische Blätter* 64, no. 1
(January 1916), 2-4.
[24]"Männer im Felde," 67.
[25]"Jahresbericht der Vereinigung der Mennoniten-Gemeinden im

After Mannhardt's death in 1927 the Danzig Mennonite congregation went on to participate in and suffer from World War II in ways that were largely the same as other Germans. At the end of the war most of the German civilian population of the area either fled in advance of the Soviet army or was deported by the new Polish government in accordance with international agreements reached by the victorious Allies.

Special Features of the English Edition
The most unique contribution of this new edition of Mannhardt's work is the epilogue provided by Gdańsk pastor Tomasz Ropiejko whose congregation now worships in the former Mennonite church building. Polish Evangelicals and Pentecostals worked diligently for decades under difficult political conditions to rebuild and preserve this piece of Mennonite heritage. On numerous occasions they have served as gracious hosts for Mennonite visitors from the Netherlands, Germany, and North America. We are grateful for Ropiejko's contribution to this volume and for the ministry of his congregation. When the church building was dedicated on September 12, 1819, Pastor Peter Tiessen Jr. preached on I Kings 9:3 "I have consecrated this house that you have built and put my name there forever." He concluded with a prayer that God take "this building into His care, may He answer the prayers that arise in it, and may He bless the holy rites enacted here with rich fruit."[26] Almost two hundred years later that prayer is still being answered in ways the congregation gathered on that day could never have imagined.

The editors have confronted a number of interesting decisions in bringing this translation to life. Victor G. Doerksen, professor emeritus since 1996 in the Department of German

Deutschen Reich über ihre Tätigkeit in den Jahren 1918 und 1919," *Mennonitische Blätter* 67, no. 11 (November 1920), 84. The best English language overview of intellectual developments among North German Mennonites in the years leading up to World War I is James Regier's "Where the Two Kingdoms Merge: The Struggle for Balance Between National and Religious Identity among Mennonites in Wilhelmine Germany" (master's thesis, Wichita State University, 2006).
[26]See page 172.

and Slavic Studies at the University of Manitoba, did the initial translation work. At a number of points, however, specific German titles and terms seemed difficult to express clearly in English. In order to make the book broadly accessible to students and readers who did not know any German, we decided to find English equivalents for every one of these terms. For example, the geographic names *Danziger Werder* and *Großer Werder* have been rendered as the Danzig Delta and Greater Delta. Where the term Vistula delta appears it refers to the entire general area. Similar equivalents have been found for professional and government titles. The results will sound odd to the reader who understands the German original provided in parentheses or footnotes, but the text hopefully will flow better for other readers.

We have largely retained the German-language place names of the original despite the contemporary location of the Vistula River in Poland. At the first mention of each place name we added the Polish equivalent wherever we could. A complete listing of German and Polish place names is provided in the appendix. Italics for emphasis represent the nineteenth-century version of e x p a n d e d   l e t t e r s for emphasis in the original. Biblical quotations were not translated directly but supplied from the New Revised Standard Version.

The destruction caused by World War II destroyed the Danzig Mennonite congregation. Its members were killed or scattered to East and West Germany, North and South America. In addition, many of the records originally cited by Mannhardt have been lost. Wherever possible, we have formatted the original footnotes to match the requirements of modern scholarship, but many citations of archival records are like dead links on a website, leading to destinations that no longer exist. The Danzig congregation, and many of the other Vistula Mennonite congregations, had rich archival collections before World War II. The vast majority of those collections were lost and likely destroyed in the last days of the war. Some records were brought to western Germany by Mennonites fleeing the Vistula Delta in 1945 and are now in the Mennonitische Forschungsstelle at Weierhof, Germany. A few other remnants were retrieved by Mennonite Central

Committee workers from North America who worked in Poland immediately after the war. These archival fragments were brought back to the United States and can now be found in the Mennonite Church USA Archives – North Newton (Mennonite Library and Archives) at Bethel College.[27] Surviving records from Danzig include two fire-damaged 18th-century

Danzig Mennonite archival records recovered after World War II, now located in the Mennonite Church USA Archives at Bethel College, North Newton, Kansas

membership books, a book listing baptisms and other data back to the mid-17th century, and other miscellaneous and fragmentary documents. Records in the Danzig city and state archives and library also suffered many losses, but the surviving

[27]Collection MCA.V.18.

records are still located in Gdańsk. Sources that H. G. Mannhardt cited as being from "Danzig City Library" would now be part of the library of the Gdańsk branch of the Polish Academy of Science (*Biblioteka Gdańska Polskiej Akademii Nauk*) and the "Danzig City Archives" sources would now be in the Public Archives of Gdańsk (*Archiwum Państwowe w Gdańsku*).[28]

At numerous points we have added editorial footnotes to explain later developments or provide additional context for Mannhardt's text. These are set off from Mannhardt's own footnotes by square brackets and end with a designation for the editors [... Ed.]. The maps were designed by the editors and produced by Bob Regier, Professor Emeritus of Art at Bethel College. The original illustrations from the German edition were all reproduced but placed in different locations than in the original in order to bring them in closer proximity to the relevant text. In some cases, clear photographic prints were available for the illustrations in the original German edition. In other cases, the editors scanned illustrations directly from a copy of the 1919 volume. The editors also added a number of photographs where relevant. New or scanned illustrations are indicated in the captions. Since the German edition had only very limited captions, the captions for this translation were written primarily by the editors.

It is a special pleasure to acknowledge the support of the Vistula Mennonite Studies Project Advisory Council. Bruce Entz, Peggy Goertzen, Karen Penner, Milton Claassen, and Tim Penner have read drafts, discussed with us issues of clarity and readability, brainstormed ideas for advancing the work of this project, and volunteered their time and expertise promoting this volume among different groups. We also thank the scholars who have readily answered our queries in their areas of expertise. At Bethel College, Dale Schrag helped us with Anabaptist sources, Keith Sprunger with Dutch translations, Dan Quinlin with Latin, and Merle Schlabaugh with German.

---

[28]The published guide to the Gdańsk archives is Czesław Biernat, *Staatsarchiv Danzig — Wegweiser durch die Bestände bis zum Jahr 1945* (München: R. Oldenbourg Verlag, 2000). An older, pre-war guide to the city library's manuscript holdings is *Katalog der Danziger Stadtbibliothek,* 6 vols. (Danzig: Stadtbibliothek, 1892-1921).

Joe Springer provided additional information on sources only available at the Mennonite Historical Library in Goshen, Indiana. Dan Riches at the University of Chicago helped with information on early modern currencies and economics.

This project would not have been possible without major donations from Tim and Faith Penner and the estate of Henry E. Jantzen. Several other donors gave smaller amounts and we thank each one of them. We plan to continue translation work on the history of the Mennonites of the Vistula region and welcome contact with and support from anyone who shares our interest in this story.

Mark Jantzen
North Newton, Kansas
November 2006

H. G. Mannhardt

Foreword

On September 14 of this year [1919] our congregation will quietly celebrate an important anniversary. Therefore it would be valuable for church members to be better informed about the past of our religious community than was previously possible. No doubt some information about the history of the Danzig Mennonites is already known. In the book by A. Brons, *Origin, Development and Fate of the Old Evangelical Anabaptists or Mennonites* (3rd ed., Emden, 1912),[1] our congregation is often

---

[1] [*Ursprung, Entwickelung und Schicksale der altevangelischen Taufgesinnten oder Mennoniten*, 3rd ed. (Amsterdam: Johannes Müller, 1912). (Mannhardt lists Emden as the place of publication for this 1912 edition, but the actual publisher was located in Amsterdam. The book's printer was in Emden.) Like H. G. Mannhardt, Brons both welcomed and advocated German Mennonites' embrace of and incorporation into German society. Both allowed that accepting military service and closer contact with German Protestants culturally and theologically were necessary, helpful steps for Mennonites to take; see chapter twelve and the conclusion. On Anna Brons see Bernhard Brons, *Frau Antje Brons, geb. Cremer ten Doornkat zu Emden, geb. 23. November 1810, gest. 2. April 1902: aus ihrem Leben* (Kaiserslautern: Buchdruckerei Heinr. Köhl, 1904); Julia Hildebrandt, "Antje Brons als Mennonitin," *Mennonitische Geschichtsblätter* 23 (1966): 41-58; and Mary Sprunger, "Anna Brons and Ludwig Keller: Partners for Historical Renewal" (BA thesis, Bethel College, North Newton, Kansas, 1984). Other historical overviews of Mennonites in the Vistula River area and Germany more broadly include Horst Penner, *Die Ost- und Westpreußischen Mennoniten*, 2 vols. (Weierhof: Mennonitischer Geschichtsverein, 1978; Kirchheimbolanden: Selbstverlag, 1987) and Diether Götz Lichdi, *Die Mennoniten in Geschichte und Gegenwart: Von der Täuferbewegung zur weltweiten Freikirchen* (Weisenheim am Sand: AGAPE-Verlag im Zusammenarbeit mit dem Mennonitischen Geschichtsverein, 2004). English language overviews of the Vistula area Mennonites include Peter J. Klassen, *A Homeland for Strangers: An Introduction to Mennonites in Poland and Prussia* (Fresno, CA: Center for Mennonite Brethren Studies, 1989); Mark Jantzen, "Mennonites in Poland – Mennonites in Prussia: A Look at Recent Mennonite Scholarship," *Mennonite Life* 47, no. 2 (June 1992): 11-14; and Horst Penner, "West Prussia," *Mennonite Encyclopedia*, 4:920-6. In contrast to much of the German-language historiography on Vistula River Mennonites, Klassen stressed their location and history in the Polish Commonwealth before the Partitions of Poland 1772-1795. For an introduction to Mennonites more broadly see Horst Penner, Horst Gerlach, and Horst Quiring, *Weltweite Bruderschaft: Ein mennonitisches Geschichtsbuch*, 5th ed. (Weierhof: Selbstverlag Horst Gerlach, 1995); C. Henry Smith, *Smith's Story of the Mennonites*, 5th ed., ed. Cornelius Krahn (Newton, KS: Faith and Life Press, 1981); Cornelius J. Dyck, *An*

mentioned, but naturally only in connection with other congregations. Dr. Wilhelm Mannhardt dealt with his home congregation in greater depth in his book *The Military Service Exemption of the Mennonites of Provincial Prussia* (Marienburg, 1863),[2] and publicized important information from the archives of the City of Danzig and our congregational records. However, given the specific focus of his work, he too could only occasionally refer specifically to the Danzig congregation.

Although I have tried to narrate the origins and development of the Danzig Mennonite congregation, I must ask for the reader's indulgence. Unfortunately, information about the early developments is very scarce. Due to the numerous fires that destroyed the homes of Mennonites outside the city walls of Danzig, some valuable accounts were lost. These included the complete lists of baptismal candidates to the year 1667, as well as the extensive correspondence of the congregations' elders[3]

Introduction to Mennonite History, 3rd ed. (Scottdale, PA: Herald Press, 1993); Harry Loewen and Steven Nolt, *Through Fire and Water: An Overview of Mennonite History* (Scottdale, PA: Herald Press, 1996; and Claude Baecher and others, *Global Mennonite History Series*, vol. 2 *Europe: Testing Faith and Tradition* (Intercourse, PA: Good Books, 2006). Ed.]

[2][*Die Wehrfreiheit der altpreußischen Mennoniten*. Wilhelm Mannhardt was the first German Mennonite to earn a Ph. D. and was an important figure in the development of the field of German folklore. His book on the history of Mennonites' exemption from military service in Prussia was commissioned by the Mennonite leadership of the Vistula Delta in 1862 in an attempt to persuade a broader public that efforts to force them to serve in the military were misguided and illegal. Mannhardt used sources from state and congregational archives that have since been lost, making his book the best single account of Mennonites in the Vistula Delta. The irony of his effort was that he himself was a staunch German nationalist who thought Mennonites should serve in the military. For additional information on the origins and impact of this book see H. G. Mannhardt, "Zur Entstehung und Geschichte der Königliche Kabinettsordre vom 3. März 1868, betreffend den Heeresdienst der Mennoniten," *Christlicher Gemeinde-Kalender* 28 (1919): 97-107; and Mark Jantzen, "At Home in Germany?" 294-9. Ed.]

[3][Mennonite congregations in the Vistula region historically had three types of leaders, all of whom were elected for life. Deacons comprised the first level. They were elected from among the male members and their primary responsibility was to administer the poor fund. The second level, preachers or *Lehrer*, were elected from the deacons. They shared in the preaching on Sunday mornings and could officiate at weddings and funerals.

with our co-religionists elsewhere. Not until the time of Georg Hansen, who was called as a preacher in 1665 and elder in 1690, do the records become more substantial. Presumably this energetic leader of the congregation saw to it that the lists of births, baptisms, marriages, and deaths were saved in several copies. He also wrote a kind of chronicle, also no longer extant, from which Elder Hans von Steen (1754-81) preserved important extracts. We also have some commentary and numerous letters from von Steen, so that the sources of our story are richer beginning with the mid-eighteenth century. In the nineteenth century, finally, the minutes of meetings of the church board, and the church chronicle which was kept starting in 1831 have abundant information. All of this applies to the Flemish, and later for the united congregation.[4] Information about the Frisian (Neugarten/Nowe Ogródy) church, however, is sparse, even regarding membership lists. It is true that we have baptismal registers starting in 1665, but these are very incomplete, omitting almost all data concerning birth, parents, marriage, and death.

We must, therefore, depend largely on the files of the Danzig State Archives and manuscripts in the Danzig City Library in order to gather the scattered facts about the first hundred years of our history. In this laborious and time-consuming task I was greatly assisted by Archivist Dr. Schottmüller, and I am very thankful to him for his expert advice and help.

The books I consulted are listed in the footnotes. Almost all of them are available in our church library.

Preachers were eligible for election to the top post of elder or *Aelteste*. The elder was the main spiritual leader of the congregation and the only one who could baptize and lead communion services. A neighboring elder typically conducted the election and installation of an elder, providing the only formal link between otherwise autonomous Mennonite congregations. These traditional structures changed earliest in the Danzig congregation in the nineteenth century in a process that Mannhardt describes in chapter eleven. Ed.]

[4][There were two Mennonite congregations in the Danzig area from the second half of the sixteenth century until 1808. The origins of both congregations are described in chapter four, the story of their unification in chapter ten. Ed.]

A small publication, *Our Church Building 50 Years Ago*,[5] was distributed in our church on September 12, 1869, on the occasion of a memorial service. Its author was my cousin, Dr. Wilhelm Mannhardt (died 1880), the son of the elder and minister at that time, Jacob Mannhardt. His detailed description of the church building has been a great help for the present work.

Due to the limited time I had available, I was not able to use all the relevant source materials. It would have been desirable to expand the present account of our Danzig church to a history of all the Mennonite churches in Prussia, but I could not and did not want to do that in this anniversary book. Our congregations, their brotherly unity notwithstanding, exist as individual congregations, and though they have shared common experiences, each has its own history, especially an urban congregation like ours.

In order to provide some broader context from the early history and events of the Anabaptist-Mennonite movement for this brief account, I have prefaced it with two chapters taken from my *Festschrift on Menno Simons 400 Year Anniversary, November 6, 1892* which is out of print.[6]

Concerning the tasks of our church in the present and our prospects for the future I ask the reader to consider the words of the last chapter.

Danzig, September 1, 1919. H.G. Mannhardt.

---

[5] [*Unser Kirchenbau vor 50 Jahren: Gedenkblatt für die Danziger Mennonitengemeinde* (Danzig, 1869). The only known North American copy of this book is available at the Mennonite Historical Library at Goshen College in Goshen, Indiana. Ed.]

[6] [*Festschrift zu Menno Simons' 400jähriger Geburtstagsfeier den 6. November 1892* (Danzig: Selbstverlag der westpreussischen Mennoniten-Gemeinden, 1892). Ed.]

1
The Oldest Anabaptist Congregations

The time beginning about 1440 and continuing beyond the middle of the next century was one of great movement, a new season of spring in the history of the world. New life was evident in all areas of human endeavor. Science freed itself from the authority of a power-hungry church; the arts created works of enduring beauty; reason devised a host of benevolent inventions, among which the invention of printing was the greatest. The zeal for action led intrepid heroes over unknown seas to the discovery of new worlds.

Even in those matters that tend to cling to tradition, in state and church, a new spirit arose. In the political realm there was no early success. The long, failed government of Frederick III (1440-1493) meant the doom of the imperial office in the Holy Roman Empire. Maximilian (1493-1519) attempted in vain to revive the old glory of the imperial title and its feudal social system. And although Emperor Charles V (1519-1556) boasted that in his lands the sun never set, his power in Germany was limited everywhere by the growing power of the greater and lesser rulers, who put their own interests ahead of those of the empire and the emperor.

But in the area of *religious* life there was a tremendous, if gradual, reversal. At first leading thinkers had distanced themselves slowly from the church. Then a longing for improvement in the church arose in the midst of the common folk where it was much deeper and more heartfelt than among the scholars. One can trace the presence of quiet sects far back into medieval times, groups who secretly followed the Gospel in opposition to the church. The influence of the mystics, of the Waldensians, of Hus and Wycliffe had stimulated a desire for reformation among the people at large. And thus, the ground was well-prepared when Luther appeared.

Luther
Like all great men, Luther did not achieve his ends only by means of doctrine, but above all by force of personality. The German people recognized that he embodied their own traits in the form of *one man*. His piety and hearty humor, his strong faith

and courage were as German as his occasional dogmatism and stubbornness. In addition, he had himself gone from being a monk, that is, from the works righteousness of the Catholic Church[1] to the *true freedom* of a Christian[2] in a serious personal struggle of his soul. Therefore, he must have been chosen to lead many thousands along the same path. His marvelous words, spoken quite in the spirit of Paul, "By faith I am a lord of all things, but by love I have made myself everyone's servant!" perfectly denotes evangelical piety.[3]

But Luther was unable to satisfy all of the legitimate religious demands of the German people and their neighbors. The firm conviction of his personal belief became a barrier to those who wanted to go further in the restoration of Apostolic Christianity than he himself was willing to go. These groups were not simply "fanatics and troublemakers" (*Schwärm- und Rottengeister*), as he liked to call them, but rather included men of the highest virtue and purest motives, whose co-operation in constituting the new church would have been desirable. Naturally all those who hoped for a church of Christian congregations and the Christian people had to be disappointed when instead they saw the new state churches arise. In these churches everything was directed by an external state organization and focused on the formulation of complicated dogma. In the resulting struggle "pure doctrine" overshadowed any emphasis on the *new life.*

It would be wrong to place the blame for this on Luther alone. The terrible political and social circumstances in

---

[1][Luther himself referred to Catholic soteriology as "works righteousness." C. Arnold Snyder, *Anabaptist History and Theology: An Introduction*, (Kitchner, Ontario: Pandora Press, 1995, 35). Ed.]

[2][Mannhardt's German here, *zu der* wahren Freiheit *eines Christenmenschen*, quotes of the title of a famous 1520 Luther tract known in English as *On Christian Liberty*, trans. W. A. Lambert (Philadelphia: Fortress Press, 1957). Ed.]

[3][The Pauline reference is to I Cor. 9:19 "For though I am free with respect to all, I have made myself a slave to all, so that I might win more of them." Mannhardt here alludes to a famous Luther quote from *On Christian Liberty*, "A Christian is a perfectly free lord of all, subject to none. A Christian is a perfectly dutiful servant of all, subject to all," Luther, *On Christian Liberty*, 7. Mannhardt has created his own paraphrase out of an amalgamation of these two sources. Ed.]

Germany proved more powerful than the great reformer. But such simple-minded blame was placed then, and still is today, on those who strove to restore Apostolic Christianity without a state church and coercive dogma. We cannot deny that in the Reformation period there was a radical and revolutionary movement that imagined original Christianity in terms of the flesh, quite differently from what it had been. It was natural for Luther to take issue with these people, especially since they cited him as an authority. After he had to preach against the Zwickau prophets and against the revolutionary peasants, he hastily took every disagreement with his teaching, even from pious and moderate men, to be a betrayal of the Gospel. In this way he turned away the noble Kaspar von Schwenckfeld, a devoted follower, because Schwenckfeld, for the sake of his conscience, had not agreed with him in all points. Luther's attempt to unite with Zwingli failed for the same reason.

Rebaptizers

But most of all, those men who were labeled Rebaptizers[4] elicited the opposition of Luther and of his followers. This name denoted almost everything that, in Germany at least, refuted or expanded on the teachings of Luther. In time the name was associated only with rebellious elements in society, because in the teaching of history to our youth no other image of the Rebaptizers was shown but that of Thomas Müntzer and

---

[4][Mannhardt used four different terms in the German original for Anabaptists. Two terms were used by the Anabaptists themselves, *Täufer*, or Baptists, and *Taufgesinnte*, or baptism-minded. The term Baptist cannot easily be used in English to convey the meaning its German counterpart has, so in this book *Täufer* will be translated as Anabaptists as will the term *Taufgesinnte*, which was more common in Dutch than German in any case. A third term, the derogative *Wiedertäufer*, was applied by the authorities to this new religious movement and emphasized the crime of rebaptism. As Mannhardt pointed out, developments in German historiography for centuries made this term synonymous with the violent events at Münster, recounted at the end of this chapter. To better convey the negative implication of this term, *Wiedertäufer* will be translated as Rebaptizers in this book. Mannhardt used the fourth term, *Anabaptisten*, only rarely; it is the German version of the Latin term for this movement. Since its connotation is more positive when he used it, we have also simply translated this term as Anabaptists. Ed.]

his ilk, and of the Münster episode. Therefore, it is necessary to remind ourselves that the actual Anabaptist congregations and their leaders had very little to do with those named above, as we shall see later in connection with the Münster prophets.[5]

It must be said that there was a profound difference between the views of the Anabaptists and the teaching of Luther, a difference which no doubt would have made an

---

[5]Earlier historians have either ignored or dismissed the Anabaptist movement of the Reformation. By contrast, in more recent works dealing with that period there is a more just assessment of the Anabaptists and their martyrs. See the works of Troeltsch, Karl Heussi, Karl Müller, Friedrich Nippold, Walter Köhler, etc.

[Ernst Troeltsch (1865-1923) was a Professor of Systematic Theology who taught at Bonn, Heidelberg, and Berlin. He worked concurrently as a high-ranking official in the Prussian Ministry of Culture in the department that oversaw the Protestant state church. He introduced principles of history and sociology to the study of religious groups, developing a widely influential typology of churches and sects where the former are all-inclusive and willing to use force to enforce their dogma and the latter are small and voluntary. For Troeltsch, Anabaptists constituted a prominent prototype of small, free-church movements. For general background see H. Beuckert, "Troeltsch, Ernst," *Die Religion in Geschichte und Gegenwart* (RGG), 3rd ed. (Tübingen: J. C. B. Mohr (Paul Siebeck), 1957-62), VI:1044-7.

Karl Heussi (1877-1961), Professor of Church History in Jena, wrote a basic handbook on church history that served as the standard for Protestant pastoral education for much of the twentieth century. His treatment of Anabaptists was objective and listed them as part of the Reformation. E. H. Pältz, *RGG*, III:307.

Karl Müller (1852-1940) was a church historian who taught in Berlin, Halle, Gießen, Breslau, and Tübingen. In 1907 he published a book on Luther and Andreas Karlstadt, who was a key figure in the emergence of Anabaptism. K. Kupisch, *RGG*, IV:1171-2.

Friedrich Nippold (1838-1918), also a church historian, taught in Heidelberg, Bern, and Jena. K. Scholder, *RGG*, IV:1498. One of his doctoral students, Gerhard Haake, was a Mennonite pastor who wrote his dissertation on Hans Denk. Abraham Friesen, *History and Renewal in the Anabaptist/Mennonite Tradition* (North Newton, KS: Bethel College, 1994), 67-8.

Walther Köhler (1870-1946) was a theologian who taught in Gießen, Zurich, and Heidelberg. He was a student of Troeltsch and a specialist in the Reformation, writing extensively on Luther, Zwingli, and the Anabaptists. Ernst Wolf, *RGG*, III:1690-1. Ed.]

accommodation between them impossible even if Luther and his followers had been more patient.

The Basic Beliefs of the Anabaptists
The following points basically separated the two groups:
1. Luther based his teaching on the doctrine of the justification of man before God without the Law by faith *alone*. What one-sidedness and exaggeration this teaching led to is well-known. The Anabaptists, without denying in any way the doctrine of justification by faith, taught with the greatest conviction that faith cannot be separated from works, indeed, that in a true Christian life faith's fruit must be evident. For this reason they placed the greatest stress on following Christ and on the fulfillment of his commands.
2. Luther denied absolutely the free will of humanity and saw human nature as completely corrupted. The Anabaptists explained that humanity has free will to choose between God and sin, and that human nature has the potential to incline toward the good. They did not deny the necessity of God's grace, but explained that it is the free will of humanity to accept or reject the grace of God.
3. Luther organized a state church, and taught that even in church matters one must obey the authorities. The Anabaptists insisted on a restoration of the early church order and opposed a state church just as they opposed a papist church. The state should not become involved in questions of faith among its citizens, but rather follow the principle of *complete religious tolerance and freedom of conscience*. All human considerations in matters of faith should also be ignored. The Bible remains the sole authority in matters of faith and life. The teachings of the Bible should not merely be translated into dogmatic assertions in order to exercise one's reason, but instead one *should believe them from the heart, love them, and live according to them*.
4. In contrast to the sacramental teaching of Luther, Anabaptists taught that baptism and communion do not mediate grace, but rather are only external symbols. But because Christ instructed that these arrangements should be followed, the church should faithfully practice them in his memory. *Baptism* should not be offered to children, but only to those who

prove their repentance by the renewal of their lives, confess their faith before the congregation, and request baptism. *Baptism is not regeneration*, but the "covenant of a good conscience before God" (1 Peter 3:21),[6] and a covenantal sign of admittance into the Christian church. Communion should be celebrated in memory of Christ's death on the cross, and as a sign that the congregation is, and will remain, "*the spiritual body, of which Jesus Christ is the head.*"[7]

These are the primary points in the teachings of the Anabaptists. Others follow as a consequence of these. Thus, church discipline derives from a view of the church as striving to be a community of saints[8] and therefore the church must be in a position to ban those who deny the spirit of Christ in their walk. Furthermore, the oath is rejected for it stands in contradiction to the express command of Christ in the Sermon on the Mount. Likewise, the nonresistance (*Wehrlosigkeit*) of the Christian is taught because it is not right for a disciple of Christ to use the sword, though this principle was not common to all early Anabaptists. Finally, they taught that everyone owes obedience to the state, since God ordained such, but no Christian should accept a state office because, in so doing, he would become the servant of revenge. The same applies to disputes over material possessions, taking matters to court or sitting in judgment of others. For it is seemly to behave as brothers within the congregation in the case of a complaint of one against the other. Also, the church must care for the poor, the widows, and the orphans in their midst, just as the congregations of the Apostles had done.

We are not concerned here with determining which teachings are more scriptural or correct. We only want to show that there were differences between Luther and the Anabaptists, which at *that time*, due to the emphasis put on *doctrine* by Wittenberg, made their positions irreconcilable.

---

[6][Modern translations do not translate ἐπερώτημα as covenant. The NRSV, for example, reads "an appeal to God for a good conscience." Ed.]

[7][See Eph. 4:15-16. Ed.]

[8]Anabaptists did not use the word "saints" in the sense of "sinless," but in the meaning of Paul, who addressed his church members as "saints."

Likewise, it was impossible to find common ground between the Anabaptists and *Zwingli* due to his insistence on a state church, Anabaptists' strict church discipline, and the controversy over infant or adult baptism.

The decision by both Lutheran and Reformed governmental authorities, supported by the leaders of the new churches, to continue the struggle against the Rebaptizers by means of physical coercion and bloody persecution will always remain a dark shadow over the great history of the Reformation, even though the majority of Anabaptist martyrs were found in Catholic lands.

The History of the Anabaptist Movement

The history of the Anabaptist movement during the Reformation had three phases, a *Swiss*, a *South German*, and a *Dutch* phase. The first two occurred in the 1520s and to some degree they merged. The Dutch period began in 1530.

It is known, as indicated above, that already in the Middle Ages there were evangelical congregations. Mainly from the time of persecution of the Waldensians, we find scattered groups of "Brothers" in Switzerland, Germany, and the Low Countries. They attempted as much as possible to stay in touch with each other, while keeping their faith secret due to persecution, and could only fellowship together in secret. Some of these "Brothers" joined Luther when he shook off the yoke of papal authority, but others did not. They hesitated because of their old-evangelical tradition. All the same, a number of outstanding leaders of the Anabaptists came from their ranks.[9]

---

[9][Here Mannhardt is following a theory put forward by Ludwig Keller (1849-1915) that more recent scholarship has discredited. Keller was an archivist who worked in the Prussian state archives in Münster and Berlin. His extensive publications on Anabaptists were among the first to point to their broader significance for the Reformation. Hans Denk was his favorite among the Anabaptists and Keller's thesis that Anabaptists learned their understanding of the Gospel from the Waldensians was controversial even in his day. Keller proposed the term "old-evangelical" as an umbrella term for the medieval sects and Anabaptist groups that he argued shared a common set of theological principles. His powerful articulation of renewed Mennonite significance in German society made him an intellectual force in

Swiss and South German Leaders are Executed
The Swiss movement began in Zurich and won adherents in all the Swiss cantons. The congregation at Zurich was led by *Conrad Grebel*, the son of a Zurich patrician, and by *Felix Manz*, who also came from a leading family. Besides these, there was the former monk, *Georg Blaurock*, and a priest, *Wilhelm Reublin*, who were active among the Swiss Anabaptists. After a failed attempt to reconcile Zwingli and the Anabaptists, the Zurich Town Council took measures to punish the Anabaptists. Conrad Grebel escaped a martyr's death by succumbing to illness as the result of a long imprisonment. Felix Manz was drowned on January 5, 1527. Both men had a good education, having studied in Paris and Basel. Manz was the first sixteenth-century Swiss martyr. With Manz' death in 1527 a long series of martyrdoms began in Switzerland and the neighboring countries, especially among the Anabaptists on account of their faith. Blaurock was driven out of Switzerland and burned at the stake in 1529 in Clausen, Tirol. The book by A. Brons, *Origin, Development and Fate of the Anabaptists*, details the stories of the Swiss Anabaptists, some of whom were led to Moravia by Jacob Hutter.[10]

Among the south German Anabaptists, who, incidentally, had close contact with the Swiss Brethren, the most important are *Hans Denk, Dr. Balthasar Hubmaier, Michael Sattler,* and *Ludwig Haetzer*. Their writings, insofar as we still have them, are worth reading, and demonstrate better than anything else that the charges hurled against them are false. Especially the noble Denk, of whom it may justly be said that in many things he was

---

German Mennonite circles in the 1880s and early 1890s. Anna Brons' history of the Mennonites, for example, owed much to Keller's ideas. See Mary Sprunger, "Anna Brons and Ludwig Keller: Partners for Historical Renewal," Christian Neff, "Keller, Ludwig," *ME* III:162-3; Robert Friedmann, "Keller, Ludwig, and the Mennonites," *ME* III:163-4; Snyder, *Anabaptist History*, 441, and Friesen, *History and Renewal*, 41-146. Ed.]

[10]It is a painful fact that in so-called "free" Switzerland the hateful persecution of Anabaptists continued the longest. As late as the eighteenth century they were sent to the galleys, and in 1811 twenty-seven children of Mennonites in Bern were forcibly baptized by order of the authorities and dragged into the state church by the police.

ahead of his time, left a number of excellent writings, among them the booklet *Concerning True Love*,[11] which was especially highly regarded by the Brethren.

Denk was also known in the North as a spiritual leader of the Anabaptists, and his writings were much read. He was born in Bavaria around 1495, and beginning in 1523 was prorector[12] of the Sebald School in Nürnberg. Driven from his post by Lutheran ministers and the city council, he went to Augsburg in 1525, where he met Dr. Hubmaier. Together they led the sizable local Anabaptist congregation. In 1526 he was expelled from Augsburg and went to Strasbourg, only to be banned to Worms. In the summer of 1527 he returned once more to Augsburg to lead a large conference of Anabaptists. He died in October of the same year in Basel at the age of thirty-two. His early death saved him from the fate of his friends who died as martyrs in succeeding years. Among them Dr. Balthasar Hubmaier was the most notable. In 1519 he had openly sided with the Reformation when he was cathedral preacher in Regensburg. Previously he had been prorector at the University of Ingolstadt. The Catholic cathedral chapter took his position away from him and he withdrew to the small town of Waldshut in Baden. Here he met the Swiss Wilhelm Reublin, and, together with a large portion of the population, joined the Anabaptists, since his evangelical outlook, especially as regards the question of freedom of the will, agreed completely with the Anabaptist position. He was soon driven out of Waldshut, and found a refuge in Moravia. Here the lord of Nicholsberg, Leonhard von Liechtenstein, joined the Anabaptists and offered them protection. In 1527 Hubmaier participated in the great synod of Anabaptists in Augsburg, which is called the Martyr Synod in the Chronicle of the Moravian Anabaptists.[13] In 1528 the emperor had him arrested and forcibly brought to Vienna,

---

[11][Available in English in Clarence Bauman, ed. and trans., *The Spiritual Legacy of Hans Denk* (New York: E. J. Brill, 1991), 178-203. Ed.]

[12][A joint administrative and teaching position. Ed.]

[13][*Great Chronicle: The Chronicle of the Hutterian Brethren* (Rifton, NY: Plough Publishing House, 1987). Ed.]

where he was burned at the stake, while his faithful wife, who had accompanied him, was drowned.

The other prominent south German Anabaptist leaders who suffered martyrdom are *Ludwig Haetzer* and *Michael Sattler*. Along with Denk, Haetzer had translated the Old Testament prophets into German, a publication that appeared in thirteen editions in three years. He was beheaded in Constance in 1529. Michael Sattler was the highly regarded preacher of the large Anabaptist congregation in Strasbourg. On May 21, 1527, in Rothenburg on the Neckar River, he was tortured with glowing irons on orders of the bishop and then burned to death. The reformer of Strasbourg, Martin Bucer, said Sattler was "a dear friend of God, although he was a leader of the Anabaptists."[14] And the other Strasbourg reformer, Wolfgang Capito, testified:

> One should not suppose of Michael and his followers that they are blasphemers of God, unless one counts as blaspheming that the poor people have resolved to avoid frivolity, heavy drinking, gluttony, adultery, war, murder, slander and living according to the lusts of the flesh and the ways of the world.[15]

Widespread Persecution

While the leaders of the movement were killed, their congregations were not spared either. And there were many of these. The movement's adherents in Germany in the 1520s, especially between 1525 and 1530, were much more numerous than one might think, because persecution in many places soon wiped out all the traces, and the movement in any case had been strictly peaceful and quiet. The well-known chronicler Sebastian Franck, who knew the leading Anabaptists personally, said:

---

[14][Martin Bucer, *Martin Bucers Deutsche Schriften*, ed. Robert Stupperich (Gütersloh: Gütersloher Verlagshaus Gerd Mohn, 1962), vol. 2, *Schriften der Jahre 1524-1528*, 253. Ed.]

[15][Letter of Capito to the council of Horb, May 31, 1527; Manfred Krebs and Hans Georg Rott, eds., *Quellen zur Geschichte der Täufer*, VII. Band, *Elsaß, I. Teil: Stadt Straßburg 1522-1532* (Gütersloh: Gütersloher Verlagshaus Gerd Mohn, 1959), 83.]

The movement spread so quickly, that its teaching soon covered the land and they had a great following. They attracted many good hearts who longed for God.... For they teach nothing but love, faith and the cross, were patient in much suffering, broke bread with one another as a sign of their unity and love, and faithfully helped each other.... They kept together and grew so quickly, that the world feared rebellion from them, of which, as I have heard, they were found innocent. And they were persecuted with great tyranny.[16]

In 1527 the great Anabaptist synod mentioned earlier took place in Augsburg. Here more than sixty respected men came together and consulted about a common plan of action and a common confession of faith. Dr. Keller assumes that this confession is contained in the booklet *Concerning True Love* by Hans Denk. But the peaceful and quiet spread of its pious and true Christian principles as outlined in this book were a thing of the past. The violence of the persecution not only precluded this, but also destroyed existing congregations in many places. That broke the blossom of the Anabaptist movement. As had so often occurred in the history of Christianity, here too secular authority was misused to suppress those who had committed no other crime but to take Christian positions on the basis of the Gospels that differed from those of the ruling church authorities. Luther gave an example in word, deed, and song of the courageous faith demonstrated by followers of the Gospels in the Reformation period and this faith also motivated the unfortunate Anabaptists. Many witnesses give moving testimony regarding the steadfastness of the multitude led to their deaths. A Lutheran preacher in the Palatinate, Johannes Odenbach, in 1528 wrote, in a *Letter and Advice to the established judges concerning the prisoners at Alzey, who are called Rebaptizers,*

---

[16][Sebastian Franck, *Chronica* (Darmstadt: Wissenschaftliche Buchgesellschaft, 1969), 3rd book, folio 193. Ed.]

You have treated thieves, murderers and evil-doers with more pity in prison than these poor ones. They have let themselves be baptized for the second time to the honor of God and to no one's harm, for the sake of a small error. If you kill them, people will say of them: 'Look at the great patience, love and devotion with which these pious people have died, how courageously they withstood the world. They have not been overcome with truth, but with force, and they are holy martyrs of God.'[17]

The noble and pious Catherine Zell, wife of the admirable Matthäus Zell, who, together with Bucer and Capito, introduced the Reformation in Strasbourg, wrote in a letter to the Protestant leaders:

The poor Anabaptists, about whom you are so angry and upon whom you set the authorities everywhere, like hunters with their hounds upon a boar or a rabbit, they but confess Christ as we do.... Should we thus persecute them, and Christ in them, whom they confess with zeal, and many among them have confessed unto misery, prison, fire and water? Instead *you should take the blame*, since we are the cause in teaching and life that they have separated from us. The authorities should punish whoever does evil, but one should not force and rule faith as you think. Faith belongs to the hearts and consciences, not to the outer person.... And that the old Mattäus Zell did not do but rather

---

[17]The intervention of this courageous man affected nothing. Once the Catholic and Protestant rulers in 1529 at the Speyer Reichstag had decided to kill all Rebaptizers, the Landgrave Ludwig [of the Palatinate] had more than 300 executed in short order. Especially his administrator of Alzey, Dietrich von Schönberg, had all the imprisoned Anabaptists, men and women of all ages, beheaded, burned, and drowned. [Mannhardt's quotation of Odenbach here is a rather free paraphrase of the original text. See Manfred Krebs, ed., *Quellen zur Geschichte der Täufer*, IV. Band, *Baden und Pfalz* (Gütersloh: C. Bertelsmann, 1951), 133-135.]

he gathered his sheep and did not disband them. He also disagreed with what was done, but watched with a sad heart and serious mien when the scholars also did the same with the authorities, and he said openly from his pulpit in the company of preachers: 'I take God, Heaven and earth as witnesses that I wish to be innocent of the persecution and crucifixion of these poor people.'[18]

But such voices were rare and echoed unheard in the storm of emotions. It is humbling to think that the confessors of the Gospel, authorities and clergy, participated in the extermination of the innocents. Only Duke Philipp of Hesse courageously refused to execute anyone in his lands "on account of their faith." Only a few Anabaptists from the blossoming congregations in southern Germany escaped the fury of persecution. They are the forerunners of the small congregations still extant there today. Robbed of their leaders, they lived separated from the world but in quiet communion with each other on isolated mountaintops or hidden in the masses of the cities, until milder times brought toleration. Some Swiss and German refugees found a new home in Moravia, where their settlements attained a high level of respect until the Jesuits drove them out,[19] together with the Bohemian/Moravian Brethren, during the Thirty Years War.

Dutch Anabaptists and the Upheaval in Münster
As they had done in Switzerland and Germany, the Anabaptists early in the Reformation founded congregations in the *Low Countries* with the same evangelical principles. There was also correspondence between these groups from early times.[20]

---

[18][Elsie Ann McKee, *Katharina Schütz Zell*, vol. 2, *The Writings: A Critical Edition* (Leiden: Brill, 1999), 209, 212. Ed.]

[19][Mannhardt is referring to the Hutterites here. Ed.]

[20]This is proven especially by a letter that the Swiss Anabaptists wrote to the Low Country brethren in 1522. [Mannhardt seems to have gotten the idea of a 1522 letter from Anna Brons, *Ursprung* (1884), 58. Brons' source for this claim is not known. Such an early connection between Swiss and Dutch proto-Anabaptists is not supported by current historical research. Ed.]

The strong desire for improvement of the church in the Low Countries was fed by the scattered Waldensians and greatly encouraged by the first writings of Luther. But under the heavy pressure of the Catholic government there could not be quick change to a new church structure. Indeed, "Protestants" were everywhere, but only a few were inclined to the church of Luther, just as somewhat later in the Low Countries the church did not become Lutheran. As early as the 1520s many were inclined to accept Anabaptist principles. But only after 1530, when in Switzerland and Germany persecution had done its bloody work, did the main arena of Anabaptism transfer to the Low Countries. Here too new leaders emerged, among whom there was soon a deep division. Around that time many Anabaptists were found in the Dutch cities. In Amsterdam and elsewhere they called themselves Confederates (*Bundesgenossen*). Others simply called themselves "Brethren," as in Germany. It is assumed that the latter name comes from the Waldensian tradition, while the former were followers of Melchior Hoffmann. He was a German Anabaptist who, after long activity in Latvia and as a preacher in Kiel, had joined the Anabaptists in Strasbourg and since 1529 had been active in Emden.[21] Melchior Hoffmann was a quiet, pious man, far removed from the violent creation of an external Kingdom of God. He tended, however, to a fantastic interpretation of the Old Testament, especially of the Prophets, and thereby confused some of his followers and left the simple foundation of the Gospel. And in the early 1530s fanatics like Jan Matthijsz of Haarlem, who held to the Old Testament and wanted to erect the Kingdom of God on earth by force, became active. Contrary to the teaching of the Anabaptists, who preached patience and suffering of injustice, these blinded ones preached that, according to the will of God, force should arise against force, and that where the authorities persecuted the "children of God," the latter should gird their loins with the sword of Gideon and overthrow them. Instead of the Kingdom of Peace

---

[21]Melchior Hoffmann, after serving a growing congregation in Emden and appointing a successor, returned to Strasbourg in 1533, where he was jailed for ten years until death released him.

of Jesus Christ they wished to establish a "new Israel" in which the revenge of Jehovah would be carried out by the elect. Beside Matthijsz, the tailor Jan Bockelson of Leyden preached in this manner. It is no wonder that this preaching was eagerly accepted by the many unsatisfied and exploited. When the same Jan van Leyden, together with his colleagues and with the help of the Lutheran preacher Bernhard Rothmann, took power in the Westphalian city of Münster, he attracted many persecuted and harried Anabaptists. Although his teaching was in almost all points the opposite of the evangelical Christian principles of the Anabaptists, perhaps this contrast had an effect on those who believed that God had removed his hand from them, and that the dark, Old Testament examples were now intended to show them the right way to battle against the powers of this world.

Around 1533 the Low German publication *On Revenge* came out of Münster, and was eagerly read.[22] And the so-called Batenburg Gang, consisting of Münsterites, began to attack Catholic churches and profane the cause of the Gospel by violence.

In contrast with these fanatics moderate Anabaptists remained firmly grounded on their principles, specifically that a Christian could not spread or defend their faith with the sword, that the Kingdom of God is a spiritual, invisible kingdom, and that disciples of Christ could only withstand the opposition of the world by patience and self-sacrifice.

In those dangerous times between 1533 and 1535 there were two men in particular who knew how to keep the brethren of Holland on the right path, namely, *Jacob van Campen*, preacher of the Anabaptist congregation in Amsterdam, and *Obbe Philips* of Leeuwarden. While *David Joris* of Delft and his followers, and some disciples of Melchior Hoffmann formed separate congregations which soon dissolved, these two pious men became the instruments through which God's hand protected the majority of the Dutch Anabaptists from the false paths of the fanatics.

---

[22]["Bericht von der Wrake." See Robert Stupperich, ed., *Die Schriften Bernhard Rothmanns* (Münster i. W.: Aschendorffsche Verlagsbuchhandlung, 1970), 284-297. Ed.]

And His spirit had already awakened the man who would become a leader and strong bulwark after the pitiful end of the false prophets of Münster and during the time of renewed persecution. Since the time of Münster, the name Rebaptizer had become synonymous with revolution. Both Catholic and Protestant authorities would take a person to court if they heard that he opposed infant baptism, even if he was the quietest and most pious Christian. But no imperial mandates, which became ever more drastic, nor torture or executions, were able to destroy the congregations. Many, indeed, went to prison and to their deaths, but they, like their brothers and sisters in Switzerland and in south Germany, bore their martyrdom with courage as noble examples of faith in God and true Christian patience (*Gelassenheit*) in suffering.[23] Many, indeed, were driven from their home and hearth, and moved from place to place in northern Germany, seeking any place where they could live quietly by the work of their hands and look after themselves and their families. And when, amidst the hardships of such a pilgrimage their courage waned, then they comforted one another with the words of Him who bore His Cross before them: "Blessed are you when people revile you and persecute you and utter all kinds of evil against you falsely on my account. Rejoice and be glad, for your reward is great in heaven."[24]

The man who became the leader of these scattered people was *Menno Simons*.

---

[23]See Thieleman J. van Braght, *The Bloody Theatre or Martyrs Mirror*, Amsterdam, 1660 and 1685, and A. Brons, *Ursprung*, 28ff.

[24][Matthew 5:11-12a. Ed.]

Menno Simons (according to Jacobus Burghart 1683)

2
Menno Simons

Against Jan van Leyden

In May of 1535 a publication appeared in Holland with the title: "A Plain and Clear Proof from Scripture, Proving that Jesus Christ is the Real, Spiritual David of Promise, the King of Kings against the Great and Fearful Blasphemy of Jan van Leyden."[1] This tract was dedicated "to all the *Brethren* and *Covenanters* dispersed here and there."[2] The author of this tract, which was read eagerly and thankfully by the Anabaptists, was the priest *Menno Simons* from the Frisian village of Witmarsum.

How did this man, who at the time had himself not become a "Brother or Covenanter," come to write such a tract in the spirit of the Anabaptists? We find the answer in his own narrative of his "Departure from the Roman Catholic Church."[3]

Menno was born in the village of Witmarsum in West Friesland in 1492,[4] and he had become a Catholic priest in the neighboring village of Pingjum in 1516. Here he worked together with two other priests, one of whom was above him in the hierarchy, while the other was subject to him. "These two men and I," he tells us, "spent our daily life in gaming and drinking and other idle pursuits with others, as is the case with such godless people."

He was awakened from this thoughtless life by the idea that occurred to him at Mass, that the wine and bread that he held in his hands could not be the flesh and blood of Christ. That seemed to him to be the voice of temptation, but he resisted it in vain. He could find no peace until he turned to the New

---

[1] [*The Complete Works of Menno Simons*, trans. Leonard Verduin, ed. J. C. Wenger (Scottdale, PA: Herald Press, 1956), 31-50. Ed.]

[2] [Thus the work was addressed to the followers of Melchoir Hoffmann, who were also known as Melchoirites. Ed.]

[3] [Often reprinted as a separate tract under this title (*Ausgang aus dem Papsttum*), it was originally published as part of "Reply to Gellius Faber" in *Complete Works of Menno Simons*, 668-74. Ed.]

[4] [Mannhardt was apparently unaware of Karel Vos' 1914 Dutch language biography, *Menno Simons 1496-1561*, that settled the debate over Menno's year of birth; Walter Klaassen, "Menno Simons Research 1837-1937, 1986-1990," in *Menno Simons: A Reappraisal*, Gerald R. Brunk, ed. (Harrisonburg, VA: Eastern Mennonite College, 1992), 185. Ed.]

Testament, which he had never before held in his hands. Now he realized that the church teaching concerning Communion was false. As he was reading Luther's early writings at the same time, he became convinced that "human laws cannot condemn us to eternal death."[5] With that, Menno's separation from the Catholic Church was complete. Naturally, his conviction was reflected in his sermons, which soon drew large congregations, since Menno became reputed as one who "preached the Word of God and was a free man." Neither he nor his hearers seemed to have been affected by the growing persecution, probably because they did not leave the old Church in spite of their evangelical views. For many, these views may only have been matters of the intellect, which did not affect their heart and life. That was the case with Menno himself, who did not even think about leaving the Church, but instead took a better position as a priest in Witmarsum, although by his further Bible studies he became more alienated from the teachings of the Roman Church.

The execution of a respected man, Sicke Freerks, caused Menno to reflect on baptism. Sicke was beheaded in Leeuwarden in 1531 for "renewing his baptism." After he studied the Bible and consulted the Reformers Luther,[6] Bucer, and Bullinger,[7] receiving different answers from each, Menno had to admit that infant baptism did not square with Scripture. Through this and other new insights he became a follower of the Anabaptists, while still unfortunately maintaining his secure pastorate, because he did not wish to be exposed to persecution. This meanwhile was becoming ever more severe. Among others, a very prominent and respected man, *Andries Claessen*, was executed as an Anabaptist and had all his goods confiscated, so that his widow with seven children was robbed of all that she had and abandoned to the misery of poverty.

---

[5][*Complete Works of Menno Simons*, 668. Ed.]

[6]Luther taught that little children should be baptized on account of the faith they already have, acknowledging thereby the necessity of faith preceding baptism, something his contemporary followers deny.

[7][Martin Bucer (1491-1551) was the most influential Reformer of Strasbourg. Heinrich Bullinger (1504-1575) led the Reformation in Zürich after 1531 when Zwingli was killed in battle. Ed.]

When the advance guard of Jan van Leyden came from Münster in 1534 and moved about with their cry for revenge against the authorities, the executions of imprisoned Anabaptists became more frequent. No wonder then that for many the fanatical call for revenge by the Münsterites generated a favorable response. These people held mighty speeches, where possible in public, in which they proclaimed their supposedly godly message, and then came secretly into the homes of these fearful ones and tried to win them with tempting promises. In vain Menno warned against these seducers; he even debated with one of them to no end. Indeed it was said afterward that he had "gracefully stopped up their mouths," but still many were blinded by passion and followed the seducers.

And thus it happened that on February 18, 1535, a crowd of 300 men with wives and children took the Bloemkamp monastery, not far from Witmarsum, and with the courage of desperation defended it against the army of the Governor of Friesland, who nonetheless took it again on April 7 after a frightful bloodbath.[8]

Confession and Conversion

This event hit Menno's soul like a ton of bricks and his conscience accused him of not having done enough to keep these blinded folk from their folly. He felt guilty before God for the blood of the victims, who included his own brother. From then on a change occurred in Menno. God led him through the depths of contrition to the heights of faith in divine grace. While in the state of self-condemnation, and humbled before the mighty hand of God, he saw his self-justification crumble, and his heart for the first time was gripped by the truth of the Gospel which to that point had only been of intellectual interest. His soul now learned to understand the words of the Savior: "Whoever believes in me has eternal life."[9] Now his life was dedicated to the true service of the Gospel; now he prayed daily to God to "create a pure heart in him and grant him

---

[8][Modern scholars refer to the monastery as Oldeklooster and date the battle to March. Snyder. *Anabaptist History*, 149. Ed.]

[9][Mannhardt's paraphrase of John 3:16b. Ed.]

wisdom, spirit, candor and a manly heart, so that he could preach His name and His holy word unadulterated and make known His truth to the glory of God."[10]

First, he wrote the article against Jan of Leyden mentioned earlier. Then he resigned his position, after he had untiringly preached repentance and renewal of the inner life from his pulpit for several months. For almost a year he lived quietly and withdrawn, in poor circumstances. He visited his followers secretly, a messenger of peace, who comforted them and gave them courage in their time of doubt. At the same time he studied the Scriptures incessantly, and also wrote several small articles in which he expressed his convictions, and which he later published.

Persecution and Flight out of Holland

In the meantime new events had taken place that would have a great influence on the fate of the Anabaptists. The kingdom of Jan van Leyden in Münster collapsed pitiably, as Menno had foreseen. The small remnant of his followers were present at a meeting of various Anabaptist groups in Bocholt in Westphalia, but the Anabaptists led by Obbe Philips wanted nothing to do with them.

Of these pious followers of Obbe Philips, some six or eight came to Menno Simons early in 1537 and begged him "to take to heart the great hardship and suffering of these harried souls"[11] and accept the role of elder for their congregation.

Menno heard this petition with a heavy heart, but he had to acknowledge that he would not be able to turn them away because these pious and faithful souls greatly desired to find a leader whom they could fully trust. Based on his experiences and writings, Menno appeared to them to be such a leader.

"In this way," he himself tells us, "I was not called by the Münsterites or any other seditious sect as it is falsely reported concerning me, but I have been called, though unworthy, *to this office by the people who had subjected themselves to Christ and His Word, led a penitent life in the fear of God, served their neighbors in love, bore the*

---

[10][*Complete Works of Menno Simons*, 671. Ed.]
[11][Ibid., Ed.]

cross, sought the welfare and the good of all men, loved righteousness and truth and abhorred wickedness and unrighteousness."[12]

He was consecrated as elder of the congregation of Groningen by Obbe Philips, and remained there until 1541. During that time he married Gertrud. He led his congregation steadily and faithfully, and soon earned high respect from other congregations, especially due to his many edifying writings, which were written in a popular style and thus found many readers. His most important colleagues at this time were Leenaert Bouwens and Dirk Philips, Obbe's brother.

Naturally, the eyes of the authorities were soon turned to Menno. Even before 1539 he was not able to teach or preach publicly, but only conduct secret visits to his own in the various areas where congregations existed. Soon several of those who had given him shelter or had been baptized by him were executed. In 1541 the court of Holland wrote to the state governor, saying: "The Anabaptists would have been long since eliminated were it not for a certain priest, Menno Simons, constantly prowling about." It was therefore proposed that imprisoned Anabaptists who showed some remorse should be released on the condition that they turn Menno in to the authorities. In the following year Emperor Charles V posted a reward of 100 Karlguilders for the arrest of Menno.

Emden, Cologne, the Baltics, and Wismar

In 1543 Menno went to Emden, where the Reformation had been introduced, and where the Duchess Anna, the ruler of East Friesland, tolerated the Anabaptists. The Brethren had called Menno for a disputation with John á Lasco, the leader of the Reformed church there. This disputation, like all such affairs, was without a successful conclusion since the opponents were unable to convince each other. Starting in 1545 we find Menno in Cologne, working among the Brethren there, who were tolerated by the local prince, Hermann von Wied, who supported Protestantism. When von Wied died in 1546, his successor drove out all non-Catholics. Menno moved to

---

[12][Ibid., 672. Ed.]

Wismar, where he found a fairly safe place of refuge with his
followers.

Menno did not remain inactive there but traveled around
everywhere where he expected to find scattered Anabaptists, in
order to gather them in congregations. In addition to several
trips to the west, to Emden and Holland, he also went eastward,
and, together with his friend Dirk Philips, visited the cities on
the Baltic Sea, where he found Anabaptists who had fled
Moravia, Switzerland, South Germany, and the Low Countries.
On October 7, 1549, he wrote a letter from Wismar to the
congregations he had gathered in Prussia, probably those in and
near Danzig, Thorn/Toruń, Elbing/Elbląg ·and
Graudenz/Grudziądz. This document, entitled "Exhortation to
a Church in Prussia,"[13] proves that Menno himself initiated the
first beginnings of our West Prussian congregations. In 1555 he
also had to leave Wismar. The six Lutheran Hanseatic cities,[14]
Hamburg, Lüneburg, Lübeck, Rostock, Wismar, and Stralsund,
decided that no one other than Lutherans would be tolerated
within their walls.

Wüstenfelde

Now the aging Menno with his followers found a last refuge
with a nobleman of Holstein, Count Bartholomäus von
Ahlefeldt, who allowed the Anabaptists to found a small colony,
Wüstenfelde, on his estate, called Fresenburg, near Oldesloe.
Von Ahlefeldt had earlier been in military service in Holland,
and had been a witness of the pious steadfastness of Anabaptist
martyrs. Here Menno was able to set up a small print shop,
which enabled him to issue new editions of his earlier writings
and several new ones. Here, too, the Anabaptist leaders from
southern Germany met with him in order to discuss matters of
doctrine and congregational polity. Unfortunately, his last years,
when he was free of persecution, were troubled by differences

---

[13]A hand-written German translation of this letter is preserved in the
Mennonite Church of Thiensdorf-Markushof/Jezioro-Markusy in
Marienburg/Malbork county.

[14][The Hanseatic League was a confederation of mostly north German
trading cities who cooperated on trade and defense issues. Ed.]

concerning the use of the ban[15] in the congregations. As painful as this must have been for him to disagree so strongly with other leaders, this nevertheless demonstrates for us the absolute independence of individuals even in the face of Menno's moral authority. Obviously he did not occupy a domineering position with regard to the Brethren nor ever aspired to such a position.

On January 13, 1559, the tired soldier of God went to his reward in Wüstenfelde.[16] His grave remains unknown to us. The prosperous little colony that Menno and his co-workers had established was destroyed during the Thirty Years' War.[17] The village of Wüstenfelde, where once these peaceful people lived from the industrious work of their hands, cannot be found. But Menno's name has not been forgotten by his followers. The congregations that bear his name are the living memorial of his work and they remember with gratitude the rich blessings that came to their forefathers from him.

From Menno's Writings
Beneath the beautiful copper engraving by Petrus Grooten, made more than 200 years ago from the oil painting of Menno Simons by Jacobus Burghart,[18] we find the following words:

On this copper plate you may read, dear reader,
What the appearance of Menno was.
But if you wish to see the gifts of his spirit,
You must go without prejudice to his works.
There you will see the finger of God without a doubt,
With which it pleased him to strengthen this worthy man

---

[15]The ban meant the excommunication of unworthy members from the congregation.
[16][The accepted death date for Menno is now 1561. Klaassen, "Menno Simons Research," 185. Ed.]
[17][1618-1648. Ed.]
[18]The plate is in the possession of the Hamburg-Altona Mennonite Church. Since Hermann Brams made a copy in Norden in 1889, the acquisition of this reproduction is highly recommended. [See also Piet Visser and Mary Sprunger, *Menno Simons: Places, Portraits and Progeny* (Altona, Manitoba: Friesens; Morgantown, PA: Masthof Press, 1996), 80-1. Ed.]

And stand by him. He was a faithful servant
In the work of his Lord, and lived simply and justly.

As stiff and unpoetic as these lines may be, they are right in pointing out to us that we should not part from this picture until we have looked more closely at his teachings and writings.

According to Professor de Hoop Scheffer of Amsterdam,[19] there were, among the non-Catholic writers in Holland before 1550, none who had written as many religious articles as Menno, and none who had achieved such a popular style. Thus Menno met the needs of his time perfectly.

In his doctrine Menno stood on the same ground as the brotherhood that he joined, and the basic principles of the Anabaptists described in the first chapter were also his. But since he was not simply a teacher, passing on accepted truths, but rather someone who had experienced a conversion accompanied by inner struggles, a conversion granted by the divine power of the Gospel to those who believe in it, thus it was natural that the center of his teaching and admonition was focused on the necessity of the *new* birth, the *new* life, and the *new* walk of the Christian. For this reason his devotional writings are more attractive than his writings on doctrine.

For only by new life and not by new teachings can such persons become spiritual leaders of others. One cannot give others to drink from the fount of eternal life if one has not dipped into it oneself and filled one's soul with the powers of healing from sin and death.

Menno was such a man. When those men of Groningen stepped into his quiet room to ask him to become the elder of their congregation, he asked for time to think and pray for certainty, as to whether it was the will of God to follow this call.

---

[19][Jacob Gijsbert de Hoop Scheffer (1819-1894) was a Mennonite pastor in the Netherlands and professor at the Mennonite seminary in Amsterdam. He published a number of articles about Menno in the Dutch Mennonite journal *Doopsgezinde Bijdragen*. Klaassen, "Menno Simons Research," 183-4. Ed.]

And indeed a voice spoke to his heart, calling to him, as it had to Paul long ago: "Woe is me, if I do not preach the Gospel."[20]

Painfully, he recognized that Luther's teaching concerning the justification of man before God by faith alone led many people of that time to continue their godless lives. "The followers of Luther," he exclaimed, "often misuse his name and teaching when they believe that faith alone can save us, without the addition of works, which must proceed from a genuine faith." "They also say: God be praised, now we have become aware that our works do not count, but only Jesus' blood and death can atone for our sins and wash them away, and they sing: The bond is broken and we are free!, and whoever sings this rhyme with them is a free evangelical person who can live as he may. But if someone comes and seeks to admonish them in love and point them to the teaching and example of Christ, he must hear that he is a 'works-saint,' a 'gatecrasher of heaven,' a dissembler and Anabaptist."[21]

For this reason it was the primary concern for Menno to use his gifts of writing and speaking to work toward a *true Christian life* and toward the root of this new life, *the new birth through the Spirit*. Already in 1538 he wrote the three small pieces: "The Spiritual Resurrection," "The New Birth," and "The True Christian Faith."[22]

God cannot save you, nor forgive your sins if you do not *repent, believe in Him, are born again in Him*, if you

---

[20] [I Cor. 9:16, *Complete Writings of Menno Simons*, 672. Ed.]

[21] [From "True Christian Faith" in *Complete Writings of Menno Simons*, 333-4. Ed.]

[22] The latter two are included in the booklet "Voices of the Reformation Period," which also includes other writings of his. Many copies of this book are still available from the church board of the Danzig Mennonite Church. [The book referred to here is *Stimmen aus der Reformationszeit: Gendenkblätter zum dreihundertjährigen Todestage Menno Symons den 13. Januar 1861*, edited by H. G. Mannhardt's uncle and predecessor as pastor, Jakob Mannhardt. The dates of authorship of the three essays mentioned are listed respectively as c. 1536, c. 1537, and c. 1541 in *Complete Writings of Menno Simons*. Ed.]

do not do what Christ has commanded, and walk as
He walked.[23]

It will be of no use to us to be called Christians and
boast in the Lord's death, blood and saving work, as
long as we live a godless life.... What will it help, if we
speak much of Christ and His word, if we do not
believe Him and strive to live according to His word.
Begin a repentant life, for Christ says: If you do not
repent, you must all die! That does not mean a
repentance as taught by the world, with hypocritical
works (fasting, pilgrimages, etc.); *we are speaking of a
repentance of vigor and deed*. (From the *Foundation of
Christian Doctrine*)[24]

For Menno a repentant life is a life lived in the mind and
spirit of Jesus Christ. Against the foolish statement that one
cannot fulfill the laws of Christ – words which provide cover
for all manner of caprice and libertinism – he says that the life
of one reborn and repentant from within consists of a constant
striving to fulfill Christ's law in the battle against sin, world, and
one's own weakness, and of following after Him. The vision of
these children of God and the goal of their strivings he
describes in the following wonderful words:

They are subjects of a spiritual king who rules them
with His spirit and word. He clothes them with His
righteousness. He satisfies them with the living water
of His spirit and feeds them with the bread of life. His
name is *Jesus Christ*.

They are the children of peace, who have turned
their swords into plowshares and their spears to
sickles, and know war no more. (Isaiah 2:4) They give
to Caesar what is his and to God what is His. Their
sword is the sword of the Spirit, which they can wield
with a good conscience through the Holy Spirit. Their
kingdom is the kingdom of the grace of God. Their

---

[23][Apparently a paraphrase of *Complete Writings of Menno Simons*, 392. Ed.]
[24][*Complete Writings of Menno Simons*, 110-1. Ed.]

citizenship is in Heaven, and they use the things of earth, eating and drinking, clothing and shelter, thankfully, for the maintenance of their lives and in willing service to their neighbors according to the Word of the Lord. Their *doctrine* is the *unadulterated* Word of God, as witnessed by Moses and the Prophets, by Christ and his apostles. They reject whatever does not agree with it. Their baptism is given to those who *believe*, according to the command of the Lord and the teaching and usage of the holy apostles. Their *Communion* is kept as a *memorial* to the good deeds, death and resurrection of the Lord, and to awaken a true, brotherly love. Their *ban* or separation is intended for all reprobate despisers, great and small, rich and poor, regardless of status, all who, after promising faithfulness and obedience to the Word of God, again fell away and teach and live contrarily – until they are found to be contrite and repentant. Their daily complaint is about their unwilling flesh, about their many false starts and struggles. They struggle inwardly and outwardly, and as long as they remain here below they do not rest in their struggle against sin, the world, and their own flesh. They strive toward the goal placed before them, and thus prove in their actions that they believe the Word of the Lord, that the strength of Christ is within them, that they are born of God and are his children.[25]

Time and again Menno returns to the admonition that the fruits of faith must be found in the Christian life. The word of the Apostle was not the just shall live because of their *faith*, but rather the just shall *live* their faith.

Some will say: Our faith says that Jesus is the Son of God and his word is true, and that he has bought us with his blood. Also, that we have been born again

---

[25]["The New Birth," *Complete Writings of Menno Simons*, 93-4. Ed.]

in our baptism and have received the Holy Spirit, and therefore we are the rightful church, the congregation of Christ! – whereupon I answer: If your faith is as you say, why do you not do as his word has commanded you? Since you are not striving to do *what He wills*, but rather *what you will*, it is obvious enough that *you do not believe that Jesus is the Son of God*, nor that His word is the truth, *for faith and its fruits must be present together*, the truth of this assertion must be granted.

Oh, you poor, blind people, do you think it sufficient that you confess Christ according to the flesh, that you are baptized, are called Christians and are bought with Christ's blood? Oh, truly no! I repeat for you: You must be born of God, so that Christ is in you and you in Christ, or you cannot be Christians. For *whoever is in Christ is a new creature*! (2. Cor. 5:17) If you truly believe in Jesus Christ, as you claim, then prove by your lives that you do believe. For the just *lives* by faith, according to the Scripture. (Romans 1:17)[26]

Similarly, as here in the article "The New Birth," Menno again and again expresses these thoughts. It was very clear to him that the true reformation must be achieved in every individual Christian, and that no external rules, no orders or regulations would contribute anything of use. His faith in Jesus Christ did not constitute a place of rest for the soul, but rather a holy spur to follow Him in life. And this faith, which to Menno was inseparable from the new life in God, gave him the unshakable courage with which he challenged not only his congregation but also the authorities and lords, the clergy of the state churches, the common folk and the misled sects with his writings to demonstrate the seriousness of their confession of faith by their deeds and to be converted to God. Naturally, much enmity came his way as a result.

---

[26][Ibid., 96-7. Ed.]

In a series of other writings Menno set out the basic elements of the doctrine to which his brotherhood subscribed. He felt the need to demonstrate the Scriptural basis of the principles that separated the Anabaptists from the other churches. This was the chief aim of his "Foundation of Christian Doctrine" or "A Foundation and Plain Statement of the Saving Doctrine of our Lord Jesus Christ," with the motto: "For other foundation can no man lay than that which is laid, which is Jesus Christ." (1. Cor. 3:11) And after his disputations with á Lasco in Emden, and later with Micron[27] in Wismar, he published writings in which he presented his views in opposition to his adversaries. Many of these became quite polemical in the spirit of the time and therefore are not on a par with the devotional writings of Menno. This is the case especially with the lengthy polemic against Gellius Faber,[28] a text he had felt under pressure to write as a result of ridiculous attacks made by this Reformed minister of Emden.

Unfortunately, Menno adopted the bad habit of the time of disputing points of doctrine with others. Others often wished to discuss the "incarnation of Christ" with him. One can hardly imagine today to what distant matters of dogmatic speculation and wordy dialectics such topics led. Menno also wrote several articles on the topic of Christ's incarnation. One is inclined to say that he would have done better to stay with the simple principle that one should not translate the Gospel into human regulations or make logical propositions out of it. In the end he admitted that we cannot with our brooding reason conceive of the miracle of the human birth of Jesus, but rather, that we may grasp the eternal life in Christ through the power of faith.

With this confession he returned to the ground of the Anabaptist principles, which did not aspire to a new dogmatic theology. This desire was expressed especially in connection with the question of Jesus' incarnation at a very important

---

[27][Menno disputed with Martin de Cleyne from Norden, known as Micron, in Wismar in 1554. *Complete Writings of Menno Simons*, 836. Ed.]

[28][Faber had been a minister in Emden when Menno was interviewed there by John á Lasco in 1544. Faber in 1552 wrote an attack on Anabaptists prompting Menno's 1554 reply. *Complete Writings of Menno Simons*, 624. Ed.]

synod of the south German Anabaptists in Strasbourg in the year 1555.

In the old city of Strasbourg, with its many historical associations for the south German Anabaptists, fifty teachers and elders from Swabia, Moravia, Alsace, the Palatinate, and Switzerland gathered to discuss that question. There were persons among them who still bore the wounds of torture on their bodies, which they had suffered in the persecution. This honorable gathering came to the following conclusion in the true spirit of its predecessors:

> since we have (regarding the dispute about the incarnation of Christ) been building what is like a useless tower, God has confused our language, so that we do not understand one another. That has probably occurred because we were so presumptuous as to claim to know more than we should.... Therefore we confess, that from now on we want to fulfill God's law by His grace, take heed of His instructions and keep them with pure hearts, walking before Him in Godly fear and truth, for in this is the blessedness and the knowledge of God and Jesus Christ, I John 2:4,5, where we read: 'To confess you is complete piety and we attest that we have confessed Him when we keep His laws. Whoever says, I know Him and does not keep His law is a liar and the truth is not in him.'[29]

Menno and the Dutch brethren heartily agreed with this when they were told of the complete statement.

In another matter Menno was not in happy agreement with the brethren, and here the South German and Dutch in greater numbers took issue with him. This, as mentioned earlier, had to do with the use of the ban by the congregation. Indeed, he had earlier, in the article "A Kind Admonition or Instruction from the Word of God as to How a Christian Should be Disposed: Also as to Shunning and Excommunication of False Brethren"

---

[29][Mannhardt is quoting here from Anna Brons, *Ursprung*, pp. 97-98. Ed.]

expressed himself mildly on the use of the ban, saying that one should not ban the weak but only the spoiled members.

> I say to you, truly as the Lord lives, there is no external baptism or communion that is valid before Him, but only the new life from God through faith, which is love, mercy, humility, peace, and truth. Therefore take care when you see your brother sin. Do not pass him by as one who does not value his soul, but if he can be healed, help him without hesitation by loving admonition and brotherly instruction, before you eat and drink, sleep or do anything else, since you seek the welfare of his soul and so that your misled brother does not grow old and go to ruin in his sins.[30]

He wrote similarly in a number of other articles.

Later, Menno tended to stricter views concerning the ban, and due to the zeal of some very strict brothers as well as through several misunderstandings, arguments arose on this matter. These differences could not be overcome, either by a meeting in Wismar in 1554, nor by a trip by Menno to Friesland and then to Cologne, where in 1558 there was again to be a discussion of this matter. Shortly after Menno's death divisions even arose among the Anabaptists over these matters that were of rather long duration.

This incomplete survey of Menno's writings may suffice here. A complete overview may be gained by reading his works. All his works and their importance are also mentioned in the book by A. Brons, as well in shorter form in the essay by Professor de Hoop Scheffer in the *Yearbook of the Mennonite Congregations in West- and East Prussia* (1883),[31] and in Professor

---

[30][Ibid., 410-12. Ed.]

[31][*Jahrbuch der Mennoniten-Gemeinden in West- und Ostpreussen*, edited by H. G. Mannhardt, (Danzig, 1883), 74-88. Originally published in *Real-Encyklopädie für protestantische Theologie und Kirche*, edited by J. J. Herzog 2nd ed. (Leipzig: J. C. Hinrichs, 1881), 9:560-6 and in Dutch in the 1882 *Doopsgezinde Bijdragen*. See also Klaassen, "Menno Simons Research," 183-4. Ed.]

S. Cramer's article, "Menno Simons" in Herzog's *Realencyklopädie*, 3rd edition.[32]

His Character

We have no particular descriptions of Menno's *character*, but it is not difficult to imagine it. After revealing himself to be somewhat irresolute, he realized the meaning of the saying: "for it is well for the heart to be strengthened by grace." (Hebrews 13:9) He was modest and humble, and did not think much of his capabilities. But he never lacked manly decisiveness and the courage for the truth when he had to stand up for his convictions, which appeared to him to be a holy treasure both granted by God and acquired by his own effort. In dealing with others he was mild and friendly, empathetic and generous. If in his writings he used strong expressions against his opponents, he nevertheless did not demonize another's opinion, and during his life was never hard against those who believed otherwise. When in Wismar a ship with families of the Reformed Church was ice-bound and could not proceed to Emden, none of the Lutheran inhabitants of Wismar wanted to help them. But Menno, together with some friends, led them to safety on land and found shelter for them with the Brethren, a deed of love for which he was badly rewarded.[33]

Among his own congregation and in all the others he thus enjoyed the greatest love and respect, which even his enemies could not deny him. And although whoever reads his writings and considers his life and work today will not agree with Menno completely, still he will unavoidably agree with him in many points and confess that it was a high ideal of the Christian faith and life that this man envisioned and sought to realize in the world, an ideal worthy of our emulation. Whether we would

---

[32]["Menno Simons" in *Realencyklopädie für protestantische Theologie und Kirche*, edited by D. Albert Hauck, 3rd ed. (Leipzig: J. C. Hinrichs'sche Buchhandlung, 1903), 12:586-94. For commentary on this article, see Klaassen, "Menno Simons Research," 185, 187. Ed.]

[33]See A. Brons, *Ursprung*, 84. [Menno got involved in disputations with the group which both sides had promised to keep secret but were in fact later published by Menno's interlocutors. As a result, governmental pressure forced Menno to leave Wismar. Ed.]

agree with him as to the value of each method Menno used to reach that goal is not as important as the unity in the Spirit that binds us together with him and with each other.

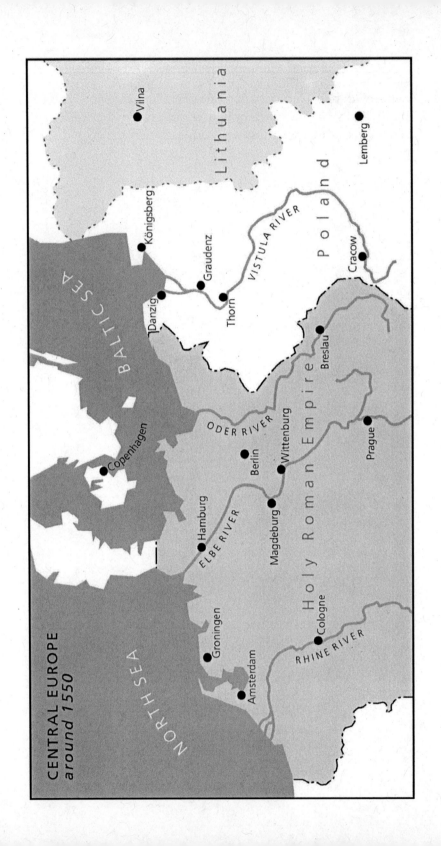

CENTRAL EUROPE
around 1550

NORTH SEA

BALTIC SEA

Copenhagen

Vilna

Lithuania

Königsberg

Graudenz

Danzig

Thorn

VISTULA RIVER

Poland

Lemberg

Cracow

Breslau

ODER RIVER

Berlin

Wittenburg

Prague

Holy Roman Empire

Hamburg

ELBE RIVER

Magdeburg

Groningen

Amsterdam

Cologne

RHINE RIVER

3
The Origin of the Mennonite Church in Danzig

Immigration from Holland

Our congregation did not emerge from the native population, but rather through the immigration of foreign Anabaptists. As early as the time between 1525 and 1529 the rumor circulated in the German Empire and the Low Countries that there might be a place of refuge in the East, in the Duchy of Prussia (East Prussia), as well as in Polish Prussia (West Prussia), for those who were being persecuted because of their Protestant faith.[1] And so it happened that first individuals and then larger groups from the Protestants of the South and West made their way eastward. The mainstream of these refugees came from the Netherlands.[2] There Emperor Charles V already on May 8, 1521, had proclaimed the first edict concerning heretics, in order to keep the Reformation out of the lands he

---

[1] [Beginning in the thirteenth century the Teutonic Order of Knights established a state in the Vistula Delta region. Early in the fourteenth century the headquarters were transferred to a new castle in Marienburg. In 1466 by the Peace of Toruń the territory was divided with the western portion ruled directly by the Polish crown and the eastern portion with the capital of Königsberg/Królewiec (modern-day Kaliningrad) ruled by the Knights who acknowledged the sovereignty of the Polish kings. The territory of the Knights was secularized in 1525 with the last Grandmaster of the order becoming the first Duke of Prussia; thus a Royal Prussia in the west and a Ducal Prussia in the east were created. The Duchy of Prussia was inherited by the Electors of Brandenburg in 1618. In 1701 the Elector Frederick III was crowned king in Königsberg because this city was outside the territory of the Holy Roman Empire whereas Berlin, his capital, was not. The Emperor did not allow new titles such as king to be created within the Empire but agreed to look the other way for Frederick's coronation outside his realm. The Elector's new designation as Frederick I, King in Prussia, became his most prominent title, thereby affixing the name of Prussia as the single most important label for his state. Only after the first partition of Poland in 1772 between Prussia, Austria, and Russia did Frederick I's grandson, Frederick II, introduce the use of the terms West and East Prussia for Royal and Ducal Prussia. Ed.]

[2] Cf. on the immigration of the Dutch: Dr. Bruno Schumacher, *Niederländische Ansiedlungen im Herzogtum Preußen zur Zeit Herzog Albrechts 1525-1568* (Leipzig: Duncker & Humblot, 1903) and Dr. Felicia Szper, *Nederlandsche Nederzettingen in Westpruisen, gedurende den Poolschen tijd* (Enkhuizen: P. Bais, 1913).

ruled directly. But only after 1530 did the persecution become so fierce as to start a larger emigration to the East. This occurred together with the appearance of the Anabaptists, whose leaders, Melchior Hoffmann and Jan Matthijsz, caused a furor among the people (see page 14). Since the Middle Ages there had been active trade and sea travel between Danzig and the Netherlands. Thus the trip to the Baltic Sea coast was not completely new or unknown for the inhabitants of Holland and Flanders. All the Protestant factions were represented among the Dutch who came to Danzig as refugees after 1530, but the majority by far were Anabaptists. They were found in other parts of Prussia too, especially in the Duchy, including Elbing, Thorn, and Graudenz, but in the upper reaches of the Vistula River there were refugees from South Germany and from the lands of the Habsburgs who there met up with their Low Country co-religionists.[3]

We do not know whether there were troublemakers or revolutionaries among these immigrants. But since many were concerned that some wild "Rebaptizers" had arrived with them, the City Council of Danzig wrote to the towns of Amsterdam, Antwerp, Veere, and Enkhuizen and asked these Low Country harbor cities not to send any dangerous emigrants to Danzig. The Dutch were otherwise gladly accepted, since they came from an economically highly developed country, and brought with them knowledge of new crafts and great energy in commerce, agriculture, and trades. Dutch farmers were especially welcome, and they were settled on the neglected lands of the Danzig Delta, where, by means of their skills in digging canals and building windmills, they turned the marshy land into productive agricultural ground.[4] Already before 1550 Dutch farmers were in Reichenberg/Bogatka, and a short time later also in Wesslinken/Wiślinka, Wotzlaff/Wocławy, Landau/Lędowo, Scharffenberg/Bystra, and Schmer-block/Błotnik. The records of these villages, which are

---

[3]Their names give the best clues to the origins of these settler families, insofar as these are known.

[4]They introduced bucket mills (*Schöpfmühlen*) for draining the marshes, which were not otherwise known locally.

preserved in the Danzig City Archive,[5] refer mainly to Dutch names like Phillip Edzema[6] for Reichenberg, as well as Phillip Albrecht, Jan Petersen, and Phillip Freesen, all names which, apart from Edzema, still occur among Mennonites of the delta. Naturally, the Dutch origin of these delta farmers does not prove that they were all Anabaptists. But that a great many of them were later known as Mennonites can be seen from the following.

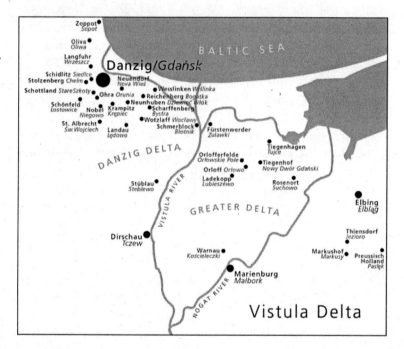

Vistula Delta

---

[5] 300-7-167a, p. 21.

[6] For the reference to these important items in the Danzig City Archives I am grateful to Archive Director Dr. Schottmüller, and a young scholar from the German Mennonite colonies in Russia, Dr. Cornelius Bergmann, who will soon, hopefully, publish his extensive archival studies under the title *Contributions to the History of the Dutch Mennonites in West Prussia*. [This book was never published. Bergmann did go on to write two books on Anabaptists, *Die Täuferbewegung im Kanton Zürich bis 1660* (Leipzig: M. Heinsius Nachfolger, 1916) and *Das Schicksal der letzten Täufergemeinden im Kanton Zürich im XVII. Jahrhundert* (Leipzig, 1916). See Kurt Kauenhoven, "Bergmann, Cornelius," *Mennonite Encyclopedia* 1:279-280. Ed.]

Mennonites in the Danzig Delta

In the summer of 1582 "The subjects of the honored Council, living in the little (Danzig or Stüblau/Steblewo) Delta, who are derisively referred to as Rebaptizers or Mennonites," directed a supplication to the administrators of the marshlands on the Danzig City Council. They complained in emphatic and dignified language about a decision of the Council that threatened all the inhabitants of the marshes with punishment if they did not attend the state church, participate in Communion, and have their children baptized. "We acknowledge that as subjects of the established authorities we owe obedience and duty in those matters which are not against the word and command of the Most High and against our conscience. In such matters, however, we owe obedience more to God than to man." Attendance at church services, baptisms, and communion could not be subject to coercion by the authorities. "And because this order and the accompanying punishment for scriptural reasons oppresses and burdens our consciences, we ask that the honorable Council not burden us with that, since we cannot nor wish to accept such a penalty, as though we had done a wrong. If punishment should come to us we will have to suffer it and leave revenge to Him to whom it belongs, who will judge all things in His own time." They then referred to the fact that the Council had been informed about their views, and that they had lived there *for thirty years* without being bothered because of their faith, which they confessed openly. They would otherwise not have accepted the land rental contracts. For this reason they requested:

> that we would be acknowledged as we had been thirty years ago, as not being any sect nor revolutionaries nor Münsterites or followers of any other group, but rather, that we desire to live in quiet and peace, and to be obedient to the authorities in all matters which are not against God and our consciences. We ask you again, with all humility, that you will not burden our consciences, nor extend your authority to our hearts and consciences, which God alone knows, and that you

will not become known for introducing such
appalling matters as a feature of your government,
but that you will leave us our free consciences, as
you too would not like yours to be burdened and
weighed down either."[7]

From this petition we can see that since the middle of the
sixteenth century there were numerous Mennonites among the
Dutch settlers in the Danzig rural territories, and also, that they
did not assume this name themselves, otherwise they would not
say that they had been called this in derision.

*The Origin of Their Name, Menno Simons in Danzig, and Jan van
Sol*

There is debate about when the name Mennonite came into
use for the non-revolutionary Anabaptists. This was already the
case in 1544 in the writings of opponents and in decrees of the
authorities, for example in East Friesland.[8] In Prussia the name
appears first in a decree of the Elbing City Council of July 16,
1572, and a year later we find it also in a decision of the Danzig
City Council.

We may assume that the name was in common use for some
time before it was used in official documents. That is not
surprising, since Menno Simons himself had visited the
scattered brethren in our area. A formal proof of his presence
in Danzig may be found in the reports of Jan van Sol.[9]

Sol was one of the Dutch who came to Danzig in the 1530s.
He then went to the Duchy of Prussia, where he owned the
Robitten estate by 1536. He returned to Danzig and then
traveled to the Netherlands to gather new settlers. As a former
follower of Melchoir Hofmann, he was accused of the crime of
rebaptism by the City Council of Brussels and interrogated on

---

[7]Danzig City Archives, VII, 167, p. 30.

[8]S. Cramer in the article "Menno Simons" in *Herzogs Realencyklopädie*, 3rd
ed.

[9]On him see Schumacher, *Niederländische Ansiedlungen*, 67f. and many other
places. [See Nanne van der Zijpp, "Jan van Sol," *Mennonite Encyclopedia* 3:82-
83. Ed.]

December 22 and 23, 1550. He was able to talk his way free by betraying his earlier brethren and saying unfavorable things about them. There is an account of this hearing in the archives of the Mennonite church in Amsterdam.[10] Here he tells much about the expansion of the Anabaptists in the "East Country," and also indicates that many of those who fled to Danzig had taken part in the revolt in Amsterdam in 1534.

As Elders who had been active here he names *Menno Simons*, Dirk Philips, and Jan de Verwer, as well as two deacons, one in Danzig by the name of Thoms Barber, born in Emden, and the other Michel Janszoon from Oosterhout in Brabant, who had lately died in Elbing.

Jan van Sol then returned to Danzig with a number of Netherlanders, but apparently was turned away here, for "since Martini, 1556, he negotiated with Duke Albrecht in order for a larger group of Dutch settlers, who had been temporarily in Danzig, to open up new settlements in the Duchy of Prussia."[11] He seems to have been a man of high social standing, probably a physician, but of unsteady character. He had no influence with the Danzig Anabaptists, and when his negotiations with Duke Albrecht were completed, he brought his followers again into the county of Preussisch Holland/Pasłęk, where he most likely remained. Hans von Wittmannsdorf, the Duke's administrator in the region of Preussisch Holland, said of him "he was truly known in Danzig and elsewhere as an untruthful and unpredictable person."[12] Several of his travel companions who did not like it in East Prussia returned to Danzig, since they feared the "Inquisition on account of the Rebaptizers." These

---

[10]For this information I am thankful to J. ten Doornkaat-Koolman, preacher in Solingen, who studied in Amsterdam in 1914.

[11]Schumacher, *Niederländische Ansiedlungen*, 67f. [Martini, or the feast day of the fourth-century St. Martin of Tours, is celebrated on November 11. Ed.]

[12]Cited from a report to Duke Albrecht dated January 22, 1558. See also Schumacher, *Niederländische Ansiedlungen*, footnote 286.

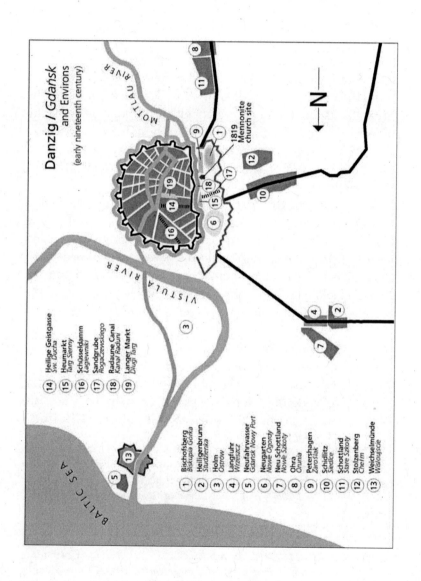

Danzig / Gdańsk
and Environs
(early nineteenth century)

MOTTLAU RIVER

VISTULA RIVER

BALTIC SEA

N

1819
Mennonite
church site

(14) Heilige Geistgasse
     Św. Ducha
(15) Heumarkt
     Targ Sienny
(16) Schüsseldamm
     Łagiewniki
(17) Sandgrube
     Rogaczewskiego
(18) Radaune Canal
     Kanał Raduni
(19) Langer Markt
     Długi Targ

(1) Bischofsberg
    Biskupia Górka
(2) Heiligenbrunn
    Studzienka
(3) Holm
    Ostrów
(4) Langfuhr
    Wrzeszcz
(5) Neufahrwasser
    Gdańsk Nowy Port
(6) Neugarten
    Nowe Ogrody
(7) Neu Schottland
    Nowe Szkoty
(8) Ohra
    Orunia
(9) Petershagen
    Zaroślak
(10) Schidlitz
     Siedlce
(11) Schottland
     Stare Szkoty
(12) Stolzenberg
     Chełm
(13) Weichselmünde
     Wisłoujście

thus were definitely Anabaptists, who sought a better connection with their brothers and sisters there and did not trust Sol.

Local Legal Arrangements

The City Council of Danzig was happy to have the Dutch settlers in their marshy villages without asking many questions about their faith, but they did not want to admit them within the city walls, as long as they were not either Catholic or Lutheran. Reformed[13] and Anabaptists were at best tolerated only in settlements directly outside the city walls. They were allowed to live in the so-called "gardens" and pursue "livelihoods," but not hold public church services.

In contrast, the Bishop of Kujavia gladly accepted the Dutch refugees in his estate, Schottland/Stare Szkoty, right at the gates of Danzig, because he hoped that these energetic craftsmen and business people would revive this area, which had been devastated by war. In Schidlitz/Siedlce too, especially on the "Nuns' Field" in Schladahl (Schlehental), a property of the Brigitta convent in Danzig, they were allowed to settle.

Menno Simons in Danzig

In settlements and villages on the edge of the city in Langfuhr/Wrzeszcz, Heiligenbrunn/Studzienka, Schidlitz, Neugarten, Sandgrube/Rogaczewskiego, Petershagen/Zaroślak, Schottland, Hopfenbruch, Stolzenberg/Chełm,[14]

---

[13]On the Dutch Reformed in Danzig around 1570 see Danzig City Library 865 ms. and ms. 134/625 as well as Eduard Schnaase, *Geschichte der evangelischen Kirche Danzigs actenmässig dargestellt* (Danzig: Theodor Bertling, 1863), 545-7.

[14]It is noteworthy what the famous syndic and historian of Danzig, Gottfried Lengnich (1689-1774) wrote in his *Des syndicus der stadt Danzig Gottfried Lengnich Ivs pvblicvm civitatis gedanensis; oder, Der stadt Danzig verfassung und rechte. Nach der originalhandschrift des Danziger stadtarchivs*, ed. Otto Günther (Danzig: T. Bertling 1900) in 1760. It shows in a few lines what the Netherlanders had achieved in those places and also what they had suffered there in wartime. Lengnich says (p.561):

"It happened that from nearby properties which had the legal standing of villages, the city profited greatly in foodstuffs, on account of which many protested. Such properties are, for example, Schottland, the Hopfenbruch

Nobel/Niegowo, and Krampitz/Krępiec on the Mottlau/Motława, Menno found his Dutch compatriots and faith family once again, and gathered them quietly in houses here and there, admonished them to faithfulness and to a pure walk according to the word of Christ, baptized those who

---

and Stoltzenberg, which lie adjacent to the city and of which Schottland belongs to the Bishop of Kujavia, Hopfenbruch to the Abbot of the Pelplinites, and Stolzenberg to the Chapter of Kujavia. Here are located breweries, distilleries, all kinds of craftsmen, open shops and storage places, so that they give the appearance of small towns without walls, lacking only mayors and counselors and receiving instead judges and jurists.

"Schottland and Hopfenbruch were previously uncultivated areas, apart from the few people who stayed there, keeping themselves by raising cattle and growing hay and garden produce, and who were protected by the dam which had been built and was maintained by the city against flooding by the Radaune. And can Hopfenbruch have gotten its name from the fact that a swamp was made arable for hops? Of Schottland the record says that in 1571 when it was under cultivation there were only six linen weavers living there, while other records have seven Scots settled there, who carried on the rope maker's trade and had given their name to the place. About Stoltzenberg one cannot find reliable information, except that it already was settled with buildings in 1520, like Hopfenbruch and Schottland, because at that time it was found necessary to set all three sites on fire for the safety of the city on the approach of troops recruited in Germany by the Grand Master of the Teutonic Knights. After its successful reconstruction, the city in 1547 and 1557 complained to the Kujavian Bishop about the craftsmen and merchants of Schottland, and asked him to banish these people from the territory, *who had increased their number by the influx of Dutch refugees.* In order to reduce the loss for the city, the authorities decided in 1565 to buy Schottland and the other lands nearby belonging to the Kujavian bishopric for 40,000 guilders, a price suggested by the King, while the Bishop had asked for 80,000 guilders. Schottland and Hopfenbruch were then again, when King Stephen expanded the territory, burned to the ground in 1576, but soon restored. The same fate hit these places in 1656 for the third time, and the city could not prevent their reconstruction, since the Bishop helped the Schottland inhabitants, while the Pelplin Abbot looked after his Hopfenbruch people, and the King did not want to allow the inhabited areas to remain barren. The fourth fire happened in 1734, when the city was besieged by the Russians, but this time too Schottland and Hopfenbruch were quickly rebuilt."

It is thus an error when Schumacher (p.36-37), and after him Szper (p.23) understand Lengnich to say that Schottland in 1565 had become the possession of Danzig. It remained the property of the Bishop, and the city, according to numerous files, tried in vain, in 1585, 1631, 1659, 1660, 1669, and 1692 to acquire it.

requested it and joined them in communion to strengthen them in faith and love. He visited Danzig several times, either alone or with Dirk Philips and Hans Sikken, between 1547 and 1552. He also visited and gathered the scattered Anabaptists in and around Elbing, in the upper Vistula valley and in East Prussia. Thus, the beginnings of our church can be traced to Menno himself, even if we can only document its lasting existence in established forms starting with the late 1560s.

Dirk Philips

Dirk Philips

After Menno's death, Dirk Philips came to Danzig again in the 1560s and lived in Schottland. (See S. Cramer's article on "Mennonites" in *Herzogs Realencyklopädie*).[15] He is considered the actual founder of the Danzig Mennonite Church.

Dirk Philips, born in Leeuwarden in 1504, together with his brother, Obbe Philips, had converted from the Catholic Church to Anabaptism. Already before 1536 he, like Menno, wrote against the Münsterites and formed a close bond with Menno.

---

[15]["Mennoniten" in *Realencyklopädie für protestantische Theologie und Kirche*, 3rd ed., 12:594-616. Ed.]

He was the most learned among the first Mennonites, and wrote a number of articles that were much read, among them *Enchiridion, or Handbook on the Christian Doctrine and Religion* in Dutch, which also appeared in German translations.[16] In Danzig and in Montau/Mątawy near Graudenz he installed elders, preachers (admonishers), and deacons. Around 1568 he traveled to Emden to settle disputes, in the company of the teachers Geert Harms and Hans Sikken. In Danzig he left as Elders Steven Vader, about whom there is no other information except that Dirk Philips greets him in his letters, and Quirin Vermeulen, as well as nine teachers and deacons (caretakers of the poor).[17] Their names were all Dutch: Cornelius van Gorcum, Cyprian Gillissen, Richert Hamerschmit, Lamert van Seven-Olden,[18] Hermann Janzen, Jan Pieters vom Gorcum, Hermann Wynes, Paul von Myllen, Geert Dirks, and Hans von Schwindern. In the years 1567 and 1568 another large group had come from the Netherlands to Danzig fleeing the tyranny of Duke Alba. Thus it can easily be understood that the other names of members that have come down to us from the early period mainly indicate Low Country beginnings: Hans von Amersfoort, Gysbert de Veer (born May 14, 1536, in Amsterdam), van Eyck, Bollaert, Beulke, van Guygen, van Almonde, van Dyck, Symons, Janzen, Mahl, van Beuningen, Fyans, van Gerynghuysen, and many others.

Dirk Philips did not return here. He was not able to settle the dispute concerning the application of church discipline between the Frisian and Flemish congregations in Friesland, and he died in Emden in 1570, where he was buried in the cemetery of the Franciscan monastery.

Schism and Quirin Vermeulen
Because of the strong immigration of newcomers from the Netherlands, the nasty schism that had appeared among the

---

[16]In our Church library there is a Dutch edition, Haarlem, 1627, and a German one, Basel, 1802.

[17]See the notes of Elder Hans von Steen in the Danzig Mennonite Church Archives.

[18][Possibly the same person as Lambert von Siebenofen on p. 49. Ed.]

Mennonites of Holland was carried here as well. The strict Flemish, who were in the majority in Danzig, could not accept the more moderate views in matters of church discipline and the so-called ban and shunning within marriages held by the Waterlanders and Frisians, who were joined by the "High Germans."[19] Thus there was another separation in Danzig into two congregations, a larger Flemish and a smaller Frisian. At the outset the vigorous Elder Quirin Vermeulen and the teacher Hans von Schwindern kept the congregation together. Vermeulen was an educated and a wealthy man. He lived here in Schottland and had beautiful, richly made Dutch Bibles printed, which became known as "Schottland Bibles." They are quite rare today, but our congregation has owned one for twenty years, one that is unfortunately not perfectly preserved. On the title page the publisher printed in Dutch: "Can be purchased at Krijn Vermeulen the younger, merchant, residing by the long wall of Schotlandt by Danzig, 1598." The notes and highlighted Bible clearly show that the editor, a true Mennonite, did not derive dogmas from the Bible, but wanted to preach a Christian way of thinking and acting. In this he seems to have put too much emphasis on discipline and strictness, for a part of his congregation resisted him and complained about his strict leadership to the leaders of the Frisian church in Holland.[20] Thereupon Jan Buschaert de Wewer and Jacob van der Molen appeared in Danzig as deputies from Holland, in order to call Quirin Vermeulen and Hans von Schwindern to account. But they had to return home empty handed since the majority of the congregation was loyal to its leaders. In 1588, though, the Montau Elder Hilchen Schmit, who headed all the Frisian congregations in Prussia, came to Danzig and in the name of

---

[19]On this question see A. Brons, *Ursprung*, 100ff, 111ff. [A main point of contention was how strictly to apply the ban. For a quick introduction to the origins of the groups mentioned here, see C. J. Dyck, *An Introduction to Mennonite History*, 3rd ed. (Scottdale, PA: Herald Press, 1993), 122-7 and Jacobus ten Doornkaat Koolman, *Dirk Philips: Friend and Colleague of Menno Simons, 1504-1568*, translated by William E. Keeney, edited by C. Arnold Snyder (Kitchener, Ontario: Pandora Press, 1998), 115-42. Ed.]

[20]In Holland the Mennonites enjoyed toleration and free religious assembly under William of Orange since 1572.

the Haarlem Frisian congregation, removed the two men, who had suffered much enmity, from office.[21] We know that Hans von Schwindern lived in Schidlitz, where he bought a house from Lambert von Siebenofen[22] for 2,374 marks (1 mark=20 Prussian groschen).[23]

Thereafter two Mennonite churches existed in Danzig, the Flemish in Schottland, later called the congregation in the city, and the Frisian in Neugarten. The latter was strongly connected with the other Frisian churches in Prussia. One of these was quite large, in the Graudenz area with a center located in Montau, while a second was located in the large Marienburg Delta in Orlofferfelde/Orłowskie Pole near Tiegenhof/Nowy Dwór Gdański, and a third on the other side of the Nogat River in Thiensdorf and its surroundings. But the Flemish congregation had a strong connection to the large Flemish country congregation in the Marienburg marshes, whose center for a long time had been Rosenort/Suchowo, as well as to the brethren in and around Elbing.

In the Tiegenhof lowland many Mennonites from both groups had settled in 1562 and the following years, invited by Simon and Hans von Loysen, the administrators of the royal lands located there.[24]

The difference between the Flemish and Frisian congregations consisted not so much of dogma, but only of the more or less strict execution of church discipline in matters of conduct and some external customs. Apart from that the two parties saw themselves as one united community when confronted by the authorities or their opponents. Here in Danzig the Flemish congregation was in the majority and saw itself as the true congregation of the genuine Anabaptists. They

---

[21]See *Successio anabaptistica*, a Dutch anti-Mennonite polemic, 1603. [Available in the Mennonite Historical Library, Goshen, Indiana. Simon Walrave, *Successio Anabaptistica, dat is Babel der vvederdopers: eensdeels in Duytsland maer principael in Nederlandt, in vvelcke de opgevvorpen oorsprong de rasende voortganck, ende bittere verstrouinge in t'cort verhaelt vvort* (Coloniae: Sumptibus Bernardi Gualtheri, 1603) Ed.]

[22][Possibly the same person as Lamert van Seven-Olden on p. 47. Ed.]

[23]*Liber fundorum villae Schidlitz*, 106 (Deeds Register), Danzig City Archives.

[24]See details in W. Mannhardt, *Wehrfreiheit*, 74f.

were in lively contact with the Flemish in Holland; indeed, a
part of these congregations in Amsterdam, Haarlem, and
Rotterdam in the seventeenth century called themselves "the
Danzig Flemish." According to Simeon Friedrich Rues'
Contemporary Situation of the Mennonites (Jena, 1743), there were
seven such congregations, who by and large were somewhat
milder than the very strict "Old Flemish."[25] It is well known that
the Flemish were called the "fine," but less so that they were
also known as "the clear ones" (in Dutch *klaar* means
unambiguous). This explains the name—which perhaps
originated in Danzig—for this group as the *Klarichen*, or
Klerichen, Low German *Klarken* or *Klerken*. This name even
appears in official documents of the authorities and in books. In
contrast, the Frisians were called coarse Mennonites or also "the
troubled ones" (*Bekümmerte*),[26] a name whose origin is unknown,
while the name attached to them in Holland, the disparaging
"manure cart" (*Dreckwagen*) appears to refer to their main
activity as farmers.[27]

---

[25][Simeon Friderich Rues, *Aufrichtige Nachrichten von dem gegenwärtigen
Zustande der Mennoniten oder Taufgesinnten: wie auch der Collegianten oder Reinsburger,
beyderseits ansehnlicher kirchlicher Gesellschaften in den vereinigten Niderlanden: samt
einer Erzehlung von den Streitigkeiten, in welche dermahlen einige der zuerst benennten
verwikelt sind: nebst verschiedenen andern dienlichen Zusäzen* (Jena: Joh. Rudolph
Crökers seel. Wittwe, 1743). Available at the Mennonite Historical Library in
Goshen, Indiana, and the Mennonite Library and Archives in North Newton,
Kansas. Ed.]

[26][Those who opposed the Flemish-Frisian schism and wished to side
with neither faction. See Nanne van der Zijpp, "Bekommerden," *Mennonite
Encyclopedia* 1:268-269. Ed.]

[27][Other sources give a more caustic interpretation of the term
"Dreckwagen." For example, Abraham Hartwich, a Lutheran clergyman,
reported in his book *Geographisch-Historische Landes-Beschribung [sic] derer dreyen
im Pohlnischen Preußen liegenden Werdern* . . . (Königsberg: Christoph Godfried
Eckart, 1722; reprint, Frankfurt: Peter Lang, 2002), p. 279, that the Frisian
faction was thought to be too willing to accept into their membership
persons from other Mennonite groups, even persons who had been banned.
Thus the term "Dreckwagen" or manure wagon, picking up the figurative
excrement of other groups. The term apparently goes back as far as Leenaert
Bouwens in the 1550s in the Netherlands. See Nanne van der Zijpp,
"Waterlanders," *Mennonite Encyclopedia* 4:895. Ed.]

After 1588 Elder Gysbert Franssen led the Flemish congregation in Danzig. He died in 1602 and was succeeded by Heinrich Pieters van den Bosch until 1607 and then Peter Schmitt until 1620. In addition, there were a large number of teachers, that is to say, preachers.

Jan Gerrits van Embden

Jan Gerrits van Embden

After the schism, the Montau Elder headed the Frisian congregation, while some "teachers" led the regular services. In 1607 the Danzig Frisians received their first elder in *Jan Gerrits van Embden*, who had served many churches in Holland with good success. He was born in Emden on April 30, 1561, and came from Haarlem to Danzig, where he soon was highly respected. He also visited the other congregations in Prussia regularly and won their love and confidence, for his manner was "fatherly, peaceful and comforting, and as a spiritual salt, he preserved the Prussian congregations in a healthy condition. The manner in which his zeal for Christian community and for the church burned can best be confirmed by those who knew him and mourned the loss of such a good teacher."[28] On April

---

[28]See also A. Brons, *Ursprung*, 238.

7, 1617, he died in his house on *In der Sandgrube*, a street on the outer ramparts of Danzig, at the age of almost 56 years, after he had personally taken leave of his friends and his sons who lived in Danzig, and by letter from his oldest son in Haarlem. One of his sons became his successor as elder, but we do not have any knowledge about him, as we have only scant information about the Frisian church in the seventeenth century.

4
Further Developments among the Danzig Mennonites to the End of the Seventeenth Century

Refused the Rights of Citizenship in the City
The Mennonites who had immigrated here were no revolutionaries or fanatics, but rather, as one could see, they were quiet, sober, and industrious people. In spite of that, they were viewed by the Church and the citizenry with great mistrust, for they could not escape the Rebaptizer label, and many an upright citizen and zealous churchman considered their humble deportment to be a hypocritical mask, behind which all kinds of evil intentions lurked. The authorities, too, who welcomed the newcomers because of their industriousness, treated them with suspicion. Indeed, they gave signs of goodwill, but they were always ready under the right circumstances to threaten the Mennonites with expulsion, or to limit their human rights and rights of citizenship severely. We have seen that the Danzig City Council accepted them into its rural territories. It also signed rental contracts with them, thereby recognizing them as having some legal standing. In Danzig itself they were forced to reside outside the city walls for a long time and never admitted to citizenship "because they did not want to swear the citizenship oath in the prescribed form." In Elbing the City Council was more tolerant. Already in 1585 it granted citizenship and permission to deal in silks, a line of trade new in that city, to Jost van Kampen and Hans van Keulen. Jost van Kampen was also allowed to build a church for his fellow believers on a piece of his land in 1590.[1]

At the Provincial Parliament (*Landtag*) in Marienburg in 1646 there was debate about these matters between representatives from Danzig and Elbing. The Danzig deputy complained that the Elbingers "had given the Mennonites citizenship without the oath." The Elbing deputy replied "that this was done for particular reasons, since the Mennonites had lived there for some considerable time, and had in time contributed to the city

---

[1]Wilhelm Crichton, *Zur Geschichte der Mennoniten* (Königsberg: Bey Gottlieb Lebrecht Hartung, 1786), 21. Mannhardt, *Wehrfreiheit*, 70.

Mennonite church building in Elbing, photographed in the 1890s. [Illustration added. Ed.]

by building several houses." The Danzigers explained that in their city "Mennonites were never given citizenship. Instead, one could show that others from different religions had had their citizenship withdrawn when they converted to being Mennonite."[2] In fact, the Mennonites of Danzig only were given the rights of citizenship in 1800. For here the old tradition obtained, "that only the adherents of the three major religions, the Lutheran, the Reformed, and the Roman Catholic, would have freedom of religion and citizenship."[3] Consequently,

---

[2]Danzig City Archives, Mm 18b, 131. Vol Rec. de Ao 1646 no 62.
[3][This stipulation was an important part of the 1648 Treaty of Westphalia that ended the Thirty Years War. Ed.]

Arians, Socinians, and Quakers, who also were not tolerated in the city, were excluded from citizenship. As far as the Mennonites were concerned, since it was well known that they did not belong to one of the three recognized religions, they were tolerated but they could not receive citizenship unless they would convert to one of the three recognized religions. In 1669 the question arose whether a Mennonite, because he was ineligible for citizenship, could own or invest in an ocean-going merchant ship, a right reserved for citizens of the city. The courts (referred to as the Second Order) and two district councils within the city were willing to grant this only for this individual, without his children being eligible to inherit his citizenship. The full City Council considered this compromise problematic, and was inclined to allow him the freedom to practice this occupation but without granting citizenship.[4] The City Council had also raised the question in 1562 and 1563, "whether it would not be good to accept the refugees from the Netherlands as citizens, but the Third Order (representatives of the guilds) would not hear of it, and the Second Order (the Courts) declared that it would not be possible to do so unless the Orders were unanimous in the matter."[5]

---

[4]Gottfried Lengnich, *Jus publicum civitatis gedanensis oder Der Stadt Danzig Verfassung und Rechte*, edited by Otto Günther (Danzig: T. Bertling 1900), 121.

[5]Ibid., 529. [The City Council of Danzig or First Order consisted of a dozen or fewer members who were drawn from a couple dozen of the wealthiest families in the city. The Council elected its own new members as needed. In addition, the Council appointed twelve judges who collectively were referred to as the Second Order. The chief judge was also a member of the City Council. Early in the sixteenth century, following riots associated with the introduction of Lutheranism into the city, a Third Order was formally established. This group consisted of 100 representatives from the commonalty who were appointed by the City Council, with the four leading guilds of the blacksmiths, the bakers, the butchers, and the shoemakers supplying two representatives each. This group was divided into four groups or districts. Both the Second and Third Orders had specific advisory functions but were explicitly forbidden to ask questions about city finances. Resolutions could pass with majority support from the Second Order and two of the four districts of the Third Order. After the middle of the eighteenth century the Third Order won changes in the city constitution and gained additional power. Karin Friedrich, *The Other Prussia: Royal Prussia, Poland and Liberty, 1569-1772* (New York: Cambridge University Press, 2000),

The Changeable Attitudes of the City Council
Thus the Mennonites at first were located in separate jurisdictions, some in a bishopric, others in lands of religious orders, or in the suburbs of Danzig, as "non-citizens" without the accompanying rights. They were allowed to earn their bread within a framework of limitations. As one might expect when people are tolerated as a lower class within the social order, they were treated not according to established principles but with arbitrary actions and conditions. The City Council of Danzig responded to them sometimes sympathetically, sometimes ruthlessly. It was favorably inclined to them when it came to economic or political issues. Economically, because they were well equipped to increase the wealth of the city of Danzig and politically, because Danzig desired good relations with the Netherlands. In communicating in 1572 with William of Orange, for example, the city referred to its good treatment of the Dutch refugees.[6]

On the other hand, the Council often took a very negative attitude towards them. This was a result of various pressures, partly from the King of Poland, partly from the citizenry and its representatives, the Third Order,[7] partly also from the churches and their public constituency.

Already on August 28, 1552, King Sigismund II Augustus had issued an edict to the effect that no "Hollander" who was not either a Catholic or a Lutheran should be tolerated in the Danzig area.

In 1561 and the following years complaints can be found in City Council records about foreigners who had taken over most of the trade. There is special mention of the Netherlanders, who lived "in the gardens," and raised foodstuffs there, and who should not be tolerated, since they were Rebaptizers and

---

63-70; Edmund Cieślak and Czesław Biernat, *History of Gdańsk*, trans. Bożenna Blaim and George M. Hyde (Gdańsk: Fundacji Biblioteki Gdańskiej, 1995), 130-42; and Max Bär, *Die Behördenverfassung in Westpreußen seit der Ordenszeit* (Danzig, 1912; Hamburg: Selbstverlag Verein für Familienforschung in Ost- und Westpreußen, 1989), 60-70. Ed.]
   [6]Paul Simson, *Geschichte der Stadt Danzig [bis 1626]* (Danzig: A.W. Kafermann, 1913-18), 2:258.
   [7]On the Danzig Orders see ibid., 2:94.

sectarians. In 1566 they were told that they would have to leave the city by the next Easter.[8]

In May 1572, and then again in April 1573, a decree was posted at the Artushof,[9] stating that all Rebaptizers, Sacramentarians, Mennonites, and other sects were exiled from the city, and all citizens were forbidden to "offer refuge to this kind of person."

At the assembly of nobles and cities in Thorn at Michaelmas[10] 1571, the representatives of Danzig complained "that on the Bishop's territory not only craftsmen had settled, but also notable merchants from many nations, and dangerous sects who are harmful not only to the citizens of this city but also to the inhabitants in general, by taking over trade and with it the bread out of people's mouths. They were taking over all the markets in the area while according to the official privileges this should be limited to those who were citizens. Therefore be it resolved to strive energetically to get rid of such *harmful, selfish, suspicious, and blasphemous* persons from the same Schottland."[11]

The City Council continued to complain unflaggingly in the following years about the foreigners in Schottland, and likewise the Third Order complained about them and about the Rebaptizers in the other suburbs. One can see plainly that although the City Council was in earnest about getting rid of these hard-working and skillful people in the bishop's territory of Schottland, it looked favorably on them in its own territory. That is no wonder since these Dutch Mennonites made both Schottland and Stoltzenberg prosper, turning these two districts into uncomfortable rivals for the shopkeepers and artisans of the city. The Bishop knew why he was protecting these people,

---

[8]Lengnich, *Jus publicum*, 529.

[9][Named for England's mythical King Arthur, the Artushof stood next to the town hall on the main square of the city, the Long Market. Several confraternities of merchants owned the building, which served as the main reception hall of the city for festive occasions and as an important gathering place for the city's elite. Ordinary persons were forbidden to enter. Maria Bogucka, *Das alte Danzig* (Leipzig: Verlag Koehler & Amelang, 1980), 93-102. Ed.]

[10][September 29, the feast day of the Archangel Michael. Ed.]

[11]Danzig City Archives, Mm. 18b, 698.

and we soon see that on their account there were bitter disputes between him and the Danzig City Council.

Enmity of the Third Order

The city guilds found the competition of the competent Netherlanders to be too intense and so they pressed strenuously for their expulsion. One of the many resolutions of the Third Order of August 4, 1578, enjoins the Council "to give heed, and see that the Rebaptizers, who had come from Friesland and Emden, should not settle here, but be turned away."[12]

How then can we explain that in spite of this determined enmity of the citizenry, the Mennonites nevertheless were able to remain there, and at times became wealthy?

As the bishop had done on his territory, likewise the Council allowed them "to pursue their livelihoods" in the suburbs of Schidlitz, Neugarten, across the Radaune, Sandgrube, Petershagen, etc., and only enforced the strict edicts mildly. Otherwise it would not have been possible for "the Dutch to live in the city, to comfortably carry on their trade, and to move into fine houses, as well as to use the Vistula River to move their wares and for trade."[13]

As early as between 1580 and 1600 the Council quietly allowed Mennonites to acquire real estate in the suburbs in question, and have their deeds entered officially in the records.[14] And in 1603 the City Council expressly passed an ordinance allowing them to do this. Thus it made sense when the City Council decided on March 3, 1633, in response to a petition from the Mennonites Wilhelm von Bulau and Jost Merschoot, that non-citizen residents "in Neugarten and other places outside the city wall, but within the city's jurisdiction, could have and possess inheritance and gardens, and could register these in their own names, and thus should not be bothered by the Prosecutor of the police court."[15]

---

[12]Danzig City Archives, 300.X.7. For similar resolutions and proposals see Danzig City Library, Ms. 206, 350 and 383.

[13]Lengnich *Jus publicum*, 529.

[14]Ibid., 45, see the example of Hans von Schwindern.

[15]Danzig City Archives, B.A.V., v.19.

The Third Order time and again attacked this decision, and on August 29, 1635, petitioned "that contrary to Danzig law, it should not be allowed that Mennonites and other like persons can register deeds to gardens and houses in their own names." The Council answered that this only applied within the city itself, "while in the suburbs of Neugarten, Petershagen, and other places outside the city walls, as long as no point of the law has been circumvented, it would be allowed that the people who earn their livelihoods there, although they are not citizens, should be allowed to own property."

The Third Order rejected "this distinction" on October 17. The City Council, which based its stand on the practice of many years, conceded that "during a coming revision of the law, something would have to be done more specifically in this matter."

Expulsion Orders and the Struggle for the Right to Own Property

Not satisfied with this answer, the Third Order returned to this matter again and again, until finally in 1650 a decision was taken "that the Mennonites and other unauthorized persons from this date forward will not be allowed to own or to register any property outside the city walls, as was previously the case, but rather the prosecutor's office will be allowed to pursue those who contravene these orders. *To that end, the previous decision of March 3, 1633, is declared null and void.*"[16]

I am dealing with these cases in such detail in order to show how insecure the situation of the Mennonites in Danzig was, as far as the matter of private property is concerned. That remained the situation in the whole of the seventeenth and eighteenth centuries. Occasionally an exception was made. For example, on October 4, 1700, the Mennonite Jacob Sommer was allowed to dismantle his house on the Bischofsberg/Biskupia Górka, and to build in the Sandgrube, and to enter "the property in the registry of deeds in his own name."[17] As early as a City Council meeting on April 19, 1666, the decision of 1650 was recalled, that Mennonites could not

---

[16]Act. i. Senatu, May 20, 1650.
[17]Danzig City Archives, B. A. V., 276.

own property in the city, but then the record says: "in Sandgrube, Neugarten, and outside the walls this is not strictly observed, but owning and purchasing property is allowed." Thus, in 1708 Hans Isaac van Beuningen was allowed to buy a house in Neugarten, "because the decision of 1650 about the houses across the Radaune was not taken so seriously anymore." Around 1713 the Mennonite Gerd Mahl was allowed to buy a house in Neugarten, and the register of deeds was instructed to register it "with the consent of the Honorable Council."

But these exceptions only prove the rule, and this rule, held by the Third Order and the craft guilds, considered the Mennonites to be uncomfortable competitors, and attempted to make their stay in the city area impossible. This would have succeeded if they would have been able to bring the City Council to their side.

Mennonites in Old Schottland and Stolzenberg or the City and the Bishop

Naturally, more Mennonites moved to Schottland and Stolzenberg where the Bishop gladly received them, something that did not please the city authorities. Those who remained in the city tried to find other means of remaining in possession of their property. This led to the unfortunate practice of registering their property in the names of citizens when they bought land or houses. The citizen would receive an interest payment from a small capital sum in exchange for granting the Mennonite owner life-long tenancy in the house. The City Council and the City Court for a long time allowed this practice to continue; many such contracts from the seventeenth and eighteenth centuries have been preserved.

The Mennonites had lived in Schottland for over fifty years without trouble, except for numerous restrictions on public worship. The attempts by the Danzig authorities to buy that area failed time and again. And all of the regulations applied by the city to counter the competition of the shopkeepers and craftsmen failed. We see how heavily this competition weighed on the Danzig representatives in the decisions of the City Council and the ordinances of the same, which for decades dealt with the "Schottland question." In the years 1629-56 there is scarcely a meeting at which complaints were not raised that the merchants from the Bishop's territory were taking all the business away from their city counterparts. In vain they attempted to rouse the Bishop to do something about this, but it was not in his interest to further the business of the city. In vain also were the appeals to the King. And even strong mandates that threatened the citizens of Danzig with a loss of citizenship if they did business with the Schottlanders had no effect. Already in 1629 one such prohibition was passed. It solved nothing, for on September 26, 1635, the Council declared, after urgent complaints from the four Districts,[18] that it did not know of any other remedy apart from a renewal of the decision of all the Orders under threat of punishment to forbid any citizen or inhabitant from daring to purchase anything from a Schottlander or sell to them, since a large part of the foodstuffs and possessions of the citizenry was going thence and being withdrawn from the city.[19]

When this also had no effect on the dealings and business of the Mennonites in Schottland, the Districts again suggested negotiating with the Bishop, and, "with the permission of His Majesty to offer him a sum of money, so that he would get rid of all those harming the city."

But then an event occurred which got rid of the bothersome Schottlanders all at once. In 1656 the Swedish-Polish War broke out, and when the Swedish army was descending on the city the Council had all the suburban areas, including Schottland, burned to the ground, so that the enemy could not occupy that area.

The Mennonites, who had achieved moderate wealth, suddenly saw themselves robbed of their homes and goods, and had to seek refuge, in part with their relatives and friends in the rural areas, in part with church members in the city. To this end, the homeless turned to the Council with the request to be admitted within the city walls. Twenty-one families, the most seriously affected, were given permission to settle in the city,

---

[18]On the meaning of the Districts see Lengnich, *Jus publicum*, 272.
[19]Danzig City Library, Ms. 208, V. 426 and 435.

where at that time some Mennonites had quietly been accepted already.[20]

The Danzig suburbs Schidlitz and Petershagen too had been reduced to ashes, and on June 12, 1656, the Council received an appeal from the Mennonites there which "with hot and almost bleeding tears begged that they should be spared the one-percent tax,[21] which had been collected from them in spite of their distress by harsh means, since they were presently living from the generosity of others." The appeal was signed: "the honorable Council's poor, ruined people, completely bankrupt and destroyed, called Mennonites." The Council thereupon decided to spare the petitioners these taxes for one year.

When the brutal Swedish-Polish War came to an end with the Peace of Oliva in 1660, Danzig did not spare any effort to hinder the rebuilding of the Bishop's villages of Schottland and Stolzenberg. In an audience with King John Casimir on July 10, 1660, the representatives of Danzig presented their case, upon which "the Great Chancellor answered that His Majesty was determined to protect the Schottlanders as his subjects, and would not be pleased to hear that they had been driven out and harassed in various ways. Even the King himself spoke to the matter and reproved the fact that the Schottlanders with their wares and goods had not been granted free passage, but rather faced confiscation of their goods at the gates. The delegates argued that the reconstruction of the two Bishop's villages would be harmful to the fortifications of the city. That did not help, however, except that the people who would build there should be warned that in a future war they should expect their houses to be razed again."[22]

The Mennonites thereupon returned to Schottland and Stolzenberg from all the places to which they had fled, and in short order rebuilt their houses. From this one may conclude that there were good living conditions for them there; otherwise they would scarcely have exposed themselves to the danger of

---

[20]Danzig City Archives, 35, B.

[21]A city tax on wealth, see Lengnich, *Jus publicum*, 427.

[22]Gottfried Lengnich, *Geschichte der Preussischen Lande*, (Danzig, 1722-1755), 7:244.

being driven from home and hearth during the next war. Although they had to start over, they were of good courage, and they comforted and helped each other as was their custom, and received support and advances of money from their brethren, especially from Holland, for the modest refurnishing of their homes, workshops, and businesses.

This applied to the Mennonites as well who had to rebuild their ruined homes in the suburbs of Danzig. They continued to feel the hatred and envy of the guilds. After the twenty-one families from burned-out Schottland had been admitted to the city, the shopkeepers guild on July 27, 1657, asked that, apart from those who had lost their homes no one unqualified should be given the freedom to open a shop.[23]

In order to prevent those who had lost their places from rebuilding their houses, the "Wide District had passed on to the City Council certain recommendations including that the Mennonites should not be permitted to build on empty lots" and that as early as March 15, 1660, when the peace negotiations had barely begun.[24]

On September 30, 1664, the Third Order passed a resolution "that the Mennonites according to an order of 1636 had only been granted the exclusive right to earn their livelihoods in the city during their lifetimes, but that they should not do business on the streets and rivers of the land, and that they should only purchase goods from citizens. They break this ordinance often, and that according to the opinion of the Districts there should be an investigation of this matter by a committee representing all the Orders, and this misuse should be corrected."[25] If this resolution had been carried out it would have robbed Mennonites of all their possessions and their freedom to do business.

The Lace Trim Manufacturers

Among the crafts that Mennonites had brought with them from Holland, the ones that flourished here above all were work

---

[23]Danzig City Archives, 35, B.
[24]Danzig City Archives, Selecta ex. rec. ord. Mm. 4, p.166.
[25]Ibid. Mm, p. 242.

in lace and textiles, and the making of brandy and fine liquors.[26] At first, the lace trim manufacturers were allowed to carry on their craft without hindrance, to train apprentices (around 1750 this training took five years), and to employ journeymen. But as soon as the native trainees had completed their programs and formed their own craft guild, they attempted to supplant their erstwhile masters, the Mennonite lace trim manufacturers. This naturally happened with reference to the fact that these masters did not have citizenship and thus could not belong to the guild. Their accusers never forgot to mention that they were Rebaptizers, who really had no right to remain there. Especially aggravating to the Danzig guilds was the fact that Mennonites both produced and sold goods, a Dutch form of business that was superior to the local tradition because it was more flexible.[27]

The attack on Mennonite lace trim manufacturers and shopkeepers became especially fierce in the 1640s. Besides many other such complaints, one by the shopkeepers' guild on March 24, 1648, came to the Council "against the foreign lace makers who are not citizens." Upon receipt of this complaint and after receiving a rebuttal from those so accused and

a completed investigation and discussion with the representatives assigned to these tasks, the City Council, after carefully considering all its aspects, has declared the following: 'Because it is not allowed for foreigners to deal with other foreigners, and there must be a difference maintained between lace manufacturers and lace sellers, therefore the lace manufacturers may not be allowed to deal in wares made elsewhere, or to order manufactures of gold, silver, or silk, nor to buy them here and sell them elsewhere. Rather, they may only sell the work of their own hands that have been made here. Likewise, the same lace manufacturers may not sell ounces of gold or silver

---

[26]They also wove cloth, dyed silk, had tanneries and other crafts.
[27]See Salka Goldmann, *Danziger Verfassungskämpfe unter Polnischer Herrschaft*, (Leipzig: B.G. Teubner, 1901), 82f.

or silk apart from the things they have made, or deal in it. What they require for their own manufacture, that much and no more they may order from other places or purchase from local citizens and not from foreigners. Those who previously visited the markets of their (former) lands, and whose forefathers enjoyed this right, shall, for certain reasons, be allowed to continue this practice, but only in order to sell their own products and with the agreement of the Council. Finally, considering the cutting of finished rolls, the lace manufacturers are to abstain from this, and also from selling small amounts by weight. They shall sell their bundles and manufactures by the piece at 96 ells as is the custom. The citizenry nonetheless will be permitted to order in advance according to need a half piece of thirty ells. Apart from this, it will not be allowed to make half-pieces and to sell them."[28]

This decision by the Council signaled a victory for the narrow interests of the guilds over the blossoming craft and trade activity of the Mennonites. If it was carried out strictly then their import activity and especially their expanding and widespread trade was threatened. The guilds made every effort to see this happen. In the Danzig City Archives we find a number of complaints by the lace trim manufacturers and the shopkeepers guilds that asked the Council and the Prosecutor to carefully follow these orders.

The Mennonites on their part did not remain silent. At first those individuals who were summoned by the court lodged complaints with the Council, arguing that their ancestors had already carried on crafts and trade in a similar manner.[29] Then all the Mennonite lace makers presented a detailed memorandum to the Council on October 26, 1666. It is located

---

[28]Danzig City Archives, Vol. 35. Act i. Senatu, March 24, 1648.

[29]For example, Hans von Buler in September 1650, Danzig City Archives, 35, Vol. 70.

in the Danzig City Archives,[30] and is entitled: "Clear Explanation concerning the Freedom enjoyed by the Mennonite lace trim manufacturers of the city of Danzig from ancient times through the goodwill of the honorable authorities, how the same were attacked by opposition parties and in what way they were protected."

Since time immemorial, says the memorandum, they had been given the freedom by the Council of the honorable city of Danzig to carry on their lace trade. But for the same time their envious opponents had sought to take this freedom from them. In 1623 these opponents had presented King Sigismund III Vasa with a document full of lies, but had not achieved anything by this. Instead, the king, with the agreement of the Council, had presented the Mennonite lace trim manufacturers with a "wonderful privilege, by His grace, that they were free to deal in and sell without hindrance their wares, in total or in part, in all places and in public markets, and also train apprentices, etc."[31] This Privilege of October 30, 1623, was then confirmed by Kings Wladislaw IV and John Casimir.

Then their opponents had attempted to bring them under their control by forcing them to join their guild. But the City Council decided that the lace makers had at all times been *a free craft*, and that the Mennonites should retain this freedom, according to a decision of the City Council, March 26, 1629. Also, they were to enroll their apprentices at the City Hall and have a certificate of apprenticeship issued under the seal of the city.

On November 17, 1632, the city had once again passed a resolution to the effect "that they may deal in silk, silk materials, buttons and goods of that kind," that they also may use streets and streams, because, according to the opinion of the City Council *their forefathers had brought such trade here*, which had been greatly increased by the contemporary Mennonite lace trim manufacturers and provided a living for many people. They are therefore not to be harassed, *so that they will not move away from this*

---

[30]Danzig City Archives, Vol. 35.
[31]See Simson, *Geschichte der Stadt Danzig [bis1626]*, 2:522.

city to other places, which are already offering such a possibility to them."

The Mennonites also referred to two documents of the Danzig City Council sent to Elbing, dated November 26, 1636, and April 23, 1637, which expressly say that the Mennonite lace makers in Danzig have the right "from time immemorial" freely to sell at all times in their own houses without hindrance the wares which they themselves make and also those which they purchase from strangers. Thereupon the Elbing Mennonites were given the same freedom as the Danzigers, which they then enjoyed in peace and quiet without disturbance.

The shopkeepers guild, with which the Mennonites had lived in peace and familiarity, was also aroused by the Mennonites' opponents and this worthy guild issued a memorandum against the Mennonite lace trim manufacturers in 1644, addressed to the City Council. They had also managed to have a load of goods stopped in Graudenz, which the Mennonites had sent to the Simon and Judas[32] market in Thorn in the same year of 1644. The goods were not released until the mayor Constantine Ferber interceded on their behalf and they had shown their royal Privilege to the royal administrator of Graudenz.[33]

In order that such things would not occur again in the future, "the Lord Syndic Heinrich Freder on instruction from the City Council secured from His Majesty Wladislaw IV the following: First, a Charter of Privilege, in which they are granted the freedom to travel with their goods unhampered through the lands of Prussia and the Kingdom of Poland, and no one shall presume to disturb them."

Apart from this, the king had included instructions to the Danzig City Council for the carrying out of this Charter of Privilege, and it commanded the Lord Mayor to protect the Mennonite lace trim manufacturers. The instructions and Charter are dated December 19, 1644.

---

[32][The feast day of these two apostles was celebrated on October 28, hence the market took place on this day and was given this name. Ed.]

[33]This seizure of Danzig goods was taken by the Danzig Council to be interference in their affairs, and thus they took an interest in the matter.

Their opponents gave them one year of peace, but then in 1646 launched a new attack, this time concerning the retail trade of the Mennonites, in particular, the cutting of the lace trim. This should be forbidden since it was not mentioned in the Charter of Privilege. The Council then named a deputation consisting of Clemens Collmer, Jacob Stüwe, and David Kämmerer, which was to hear both sides and if possible satisfy them. But no representatives of the Mennonites were called before this enquiry, and so the Mennonites were suddenly surprised by the order of the City Council, which delivered them a crushing blow (see above, p. 64). A copy of this decision was only delivered to them in November 1648. No answers were given to their objections. Instead, they were told to come to terms with their opponents, and Heinrich Freder, who had in the meantime been elected mayor, warned them in harsh language that if they did not give in they would be subject to force. Then an agreement with the guild was achieved in sixteen points, on condition that the Mennonites would revert to the Council order of 1629 in case the opposition did not strictly observe the sixteen points. That party agreed with "solemn words," but soon broke faith and their respect for God by influencing the Lord Mayor to add points seventeen and eighteen, which once again were directed to ruining the retail trade of the Mennonites.

All objection to this failed, and the victorious opponents set about placing guards at the gates, and wherever a piece of lace was sold, the poor seller, who depended on such sales, was charged and fined large sums by the Prosecutor's office. Finally the City Council, reacting to a request of December 13, 1658, took pity on them and instructed the Prosecutor not to molest them. Then there was peace for a while, until in 1663 one of their own, Karl Symons in Schidlitz, was forbidden to trade due to a complaint of the leadership of the shopkeepers' guild.

On October 26, 1666, the Mennonites made an urgent request of the Council, referring with gratitude to its previous goodwill, asking that the order of May 24, 1648, be changed, signing themselves as the honorable Council's ever-dutiful subjects, the lace trim manufacturers known as Mennonites.

Conclusion

The lace trim manufacturers dealt with here in such detail are only one example of the lack of freedom the Danzig Mennonites suffered. In the following time they appear to have been left in peace in terms of their trade, but as soon as trade generally decreased they were again limited and opposed, and thus constantly lived in danger of being suddenly cut off from their living, whenever it appeared useful to the authorities to apply strict measures against them. They remained the "tolerated," and not the "entitled" and instead of being free citizens they were *foreigners and residents without rights*, inhabitants of a second class, like Jews and Gypsies.[34] This was not because of any moral or economic inferiority (in this respect they had a high standing), but rather because they could not become citizens on account of belonging to a faith considered a "sect."

The next chapter will confirm this further.

---

[34]See on this comparison Lengnich, *Geschichte der Preussischen Lande*, Vol. 9, Bericht über den Landtag in Marienburg am 25. August 1770.

5
Caught Up in Royal and City Politics[1]

The Polish Kings and the Mennonites

The Mennonites' lack of protection extended to the exercise of their religion as well. That they could only worship together in private homes has been mentioned already. The religious Charters of Privilege given to the city by the Polish king (the first by Sigismund II Augustus, in 1557) only allowed Lutherans and Roman Catholics freedom of religious practice. In the Confederation of Warsaw of 1573 some freedom was allowed to dissidents, but these did not include the Mennonites. This was expressly confirmed at the Imperial Diet of Warsaw in 1648. When it was decided here to add the Calvinists to the Lutherans who were granted freedom of worship, neither the Arians nor the Mennonites in Poland were granted this freedom. At the diet in Marienburg on September 15 of the same year their exclusion was emphasized when there was talk of the Mennonites living in the Vistula lowlands and in the towns.[2]

Thus, they were always dependent on the mercy of the current ruler in the Kingdom of Poland, and there was no lack of expulsion orders or Charters of Privilege. The latter were only valid for the reign of the bestowing monarch. In 1556 King Sigismund II Augustus proclaimed a strict edict against the Rebaptizers who had found refuge in Prussia. Each new king repeated such edicts. Wladislaw IV (1632-48) wrote to the Danzig Council on April 30, 1633, that the Mennonites would have to take the oath to the king or emigrate within four months. And on January 29, 1636, a new message from the king was read, to the effect that "the Dutch and Mennonites should not be allowed to buy grain, and also, that the Mennonites should all be driven out of the jurisdiction." Now it was fortunate for the Mennonites that the Danzig Council

---

[1][Mannhardt's original title was simply *Continuation*. The editors created this more descriptive title. Ed.]

[2]Lengnich, *Geschichte der Preussischen Lande*, 7:19. King Michael in 1676, too, declared in the Religious Privilege which he signed for Danzig that the Mennonites were not included, Danzig City Archives, Mm. 18b, 131.

considered such decrees as interference in their rights, and thus disregarded them.

Haxberg

But a royal chamberlain, Willibald von Haxberg, used the ignorance of the king, as well as his enmity toward the Mennonites, to blackmail them in a shameful manner. He managed to obtain letters patent from the king which stated: "Since the sect of Rebaptizers, called Mennists, are mightily infesting the land, and without royal permission are doing great harm to trade, therefore their goods – wherever they may be found, especially in the cities of *Danzig* and Elbing – and all their movable and immovable goods – shall be confiscated by the Crown."

The king granted these goods to his chamberlain Haxberg who hastened to announce this royal command in the Marienburg Delta. He did not dare go to the cities. The Mennonites refused to leave their possessions, and showed their contracts that documented that they and their forefathers in some cases as long ago as 1562 had settled in the Tiegenhof and Marienburg areas. But Haxberg used the military to expropriate what was due and by this means extorted from them 80,000 florins or 150 florins from each *Hufe* of land.[3]

Haxberg's activities were stopped by a decision of the Prussian parliament in Marienburg on May 12, 1642, which forwarded a complaint to the king and defended the Mennonites. At the same time, the Mennonites petitioned the king themselves, showing him their earlier Charters and presenting him with a sum of money to be used at his discretion. Thereupon they received the Royal Privilege of King Wladislaw IV, dated December 22, 1642.[4]

---

[3]Mannhardt, *Wehrfreiheit*, 79f. [One *Hufe* equals roughly 2.2 acres or 0.9 hectares. Ed.]

[4]The original, previously in possession of the Orlofferfeld Mennonite Church of Tiegenhof, is now in the Danzig City Archives. It is reprinted in Latin in Mannhardt, *Wehrfreiheit*, LXf. The official translation by the Danzig Assessors Office is in ibid., 80.

Charters of Privilege

In this document he renewed for the Mennonites near Marienburg in the Greater and the Elbing Deltas the Charters granted by his predecessors Sigismund II Augustus (1548-72), Stephen Bathory (1576-86), and Sigismund III Vasa (1586-1632), and their gift of "freedoms, rights, and justice" and promised "to protect and preserve them." He emphasizes that they had at an earlier time "come to wild, swampy, and unusable places in the lowlands and had made these useful and fruitful by much work and at great cost, by clearing the land and building the necessary mills, etc., and had thus left their heirs a good example of industry, work, and sacrifice which they should follow." Thus there had been similar Charters of Privilege granted by earlier kings, whose terms, however, we do not know.

Although the Charter of 1642 applied only to the Mennonites around Marienburg by name, it was appropriately applied to the rest of them in Polish Prussia. This did not stop the king from again issuing a strong edict *against* the Mennonites on June 10, 1647, a year before his death. These Mennonites had been falsely accused of converting persons from other confessions. The king declared: "that the sect of the Rebaptizers and Mennonites are highly dangerous to the souls of Catholics and dissidents,[5] and because their slanderous mouths deny the divinity of the only begotten Son, they are much hated by the Catholic Church and are greatly loathed." Therefore, this edict should "set a bulwark against them, whereby we, with all strictness and harshness toward every and all sectarians of the Mennonite faith in our realm and especially in Prussia, where they have been able to settle due to the indulgence of magistrates, command that they do not let it occur that a Christian Catholic or dissidents of this religion should be drawn over to their sect, *on pain of hanging, the confiscation of their goods, and immediate expulsion of the whole sect out of all royal lands.*"

No sooner had King Wladislaw died than Haxberg began his extortions again, not only at Marienburg, but also in the Graudenz area. He demanded of all Mennonites two guilders

[5][Meaning Lutherans and Reformed. Ed.]

for each *Hufe* and promised to secure freedom of religion for them in return. The new king, John Casimir (1648-68), answered the complaints of the Mennonites with a denial of Willibald von Haxberg's demands, and with two new Charters, one of which, in July 16, 1650, was directed to the Dutch and Mennonites in Marienburg, and the second of November 28, 1650, for those in the Graudenz lowland, which confirmed all the promises of his predecessor from the year 1642.

Complaints and Investigations

In spite of this, the situation of the Mennonites remained precarious and threatened. The last edict of Wladislaw of 1647 had long-term negative consequences. Soon various people accused Mennonites of proselytizing and rebaptizing. At the same time the Mennonites were suspected of sharing the belief of the Arians and Socinians, who were opponents of the Trinity, and who were expelled from Poland by a decree of 1658. Some officials also began to apply this edict to the Mennonites. But because the king received quite substantial rents for their lands, for example, from the estate of Tiegenhof alone 20,000 florins,[6] he intervened on their behalf, and in a letter of November 20, 1660, he declared that the law against the Arians of 1658 had no bearing on the Mennonites.[7]

A half year earlier something had happened in Danzig that had brought the congregation into great confusion. The following quotation on this matter is taken from a letter from the king of April 20, 1660, and may be found in our archive.[8] In German translation the letter reads:

---

[6]Lengnich, *Geschichte der preussischen Lande*, 7:118. [When the Polish crown won this area from the Teutonic knights, the crown assigned the rents from the Tiegenhof estate to cover the costs of the court, hence the estate was known as a *Tafelgut* or estate of the banquet table. Mennonites leased this land from noble managers and thus indirectly paid for a portion of the feasts and banquets of the Polish crown. Ed.]

[7]Reprinted in detail in Mannhardt, *Wehrfreiheit*, 84f.

[8]The original is a parchment document in Latin with an attached royal seal of red wax in a tin capsule.

With this letter we advise everyone that the congregation of the Rebaptizers and Mennonites within and without the city of Danzig is accused of maliciously, through its leader, rebaptizing a Catholic person named Susanna Bauer and taking the liberty of accepting her into their congregation. Whereby they have grossly sinned against divine and human laws, particularly against the capital mandate of King Wladislaw IV, by their disrespect and abuse of the sacrament of Holy Baptism, and according to the law deserve capital punishment, the loss of all goods, and expulsion from our lands for themselves and their heirs. According to our command, because of the aforementioned pillaging of the church by rebaptizing, the persons of the named Mennonite congregation, with their goods, monies, and rights have become the property of the crown, and confiscation decrees have been issued by our office for several persons. However, after this case was taken up by the Church Judge[9] of Danzig and Pomerania, Lorenz Ludwig von Demuth, and the aforesaid Susanna Bauer denied the rebaptism while under oath and thus proved the innocence of the Mennonites, we, on their request have decided that the confiscation of the goods, monies, and rights of the Mennonites in and outside Danzig should be revoked and denied, so that no one may make any claims thereupon. Rather, we confirm for the Troubled (*Bekümmerte*) Mennonites that they shall maintain their possessions in peace, tolerance and security, wherever they are, within or without Danzig. But the same congregation of Troubled Mennonites shall not violate the mandate of Wladislaw IV,

---

[9]Official or the Representative of the church court. [Bär, *Behördenverfassung*, 52-3, refers to them as church judges. The state churches had their own court system to judge matters of theology, heresy, and canon law. Ed.]

which is hereby confirmed, by presuming to draw in Roman Catholics or Dissidents by rebaptism and to incorporate them into their community. This declaration shall not apply to the other sect of Mennonites, called the Clarists, who have been accused of the same sacrilege.

Given in Danzig, April 20, 1660.

John Casimir, King

What exactly happened in this dangerous matter we can no longer determine with certainty, because we lack all sources from that year concerning the Mennonites who would have been most directly involved. From the above document we can see that for the time being only the Frisian congregation (the "Troubled") was absolved, while the Flemish (the Clarists) remained under criminal prosecution.[10] The latter turned to the City Council, which in such cases always took their side when it sensed that either royal or bishop's officials were interfering in their own jurisdiction. On April 23, 1660, the City Council advised the Flemish Mennonites "who had been summoned before the Royal Court to answer the accusation of having misled Roman Catholics to their own sect" that the Council would communicate with the Lord Chancellor on their behalf, "but they should do their part, be quiet and halt their public meetings totally, in the hope that they would then no longer be molested."[11]

This hope came to naught and upon further requests by the Mennonites the Council on May 3 answered them as follows: "that they were free to settle things amicably. If new difficulties should arise, the Council would address these matters in defense of public law."

---

[10][On the origins of these names refer to the subheading Schism in chapter 3. Ed.]

[11]Danzig City Library, Ms. 499 Folio 430.

How the matter came to rest cannot be determined, most probably by means of a voluntary tax.[12] But the Danzig Mennonites did not find peace in that year of 1660, for on November 12 the Council passed the following resolution: "that the Mennonites, whether the Frisian or Troubled ones, or those called the Clarists, should not be allowed to practice their religion, but rather that they should be seriously admonished not to spread their confession in this city and its jurisdiction, and that since they hold conventicles and meet in private homes, these meetings should be disturbed and prevented."[13] This unhappy decision was communicated to the Mennonites in answer to a request on their part for a place in which to hold their religious services, since their meetinghouse had been destroyed in the war.

King Michael and the City Council of Danzig

A new Polish king came to the throne, Michael Korybut Wiśniowiecki (1669-73). We do not know which influential persons at the court drew the king's attention to the Mennonites. It is not improbable that the intention was to damage the interests of both the city of Danzig and the Mennonites at the same time.

Thus in the summer of 1670 the Canon of Cracow, Zebrydowski, requested in the name of the king that the Danzig City Council collect a donation for the king from the Mennonites. They were "to offer a gratuity to the king without delay." By means of some information from the Council about the same Mennonites he apparently allowed himself to be dissuaded from insisting on the payment.

Suddenly, on September 17, another dignitary of the Polish court appeared in Danzig, the Warsaw Canon Stanislaus von Zboczin Zbonski. He went immediately to the presiding mayor Adrian von der Linde, to whom he brought two documents prepared by the king. The second was a royal decree of

---

[12][Marginalized groups in early Modern Europe often found themselves paying "voluntary taxes," or bribes, to smooth their negotiations with the state. This practice was not limited to Mennonites or Poland. Ed.]
[13]Danzig City Library, Ms. 499. Fol. 430.

September 5, directed against the Mennonites, and which named Zbonski as royal commissioner with the task of investigating by what right they presumed to remain in the land of Prussia and to spread their poisonous teachings, which were comparable to those of the Arians. The king did not wish to suffer this sect any longer. When the mayor presented this document at a Council meeting on September 23, they were united in feeling that the wish of the king impinged upon the rights of the City Council, and they sent the syndic[14] to the royal commissioner to defend the rights of the city. But Zbonski had already sent a summons in the name of the king to the Mennonites Cornelius and Behrend de Veer, Abraham van Beuningen, Johann Siemons, Isaac Wienhold, Erdmann Stobbe and Dietrich Radtke, demanding they appear before him. Now it became a matter of state. The summoned Mennonites asked the City Council for advice, and the Council forbade them to appear before the commissioner. Zbonski had to return without accomplishing anything. The City Council now wanted to send a message to the king, but could not because the Third Order repeatedly criticized the text to be sent. Indeed, they agreed that the City Council should protect its prerogatives, but there was strong objection to the inclusion in the text of much praise for the Mennonites. The Third Order declared that one should be grateful to the king for wanting to rid the country of the Mennonites. It was entirely unnecessary for the City Council to use this opportunity "to agree with Mennonites, to speak of their rights, to excuse their religion and further their cause, for they were clearly people whom it was unfortunate to have around as they were injurious to the citizenry and the commonweal."[15]

By the time the text of this "Information to the King" was approved by all the Orders, after many futile meetings, December had arrived. In the meantime, the king, after receiving the report of his commissioner, had already on October 26 issued a sterner edict against the Mennonites in and around Danzig. In it he suspended all their rights and privileges

---

[14][Their legal counsel. Ed.]
[15]Danzig City Library, Ms. 211, fol. 336ff.

because their presence was illegal in his kingdom. He declared their movable and immovable goods to be confiscated and banned them from the land, since their number was far too great, especially in Danzig. Also, they had by smooth talk misled others to their pernicious sect, had held secret meetings and carried on trade to the great harm of the citizenry, had bought lands, and otherwise presumed on the freedoms enjoyed by other inhabitants of the realm. Finally, they did not want to acknowledge the king as their lord, since they refused to swear an oath to him.[16]

At the same time a new summons was issued to the aforementioned six Mennonites, in which they "as well as all the other members of the Mennonite and Rebaptizer sect, men and women in the city of Danzig and its territories were invited to appear before the Royal courts." The king informed the Council of his royal rights on November 22, 1670, with the addition: "that these people shall appear in the presence of the royal law within four weeks to see and hear that they are held to be traitors to the previous commission, injurious to the royal authority, and subject to banishment. Those named shall be condemned to death, and the others to confiscation of their goods."

The summoned Mennonites now again turned to the Council, which again forbade them to follow the summons. It now sped up the process of sending its "Information" to the king, which was finally approved by all the Orders and immediately sent to the Subsyndic (Danzig's representative at the royal court), with the explicit instruction "to personally seek by all means with the senators and the Vice-Chancellor to prevent the matter from becoming officially registered as law, even if it were necessary to provide the latter with 1,000 florins. If that were not successful, he should promise the Vice-Chancellor a real gratuity if he could see to it that the Council could be granted several more weeks to hand in a new request."[17] This was sent to Warsaw on December 24 and the

---

[16]Danzig City Library, Ms. 211 and Ms. 499, p. 430a.
[17]Danzig City Library, Ms. 499.

negotiations with the Vice-Chancellor quickly reached their goal.

After the Mennonites had come up with the funds promised by the Council and had sent them off, the summons were recalled, and in January 1671 a new decree was issued, in which King Michael suspended the previous decree, "which had been presented to him under false pretenses by irresponsible advisors."[18]

Apparently many such acts of oppression against the Mennonites were no less than extortion, by which the higher or lower authorities enriched themselves. In any case, "donations," "gratuities," and the like played an important part in the reversal of difficult and impossible demands.

We can see how the Mennonites groaned under these lawless conditions in the reports[19] written by Georg Hansen, who recorded and commented on important events beginning in 1667.[20] In 1665 he was elected a deacon and then a teacher in the congregation, and then from 1690 until his death (January 16, 1703) he was elder of the Flemish congregation. He must already have been the real spiritual leader under the Elder Wilhelm Dunkel (1667-90). By trade a shoemaker like Jacob Böhme,[21] he was a well-read man, articulate and a good writer. He wrote a short report about the unrest brought about by the actions of King Michael in which he simply and faithfully tells what happened. Here and there the calm objectivity is enlivened by a certain humor. So, for example, when he says at the mention of Zebrydowski: "On August 8, 1670, we received a royal decree, with a call to honor the king (with a gift) according to long-standing tradition. But since *such an ancient tradition* was

---

[18]Danzig City Archives, 300, H.Vv. Bl. 435.

[19]Archive of the Danzig Mennonite Church, vol. LI.

[20][On Hansen see Harvey Plett, "Georg Hansen and the Danzig Flemish Mennonite Church: a Study in Continuity" (Ph.D. diss., University of Manitoba, 1991 and John Friesen, "Theological Developments among Mennonites in Poland in the Sixteenth and Seventeenth Centuries," in *Anabaptism Revisited: Essays on Anabaptist/Mennonite Studies in Honor of C. J. Dyck,* Walter Klaassen, ed. (Scottdale, PA: Herald Press, 1992), 120-1. Ed.]

[21][Jacob Böhme (1575-1624) was a cobbler and famous mystic writer from Görlitz in Silesia. Ed.]

not known to us, we did not fall for it but instead appealed to the City Council, which immediately protected us."

In conclusion there is the following about the gift of money: "Since this matter involved considerable expenditures, a collection was made on Shrove Tuesday and the sum of 2,466 florins realized. The Schottlanders were not included since they had their own burdens to bear. . . . What we learned as a result of all this is that as long as our nation[22] has been in Poland the royal court has never been more serious about these matters. And therefore, after the successful conclusion of the matter, we have reason to thank the City Council of Danzig, but especially our Lord God:

Hitherto has the Lord helped us -
May His holy name be praised forever!"

An Anonymous Polemic

It was fortuitous that the congregation had an energetic and intelligent man in its leadership at that time, for the tribulations seemed to have no end. Among the manuscripts of the City Library[23] there is a lengthy manuscript with the marginal note: "This writing was circulated anonymously in 1675 in order to raise hatred against the Mennonites." The title is: *Informatio contra Mennonistas*. The whole thing is a collection of all the usual accusations, to which the author adds a few that are particularly hateful. He begins with a Latin sentence to the effect that they should not be tolerated on account of their damned religion, which is forbidden in the Constitution. Then follow the well-known suspicions about their trade, by which they cheat the citizens with imported Dutch goods and lend them money at usurious rates. "In conclusion, not only is *all* trade in Mennonite hands, but in addition many artisans, like lace trim makers, tailors, shoemakers, and the like, who are tolerated here because authorities turn a blind eye, rob the citizenry of their livelihood.

---

[22][Hansen uses nation in the older sense of people here, referring hence to the Mennonite "nation." The burden of the Schottlanders was presumably the sack of their settlement fifteen years earlier, see the account in chapter four. Ed.]

[23]Danzig City Library, Ms. 449, p. 423f.

The citizens must become the Mennonites' slaves. The citizenry also sees the decline of its livelihood in the fact that the Mennonites have the best and wealthiest localities and houses in the city."

Then they are even accused of high treason because they "make known in foreign places everything that happens in the Kingdom of Poland, something that is proved in the newspapers, which often take information about the king or the city out into the world to be used against us." So, for example, they are supposed to have given advanced warning of the attacks carried out by Danzig against the city of Elbing during the Swedish wars.

They are also accused of having their own court, even for divorce, and thus interfering in the jurisdiction of the royal, city, and church courts. They also convince their servants "to accept their damnable teaching." The pamphleteer does not concede that the Mennonites have cultivated the delta; instead he insists that they let their farms go to ruin, did not pay their taxes and dues, etc. Settlers from Pomerania would be preferable; they would do everything better.

Finally, he even presumes to accuse the Mennonites of generating conflict between the City Council and the citizenry for their own benefit. They defy authority. They would even spend 100,000 florins *to raise an army against the government*, for which they are guilty of high treason. In conclusion the author makes suggestions about how these people could be eliminated or at least brought under strict control. He hints mysteriously that there are more points which could not yet be publicized, but which would be "shown to the king at an opportune time."

Given the unlimited hatefulness of this concoction and the obvious misrepresentation of the facts, we assume that it did not have a great effect. But it is an example beside numerous others of the fact that the Danzig Mennonites had to contend with many opponents, some of them quite wicked, who did not fight freely and openly, but only with poisoned weapons in the dark.

At least the attack in 1676 at the Prussian Parliament of Marienburg by the Woywode of Pomerania[24] was done out in the open when he demanded their expulsion. He accused the city of Danzig of coddling this sect, thereby probably provoking God's harsh punishment of Poland in the form of dam breaks along the Vistula and Nogat Rivers. The nobility agreed with him and wanted to expel all the Mennonites. Then the county parliaments, who knew the Mennonites well, defended them warmly. First the administrator of the royal estates[25] of Marienburg, Kitnowski, spoke up and then another elected representative[26] to the lower house of the Polish parliament from the Marienburg area. Both agreed that the Mennonites were hardworking farmers who kept their houses and lands in good condition, that they did the greatest service in the maintenance and improvement of the old dams and building of new ones, and in general worked for the benefit of the country and especially the lowlands. One could easily see where a lazy, drunken peasant lived or a hardworking and sober Mennonite. They therefore did not want to participate in the expulsion of this sect, but rather advised that more such people should be brought into the land. In spite of this, the nobility would have passed its motion if the representatives of the cities, especially Danzig, had not vigorously defended the Mennonites.[27]

At the national Parliament of Warsaw in the same year the Woywode of Pomerania again tried to pass another such motion, but now he was opposed by the Chief Provincial Court Judge[28] of Lauenburg/Lębork, Prebendowski, who made clear

---

[24][The Woywodes were nobles appointed by the king to oversee the provinces of the Polish Commonwealth. They were given control over state-owned estates in the province and used that income to cover their own and state expenses. Bär, *Behördenverfassung*, 35. Ed.]

[25][*Ökonomus*, the appointed noble manager of the territory (*Tafelgut*) around Marienburg that provided direct income to the royal court. Many of his tenants were Mennonites. Bär, *Behördenverfassung*, 46-7. Ed.]

[26][*Landbote*. The Polish Parliament had two houses; the 180 representatives of the lower house were elected from the nobility by the provincial parliaments. Bär, *Behördenverfassung*, 29. Ed.]

[27]Crichton, *Zur Geschichte der Mennoniten*, 25. Lengnich, *Geschichte der preussischen Lande*, 8:126.

[28][The *Landrichter* was the chief judge of a provincial or district court that

to King John Sobieski (1674-96) what harm would be done to his land by the expulsion of the Mennonites and that the Woywode was only interested in confiscating their property. The king thereupon rejected the declaration directed against the Mennonites and gave them a letter of protection in 1678, which was confirmed in 1694 by a new, solemn Charter of Privilege.

Examined by the Bishop

And so this danger, which threatened all of the Mennonites in Polish Prussia, was avoided, and one should think that now finally more peaceful times had come. But in the same year of 1678 the examination of Mennonite doctrine regarding *Arian heresies* that had been threatened earlier took place.

Since in time the term Rebaptizer began to lose its negative connotations, the opponents of the Mennonites concentrated on associating them with the Arians or Socinians.[29] Since these people were not tolerated in Poland, the attempt was made to apply the same law to the Mennonites.

In 1678 a religious interrogation of the Mennonite preachers of both congregations was conducted by order of the king and held before Bishop Stanislaus Sarnowski and his church judge, Joachim von Hirtenberg, as well as a few Catholic theologians "in the house of Jacob Gorley on the Langenmarkt, near the Junkerhof."[30] It was a remarkable scene. Simple shop keepers and craftsmen, who represented their embattled congregations, appeared before high church dignitaries and answered some forty or fifty dogmatic questions about the nature of the Trinity, about God, Christ, and the Holy Spirit, about the incarnation, personage, and the two natures of Christ, about baptism and communion, the forgiveness of sins, eternal life, etc. It would be

---

settled civil cases involving the nobility. Bär, *Behördenverfassung*, 43-6. Ed.]

[29]Socinianism had earlier been tolerated in Poland, and flourished in the first half of the 17th century. Since 1658 it was forbidden in Poland and its adherents expelled. Among the Socinians were very respected and highly educated people. [Socinians had roots in the Reformation and out of a combination of spiritualist and rationalist impulses denied the doctrine of the Trinity. Ed.]

[30]Archive of the Danzig Mennonite Church, Vol. LI.

tempting to repeat the questions and answers from the protocols, but I cannot do that here.

First of all, on January 17 the Frisian Elder Heinrich von Dühren, a spice dealer in Schidlitz, appeared and answered forty questions, generally clearly and simply. Only at question 7, "whether the flesh and the blood are the eternal Word?" and question 8, "whether the visible flesh and the humanity of Christ are the godhead or God?" we find the comment in the protocol: *hallucinatur* (he's talking nonsense). The same comment appears for question 14, "whether Christ were a creature according to human nature," and at question 19: "whether the divine nature had been incarnated in human nature, and in which form?"

On January 20 the pastors of the Flemish congregation had their turn. Here it was not the Elder Wilhelm Dunkel, but pastor Georg Hansen who spoke, and answered the forty-eight questions put to him with great assurance and openness, without taking offense. Georg Hansen, who had in 1671 published a booklet *An Account of Faith for the Youth, by a Lover of Truth, and Brought to the Light*, after the interrogation soon published a second booklet, in Latin and German, *Confession, or Brief and Simple Confession of Faith of the Mennonites in Prussia, called the Clarists*. Apart from that he published a substantial book in Dutch that he completed in 1699. It appeared in 1705 in Dutch with the title *Mirror of Life, written by George Hansen, Elder of the Church of God in Danzig Now Published by Some Lovers of Truth for the Honor of God and for the Edification of Their Fellow Men*.

In the short hand-written report that Georg Hansen left concerning the interrogation, he says in conclusion: "By this we were freed from all suspicion. This time too it cost us a serious amount of money which was very hard for us to raise, but God helped us to overcome it all." For the same reason Hansen's notes about these matters almost always conclude with the dry comment: "The price was 287 florins" or "the expenses amounted to 35 ducats." Once he wrote: "They let us know that they needed something, especially because I had asked for their favor and said we would show our gratitude. At first they acted as though they wanted nothing from us, but then they sent to

Willem Dunkel and asked for a demonstration of our gratitude, which amounted to 210 florins."

In one matter Georg Hansen proved to be puritanically strict and narrow. The well-known artist Enoch Seemann was banned by him, that is, separated from the congregation, because he painted portraits, and the Flemish congregation at that time considered that to be sin. Seemann protested in vain and finally wrote a very hateful book, *Revelation and Punishment of Georg Hansen's Folly, Published as a Brotherly Admonition and True Warning by a Lover of Truth, Stoltzenberg, 1697.* But he could not prevail against the will of the congregation, which stood unanimously behind its elder. He apparently emigrated to Holland, where at that time there was more tolerance and love of art in Mennonite circles.[31] Soon the Danzig Mennonites did not object to portrait painting anymore, as can be seen from the pastel portrait of Elder Hans von Steen from the middle of the eighteenth century that our church has in its possession.

Around 1700 we see the Danzig Mennonites still in a threatened condition. Without civil equality and limited to certain occupations, they always had to be prepared to suffer the arbitrariness of officials or the envy of the guilds. It is true that the authorities, especially the Danzig City Council, showed them good will and protection, especially when its own rights were at stake. But basically they had to fend for themselves; they had to be patient in suffering injustice, and they had to rely on their faith in God and in their own untiring industry. And the less the world wanted to know of them, the more firmly they held to each other, in their families and in their congregation.

---

[31]See Georg Cuny on Enoch Seemann, "Die Maler Deneter und Seemann," *Mitteilungen des Westpreussischen Geschichtsvereins* 12 (1913), 48.

Hans von Steen, elder of the Danzig Flemish congregation 1754-1781. [Scanned from 1919 edition. Ed.]

6
The Eighteenth Century to the End of Polish Sovereignty

The Congregation's Situation Around 1700

Twice more the attempt was made to deal with the Mennonites in terms of the law against heretics and to expel them from the country. At the Provincial Parliament in Marienburg in 1696 the Bishop of Ermland zealously took up that cause but without success; instead, the new King Augustus II at his coronation in Cracow on September 20, 1697, confirmed all the previous charters. Likewise, the Vice-Woywode Kaminczynski of Pomerania had no success with a similar application at the parliament of 1700. The Danzig representatives stated firmly *"that the Mennonites could not be driven out of Danzig without great harm."*[1]

It may appear that the City Council of Danzig defended the Mennonites more warmly in the provincial assemblies than at home against the guilds. But here, too, it sometimes defended them with firmness. So, for example, in a resolution given to the Third Order on October 30, 1677, which states: "Concerning the Mennonites, the Council, without approving that religion, communicates to the honorable Third Order that the number of them who suffered fire damage or had otherwise been allowed to take up residence here is not great. In wartime these people have helped to carry the burden, and supplied the city with not inconsiderable means. Not only did they draw business to the city, but also brought various manufacturing specialties here, which would undoubtedly cease if they departed. The Council is not cognizant of any special privileges that they may have received from the city, *apart from individual instances* when someone with experience in construction was of help in working on the city's buildings."[2]

---

[1] Crichton, *Zur Geschichte der Mennoniten*, 31.
[2] Danzig City Library, Ms. 212, fol. 442. From this resolution we can see that among the Dutch builders summoned by the city there were also some Mennonites who were given citizenship as an exception. I can not document individual cases, however.

Around the year 1700 the attempts to drive the Mennonites out of the land ceased, and the public complaints concerning their heresy stopped. On June 19, 1699, after they submitted their confession of faith in Latin and Polish, the bishop's office ruled that they were not to be considered the same as the Arians. Indeed, according to a note by Georg Hansen, the authenticity of which I cannot prove, the bishop's representative in Danzig is supposed to have said the following about the Mennonites about two years after the doctrinal examination: "When your two congregations had submitted their confession along with the questions and answers given before the bishop here, they were sent to the Pope in Rome, as is the custom in such cases, and the Pope thereupon stated that, according to the submitted confessions, the Mennonites could be counted among the Christian religions."

The Great Northern War

In spite of that, times did not improve in the eighteenth century. The world was filled with war and calamity. Here in the East the Great Northern War was raging, fought by Charles XII of Sweden against Russia and Poland. The city of Danzig was not involved as a combatant in this long-lasting struggle, which only ended with the Peace of Nystadt in 1721.[3] Foreign troops, however, were often quartered in the city, and the Russian soldiers of Peter the Great did not refrain from pillaging in the city and surrounding area. During this long period of war the trade and commerce of the city suffered, and the wealth of the inhabitants declined. This naturally affected the Mennonites, who mainly depended on trade and crafts for their livelihood.

The Number of Mennonites in and around Danzig

A word might be said about the numbers of Mennonites. We do not have accurate information from the early period. The elders avoided mentioning numbers to the authorities because they feared that these would be considered too high. But they

---

[3][The Great Northern War lasted from 1700-1721. Russia's victory in this war marked its rise to the status of a major European power and gained Peter I the outlet to the Baltic Sea that he desired. Ed.]

did keep records of baptisms, marriages, and deaths, which have been preserved since 1667, as mentioned above.[4] There was certainly a firm core of families settled permanently in the city and suburbs from the earliest time, but well into the eighteenth century there was a coming and going of Dutch co-religionists, which kept the numbers fluid.

From the year 1681 we have a "Register of Mennonites within and outside the City," which was compiled by order of the authorities.[5] This is not a complete listing of each individual, but rather of the number of households in the area of the city's jurisdiction. The list includes 124 names and was not carefully prepared. Also, it does not include the families living on the Bishop's lands or on the city's rural territory.

According to the baptismal registers of the Flemish congregation, there were on average twenty-two baptismal candidates in the years 1700-1750. The marriage register records an average of fourteen marriages. Accordingly, the congregation must have encompassed some one thousand people, including the children.

The Plague Year 1709 and a Difficult Elder Election
In 1709, the year the plague ravaged Danzig, 160 baptized persons, 70 men and 90 women, as well as 249 non-baptized persons or children—altogether 409 persons—died. There must still have been immigration from Holland in those years, since the baptism register every year has an appendix of persons who had been baptized in Holland. The number of marriages rose to 42 in 1710, while the number of baptismal candidates in the

---

[4][These records concern only the Flemish congregation. The originals are now in the Mennonite Library and Archives, North Newton, Kansas. Glenn Penner has made the baptismal records available at http://www.mennonitegenealogy.com/prussia/Danzig_Baptisms_1667-1800.htm. A published version of the earliest part of the records also exists: Konrad von Beuningen, ed., *Das älteste Kirchenbuch der niederländische Mennonitengemeinde zu Danzig/Gdansk* (Altona, Germany: Firma Sofortdruck Altona, 1990). Ed.]

[5]Danzig City Archives, Vol. 78, Nr. 40. [This list is reprinted in Penner, *Mennoniten*, 1:469-471. Ed.]

following years was above average. From this we can gather that the community soon regained its earlier numbers.

Among those who had died in the plague was also the elder, Christoph Engmann, who had been elected in 1703 to succeed Georg Hansen. He died on September 9, at age 68. To make it possible for the orphaned congregation to elect a new elder, Elder Dirk Siemens of the Greater Delta congregation[6] stayed the night in Neuendorf and then entered the church on city territory through the garden and the back door. In spite of the raging plague, 153 brothers met to elect a new elder. Anthony Jantzen was elected with 139 votes, and on the following day Dirk Siemens laid hands on him and installed him in his office. Since Siemens was not permitted to enter any house in the city, he returned to Neuendorf and from there to the Delta.

A more careful enumeration of the congregational members was undertaken on instruction from the Council in 1749, and this gives us a good picture, at least of the Flemish congregation, according to the account of Hans von Steen. There were 229 households, 137 wealthy and 92 poor, i.e. those who earned their living as artisans and the like but had no surplus. Finally, there were eight old couples and sixteen single persons living in the congregational alms house.[7] Thirty-eight families lived within the city walls, on unincorporated city territory 24, in Petershagen 12, in Sandgrube and at the high gate 10, in Neugarten 11, Schidlitz 18, Ohra/Orunia 10, Schottland 33, Stolzenberg 31, Strieß and Heiligenbrunn 4, Langfuhr/Orunia 7, Neuschottland/Nowe Szkoty 3,

---

[6][In the sixteenth century there was only one Flemish congregation with one Elder. In 1639 the Mennonites of the Greater Delta elected their own Elder to reduce the amount of travel required of the Danzig Elder. By the nineteenth century this one congregation had evolved into four independent congregations, Rosenort, Tiegenhagen/Tujce, Ladekopp/Lubieszewo, and Fürstenwerder/Żuławki. See Horst Penner, "West Prussia," *Mennonite Encyclopedia*, 4:920-6. Ed.]

[7][The alms house (*hospital*) was home to elderly or poor church members who otherwise had no place to live. Both room and board were provided here at the congregation's expense. This institution is described more fully in chapter 8. Ed.]

Mennonite banker Abraham Dirksen, from
Daniel Chodowiecki's *Reise von Berlin nach
Danzig 1773*

Oliva/Oliwa 2, Schönfeld/Łostowice 2, on the Holm/Ostrów
2, and in rural territory 20.

Occupationally most were shopkeepers and brandy distillers,
or ran a small grocery shop or inn (*Hakebude*). Of those living in
the city, ten were listed with the occupation of businessman,
one as teller (the banker Abraham Dirksen). Other professions
included a number of lace trim and textile makers, as well as
brewers, dyers and tanners, a "great master of weaving," several
brokers, groats makers, spinners, and harness makers. Among
the artisans most were shoemakers and tailors, but there were
also linen weavers, bakers, coopers, and plumbers. Finally,
mention is also made of gardeners, bleachers, cowherds and
dairy peddlers, some vinegar makers, leather workers, owners of
silk mills, cap makers, and listed individually a carpenter, a cook,
and a skinner. In a number of the listings there is an addendum:
"his wife makes bonnets." This apparently referred to the
strictly observed custom that the women in the Mennonite
church did not wear hats but rather coverings or bonnets, so
this was a quite lucrative business.

We can see from this compilation that one cannot really
speak of *wealthy* people. Those who were better off, however,
had to use their income and wealth not only to support the

church and the poor, but also many other expenses which were previously mentioned.

Protection or Exemption Money

The Danzig Mennonites felt that the so-called *protection or exemption tax (Schutz- or Schirmgeld)*, which the city imposed for the benefit of the city poor fund, was especially burdensome. Apart from that, they also had to pay excise taxes, which were charged at the city gates on many wares, at the double rate.

The protection tax was actually a tax on foreigners, for "all who enjoy the local public amenities." But starting in 1663 the city authorities, due to a great lack of funds, started looking for new taxes and were encouraged to apply this "foreign" tax to the Mennonites. On October 24, 1674, the Third Order proposed: "that since it was not only unreasonable but also irresponsible to spare the Mennonites more than others, even though they profess an illicit religion and do considerable harm to the citizenry, therefore all districts maintain the considered opinion that the most prominent of these should be taxed at 100 Reichsthaler annually, the lesser according to their possessions."[8] Thereupon, on August 29, 1675, a resolution of all Orders determined that the "Mennonites who have a household" will be taxed 300 florins.

The collection of this Protection Tax ran into difficulties. The Mennonites constantly complained that they were not foreigners but well-established residents who paid all the taxes of other inhabitants.[9] They received the reply, however, that if they did not want to acknowledge this tax as a foreign tax they could consider it a "livelihood tax" on Mennonites. In the meantime these Mennonites had complained to their friends in Holland about this unjust tax, and these friends had caused their government to take action on behalf of the Danzig Mennonites. And indeed, on May 4, 1681, a letter from the Estates General of the Netherlands[10] on this matter arrived at the Danzig City Council and the Dutch consul Pels intervened personally for his

---

[8]Danzig City Library, Ms. 211, 705.
[9]Danzig City Archives, Vol. XXXV, 70.
[10]Danzig City Archives, Mm. fol. 159.

countrymen. The City Council was inclined to give in and communicated to the Orders that "what has come in from the Mennonites does not amount to much and was gained with much effort and unpleasantness." Nonetheless the Second and Third Order stayed with their earlier decision. According to the account of the alms fund,[11] in 1681 the sum of 4,964 florins protection tax money was collected. In 1690 it was 4,727 florins and in the next year it fell to 1,553 florins, rose to 3,037 florins in 1692 and 4,377 florins in 1693.

Then, for unknown reasons, the City Council and the representatives of the alms fund neglected to collect the tax in the following two years. When they were severely admonished by the Orders, the City Council answered on July 18, 1696: "Since the Protection Tax funds from the Mennonites were reckoned among the miscellaneous items and were much bother and of little use to collect, therefore the City Council has not wanted to pursue this avenue, since it is *not a favored method in the long run*, and would prefer that this might be dealt with by negotiation." The Third Order answered on July 23, 1696, that there was no reason to spare the Mennonites this Protection Tax, "who are not here as refugees, but in most cases have been inhabitants for many years, and live and intend to die here. Especially since they do not belong to any nation or territory, but are bound together by their religion, which is only tolerated in a few places, they live well here and are doing better than many leading citizens."[12]

In the following years the tax was collected again, bringing 3,305 florins in 1696, and remained at that level for the next ten years. In 1708 the Mennonites again presented an urgent petition "to be spared payment of the Protection tax and offering instead to delay interest payment on the sum of 12,000 florins loaned to the city earlier for a period of twelve years on condition that they should not be subject to the Protection tax for that period of time, and that after that time the capital would

---

[11][The alms fund (*Hilfsgelderkasse*) was used to cover the expenses of the alms house as well as other needs of poor members who did not reside in the alms house. This fund is described more fully in chapter 8. Ed.]

[12]Danzig City Archives, Mm. 4, 340.

be returned to them, or that they would be freed from the tax for thirty years and the money would then be donated to the city."[13] The Council voted for the acceptance of this latter offer, but the Third Order did not agree, and demanded that after twelve years both capital and interest should be given to the city. A compromise proposal by the Council to agree to a period of twenty years was defeated at first but may have come into force, since there is no more mention of the Protection Tax in the following period. But then it reappears very emphatically in the year 1750, as we shall see.

Donations within the Congregation

If the Mennonites had to pay considerable regular taxes and occasional levies to the State, the maintenance of their church also was a large annual expense. The church building had to be maintained, and especially the poor had to be supported. *But there was no coercion in the matter of church finances and everything depended on donations and self-taxation.* The offerings sufficed to cover the regular expenses, and these were collected in the church leaders' gathering room after the sermon or in the homes by the deacons. Not until 1734 were collection boxes for the church and the poor acquired, a practice continued even today.

When extraordinary expenses arose, the church leadership announced on Sunday through the elder what it was about, and asked for voluntary contributions, or a congregational meeting was called when there was a particularly urgent need.

For example, in 1707 the congregation of Elbing asked for a "brotherly helping hand," because they could no longer support their poor. Deacon Schroeder advanced 500 florins and the congregation in the Greater Delta 600 florins. In the notes of the later elder Isaac de Veer we read: "After a talk by the honored Elder Christoph Engmann, the Elbing letter was read before the gathered brethren, and it was unanimously decided to give what help we could. Hereupon the church leadership met in their separate room and the brothers then went in one by one and told the amount of their free gifts. At this brotherhood

---

[13]Danzig City Archives, Mm. 4, 327.

meeting and in the following meeting with other brothers who had not been at the meeting, the sum of 3,019 florins was gathered, of which 1,000 florins was immediately sent to Elbing."[14]

In 1709 during the plague there was a general collection for the benefit of the poor, "especially for those who had become poor during this time without nourishment, to support them and to look after their funerals." In spite of the bad times 2,551 florins were collected. There was also the good custom, which has been maintained into modern times, of leaving bequests for the care of the poor. And so we read in the notes mentioned above: "Because so many departed from us in this year of the plague, various bequests left 15,890 florins to the poor. But in the same year 12,011 florins were also spent for support."

In the previous year, 1708, 1,054 florins had been gathered for those suffering in the Marienburg Delta. And in 1713, when a dike burst on the Nogat River and submerged the Elbing lowlands, the Danzig Mennonites collected 2,777 florins in three days for the inhabitants who had fled to Elbing.

In the case of necessary construction, the expenses were collected in advance by voluntary gifts of the congregation. Thus, in 1714 when the alms house was in bad condition and threatened to collapse, the individual members committed themselves in writing in the leaders' room to the amounts they were willing to give. 175 members signed for the amount of 3,871 florins. The individual donations varied between one and one hundred florins. The one-story brick building cost 4,275 florins.[15]

"In 1715 the congregation was told that given the current famine there were many poor homes which needed support, and it was decided to have a special collection. The two deacons collected over 2,000 florins in members' homes."

---

[14]Archive of the Danzig Mennonite Church, L., I., fol.13.

[15]To allow comparison with today's prices [1919] it should be noted that according to the bills, 35,500 bricks cost 708 florins and 4,604 roof tiles cost 192 florins.

Donations Outside the Family of Faith
Thus it went year after year. And it was not a matter only of collecting for their own congregation or for their co-religionists elsewhere. True to their principle of "brotherly love" they extended their help to others. Here are two examples from the notes of Georg Hansen, which lie before me:

"In 1687 the Jesuits asked our congregation to build a tower for their church and put the clock in the tower. A collection was held and the sums of first 120 florins and then 80 florins were sent to them."

"In April 1688 we were approached by the Mayor Schumann, the administrator of the City highlands, to give a small contribution to the construction of a Lutheran church in Ohra. 300 florins were collected and were accepted with great gratitude."

In 1732 several hundred expelled Salzburg Protestants moved through Danzig en route to East Prussia. All the Evangelical churches raised collections for them. The Mennonites collected 1,015 florins in the city and 400 florins in Neugarten.[16]

Flemish Connections
The Danzig Mennonites were in active contact with fellow Mennonites near and far. The three large Flemish congregations in Danzig, Elbing, and in the great Marienburg Delta[17] held faithfully together and helped each other in all matters. Their contact with the Dutch mother congregations was also very active, as has been mentioned. The well-to-do families liked to

---

[16][At the same time, the organizer of this resettlement, King Frederick William I of Prussia, was expelling Mennonites who were no longer needed in Ducal Prussia, since the Salzburg Protestants could now be settled there. Mack Walker, *The Salzburg Transaction: Expulsion and Redemption in Eighteenth-Century Germany* (Ithaca: Cornell University Press, 1992), 86-7. Those Mennonites expelled from Ducal Prussia founded a new congregation in Tragheimerweide just south of the Vistula Delta region. Ed.]

[17]The congregation there eventually became so large that it had to be divided into two. Thus, in 1728 the Heubuden congregation came into being with its own elder and preachers, alongside the so-called Grosswerder congregation.

send their sons to Amsterdam, Rotterdam, or Haarlem to learn business there. In many cases they were then also baptized there and returned to Danzig later.

In 1725 the so-called "Danzig" congregations in Amsterdam and Rotterdam wrote letters to their Danzig brothers and complained that they were orphaned after the death of their Elder Adrian van Gamern. They asked for an elder to be sent from the Prussian Flemish congregations, one who was already in office here. Since the Elbing and Marienburg Delta congregations could not release a suitable candidate, it was decided in Danzig to draw the lot among the active preachers for one who would be sent to Holland. Each of them in advance had agreed, perhaps with a heavy heart, to follow the call. The lot fell on Dirk Jantzen, the brother of Elder Anthony Jantzen. The chosen one was ordained, and traveled to Amsterdam on September 7, 1725, with his family. He had, however, stipulated that he would be allowed to return as soon as this was possible. Since his brother Anthony died a few months later in Danzig, there were many in the congregation who wanted to recall him immediately. But he remained in Amsterdam for eight years, returning to Danzig only on November 1, 1733. In the meantime Isaac de Veer had been elected elder in February 1726, and so both men served as elders until Isaac de Veer retired due to ill health in 1739. He died in 1745, and Dirk Jantzen in 1750.

The Russian Siege of 1734 and Its Tragic Consequences

The year 1734 was a year of terror and the ravages of war for Danzig. The battle for the throne between Augustus III and Stanisław Leszczyński was an evil portent for the city.[18] Danzig had recognized King Stanisław and received him within its walls

---

[18][Loius XV of France backed his father-in-law, the Polish nobleman, Stanisław Leszczyński, for the Polish throne, while Austria, Russia, and Saxony backed Augustus III, the king of Saxony and son of the previous Polish King, Augustus II. The Polish king was traditionally elected by the Polish nobility, but in the eighteenth century this "election" was, in fact, controlled by foreign powers, especially Russia. The War of Polish Succession lasted from 1733 to 1735 and resulted in the coronation of Augustus III. Ed.]

in 1733. In February a Russian-Saxon army under General Lascy moved toward Danzig, and on March 16, after Field Marshall Münnich had taken command, the siege began. In spite of a brave defense by the Danzig troops, the city capitulated on July 9. On that occasion there were 40,000 men of the Russian and Saxon army besieging the city, which was hit with 4,430 bombs. 1,800 houses were destroyed and damaged; 1,500 inhabitants were killed or wounded.

The Mennonite congregation suffered terribly. In the chronicle of Hans von Steen we find:

> On February 25, 1734, Dirk Jantzen preached, and while we were singing the 139th Psalm after the sermon, the Russian Cossacks appeared at the customs barrier of Ohra, and since they were shooting at them with cannons, everyone became very nervous and the congregation quickly dispersed.
>
> On March 21 there was supposed to be a church service, but since already on March 20 the Moscovites approached, the service had to be cancelled, since the congregation members from outside the city walls fled to the city with their most precious personal belongings.
>
> On March 28 again there was no service, since *by now they were all in the city*. Likewise on April 4. But the brethren were called to the place of Jacob Momber in the Frauengasse/Mariacka at 6 p.m., where the Elders Isaac de Veer and Dirk Jantzen told them that now, as was known, many had been ruined by the war and the poor of the congregation should be sent to the Greater Delta in the company of a preacher, where they could be looked after better than was possible here. This plan found general agreement.

On April 4 a service was held in the Fahnen granary between the Thorn and the Cow Bridges, but because the space was quite unsuitable, they rented "a large hall and a room in a grey house on the Steindamm/Kamienna Grobla" for the following Sundays and for Easter. The sermon was repeated in the afternoon, since the whole congregation could not be accommodated. On Easter Monday this plan had to be given up as well "because the cannon balls from the Judenschanze[19] were landing near that place. It was not possible to hold church services anywhere in the city, apart from the churches of St. Barbara and St. Jacob."

After the capitulation, when the city gates were open again, the degree of destruction in the villages outside the walls could be seen. Petershagen, Neugarten, all of Schidlitz, Nonnenacker, Schlapke,[20] and Jacobsacker as well as most of Stolzenberg and Schottland had been razed, and both Mennonite congregations had suffered heavy damage. There are no details about the Frisian congregation, except that their meeting place and alms house were destroyed. Because they received the same amount of 3,000 florins as the Flemish congregation from the Dutch relief, there must have been an equal number of those who had lost their homes. In the Flemish congregation there were 82 families listed by name that had lost their homes and movable goods. In addition, the buildings left standing were in such bad condition that they could not be inhabited. This applied also to the Flemish Mennonite church on city territory and the alms house that had been rebuilt only twenty years before. The Russians used this building as a horse barn, and all the wood in the church—benches, windows, and doors—had been torn out and the roof uncovered. Its rafters had been removed and the roofing tiles lay broken on the ground. The flooring had been ripped up "to see whether anything was hidden beneath it." The large tile heating stove had been upended. This picture of destruction presented itself to the eyes of the congregational leaders and members when in July they could finally go out there. But the reconstruction began immediately under the

---

[19][A part of the fortifications of the city. Ed.]

[20][Schlapke was located at the edge of Schidlitz. In 1814 in the wake of the Napoleonic wars all of these settlements were incorporated into an expanded Danzig municipality. Bär, *Behördenverfassung*, 151-2. Perhaps this is the reason we have been unable to find a Polish equivalent. Ed.]

direction of the master carpenter Gerdt Wiens. The church was restored in its previous simple form and a second floor was added to the alms house, since the number of poor had increased considerably. The construction cost over 4,000 florins, which was raised in part by means of a loan. In October 1734 the administrator of the construction, Deacon Gillis Claassen, died, followed in February 1735 by his wife. They left 6,000 fl. to the congregation, which enabled it to settle the debt.

Now they turned with redoubled energy to the reconstruction of their individual houses and businesses. Some of the members had to start from scratch, but with faith in God and untiring effort they took up the work, and some again achieved moderate wealth. But most had to limit themselves strictly. Not without reason did Hans van Steen, who had been elected as a deacon on June 15, 1738, complain "that in the time of my service as a deacon, which lasted until 1743, the alms fund was very low, so that we had to take collections once or twice a year and make visitations in the home. The deacons usually had to advance several hundred guilders. In addition we had to borrow with interest 1,000 florins for the benefit of the poor. However, in 1742 Hermann Schroeder died and left 3,000 florins for the poor. The debt could be paid leaving a balance in the fund. In addition a special collection was held for impoverished families, which brought in about 1,000 florins, which was distributed to ten poor families, who received 50, 100, or 150 florins."

Soon new tribulations would be visited on the Mennonite congregation.

7

Congregational Life and City Politics in the Mid-Eighteenth Century[1]

Hard Times and Disturbances among the Citizens

After the war of 1734 economic life in Danzig remained at a low point. Trade continually decreased and general poverty set in, lowering the standard of living of the citizens noticeably.[2] The political struggles grew worse and beginning in 1748 resulted in a reformation of the city administration in a democratic sense. Because of its failed policies in the War of Polish Succession, the Council had brought the city into a difficult situation. The indemnity paid to Russia and to King Augustus III of Poland made the debt load almost unbearable. Danzig's old position of power was gone. If the earlier Polish kings had set great store on good relations with Danzig because of its financial and military assistance, Augustus III no longer needed to bother. What indeed could the impoverished city offer him? Its influence in politics and trade, its connections with the powerful states of Western Europe, these were only a beautiful memory of an earlier golden era. Russia, which was the rising eastern power, naturally wanted to displace Danzig as the dominant power of the eastern Baltic region.

These problems were stirred up even more by the finance policies of the City Council, which met with strong opposition among its citizenry. Danzig, like other jurisdictions, raised most of its revenue by *a customs tax charged at the city gates*, an indirect tax on all manner of things, including also necessary foodstuffs. Since such indirect taxes impinge more upon the mass of society by raising their cost of living than upon the wealthy, this was seen to be a particular injustice, especially in a time of general need. But the City Council did not want to change its tax policy, because those taxes were easy to collect.

---

[1] [Mannhardt originally titled this chapter simply "Continuation." We have supplied a more descriptive chapter title here. Ed.]

[2] See Simson, *Geschichte der Stadt Danzig* (Danzig: L. Sauniers Buchhandlung, 1903), 105, and especially Goldmann, *Danziger Verfassungskämpfe*, 90ff.

Now the Third Order, as the legal representatives of the citizenry, united with the unhappy merchants, the guilds, and all those who justly desired a fundamental reformation of the city's political structures. And when they could not win the City Council over to their plans, or only received half-hearted concessions, they took the fateful step of taking their case to the king. Augustus III naturally used the occasion to limit the autonomy of the city and he received the deputation from the Danzig citizenry very benevolently when it appeared at his court in December 1748.[3]

The Third Order Again Attacks the Mennonites

The Mennonites, of course, were also drawn into these battles through no fault of their own. The Third Order had always seen them as an object of complaint. Finally the time had come, in the opinion of the guild representatives, to get rid of their hated competition in production and retail.[4]

Thus the matter of the Mennonites occupied the Orders from 1748 to 1750 without interruption. In 1748 King Augustus III had confirmed the traditional freedoms of the Danzig Mennonites. In petitions of the Third Order of May 10, September 2, 1748, and again on September 8 and 17, 1749, it was declared that the freedoms granted by the king only applied to the manufacture of lace trim, while in the meantime the Mennonites had gotten into all the other branches of the crafts and trades, as, for example, the spice trade and the widespread selling of honey. The City Council had allowed this and continued to allow Mennonites, Jews, and other such "non-citizens" to settle outside the city walls, so that the city villages and rural areas such as Ohra, Langfuhr, unincorporated city territories, Petershagen, Sandgrube and the two Neugartens

---

[3]See Goldmann, *Danziger Verfassungskämpfe*, 94ff., for further developments in these important political struggles.

[4][For similar reasons the Third Order also proceeded during this time against the Jews of Danzig, This upheaval in Danzig was part of a wider push by the merchants and guilds of the Third Order to gain more power. They turned to the king for assistance, who was only too glad to use the occasion to reduce the autonomy of the Danzig City Council since they had opposed his election. Cieślak and Czesław, *History of Gdańsk*, 247-61. Ed.]

were becoming cities, while the actual city was going to ruin. They claimed *the Mennonites were foreigners*, no matter how long they had been in the area, since according to their religion they could not swear the oath of citizenship nor bear arms. Therefore *they should be treated as foreigners when it came to applying those laws to them.*[5]

It was no wonder, then, that among the complaints that the representatives of the Third Order presented in Warsaw in December 1748, the Mennonite question played an important role in addition to the demand to change the composition of the City Council and to cancel customs taxes. The king[6] was told "that the Rebaptizers or Mennonites of Danzig, who were not eligible to become citizens, should not be allowed to carry on crafts and trades reserved for citizens, much less work as master artisans and merchants, nor should they have a royal charter or decree, but they have a *biased and self-interested* magistrate on their side."[7]

Gotthilf Wernick and the Renewal of the Protection Tax

The king sent two plenipotentiaries to Danzig, the Bishop of Ermland/Warmia, Grabowski, and the Saxon Court Counselor von Leubnitz "to investigate as to what had crept in to work against the royal decrees and to the disadvantage of commerce and the common good." These two worked together with the opposition for a year to limit the influence of the City Council, and in this they were supported most of all by the leader of the Third Order, Gotthilf Wernick. As in all radical changes, it is as easy for dishonest as for honest people to rise up from anonymity and attain power and prestige. Thus this Wernick, a clever but unscrupulous agitator, quickly made himself the spokesperson for all the dissatisfied, and ruthlessly attacked the stiff, inflexible, and undiplomatic City Council. He managed to secure the sympathy of the Saxon-Polish court. On August 9, 1749, as a result of the report by the plenipotentiaries and the

---

[5]Goldmann, *Danziger Verfassungskämpfe*, 85.

[6]Danzig City Archives, Misc., Vol. 23, 1.

[7]Augustus III did not pay any attention to these matters, but turned them over to his powerful prime minister, Duke Brühl.

actions of Wernick, a royal decree was issued according to which a part of the city's customs tax was cancelled and in its place a number of other taxes were to be raised. Among these new taxes was a 5,000 florins *protection tax*, which would be collected from the Mennonites in the city and surrounding area. So the earlier protection tax was revived, after having been all but forgotten.[8] But this time it recurred in a more onerous form. Earlier the city had been responsible for its collection from individual Mennonites. Now it was assessed on the two congregations and left up to them to assess and collect from their own members.

The Council was forced to collect the new taxes for better or worse, and on January 14, 1750, the mayor summoned Elder Hans von Almonde and read him the edict, according to which, by a decision of all the Orders, the Mennonites living in the city and surrounding territories would have to raise the annual sum of 5,000 florins as a protection tax. The first payment had been due in December of the previous year, and thus would have to be raised as soon as possible—February at the latest. In the future, 5,000 florins would have to be deposited in the city poor fund each December. From this we see that the protection tax, just as before, was raised by the city from the Mennonites though now on the king's command, and that it was based on the right to tax strangers.[9]

Wernick attempted in vain to move the royal court to restrict the Mennonites with new and more serious limits. In a petition of January 26, 1750, he claimed that the Mennonites, "who were only the favorites of the Council because they bribed individual

---

[8]Hans van Steen writes: "I wanted to find out about the protection tax, which had been collected many years ago, but I could not find anything in the written records. Only the eighty-year-old Cornelius Grauert knew enough to tell me that in his father's day some 3,000 florins had been collected, and that thereafter they had been freed from it after much petitioning and donating. " Cf. above p. 94.

[9]W. Mannhardt, *Wehrfreiheit*, 109, let himself be confused by a remark of Hans van Steen in a letter from the year 1768, to the effect that the protection tax was a payment for the freedom from the oath and military service. And Szper, *Nederlandsche nederzettingen in West-Pruisen*, 225, seemed to assume that it was a tax paid to the king for freedom from military service.

members," were the real cause of the enmity between the
Council and the Third Order. Mennonites were "thieves of
food, *who because of their religious rules could not be proper citizens,*
since they reject the oath and *consider all authority coercion.*
Furthermore, by combining craft production and retail sales,
they have assumed more freedom than the regular citizens
have." Now one had to endure the plan of the royal court to
allow them another five years without additional penalties to
wrap up their affairs. Such a postponement seemed tantamount
to a cancellation of all the measures taken against the
Mennonites.

The fact that Wernick was not able to achieve his goals
against the Mennonites may be due to the fact that they had
once again complained to their co-religionists in Holland, and
the Dutch representative had therefore put in a good word for
them at the Polish court.

Nonetheless Wernick had already used his great influence
with the Danzig Orders earlier to bring about an edict on
November 10, 1749, with the following items directed against
the Mennonites:

1. That the sellers of hard liquor, textile dyers, textile
finishers,[10] and linen weavers who make their livings outside of
city walls must desist from *producing their own raw materials,* and
must purchase what is necessary for their professions from the
local citizens.

2. That in Petershagen only a single general retail shop[11] may
be allowed inside the gate and one outside. Also there may *only
be one such shop*[12] in each village of the City's highlands area[13] that
must conform to city regulations. These may sell – at the correct
measurement and weight – market baskets,[14] tar buckets,[15]
shovels, and brooms, but must desist from selling any other

---

[10][*Presser.* The technical term for pressing linen cloth is calendering. These
presses, or calenders, were also used to produce embossed finishes on cloth.
Ed.]

[11][*Haakwerk.* Ed.]

[12][*Hakenbude.* Ed.]

[13][The Danzig highlands, in contrast with the lowlands or delta area. Ed.]

[14][*Lüschken.* Ed.]

[15][*Theerpaudeln,* carried on the back of a wagon. Ed.]

crafted items on pain of severe punishment, and that no *Mennonite* will be allowed to have such a shop.

3. That in Petershagen, on the city territory, and in Ohra farriers or general blacksmiths, harness makers, wheelwrights, tailors, shoemakers, and barbers will be tolerated, one of each of these outside the gate at Petershagen, one on the city territories, and one in Ohra. These will be subject to the masters of their craft and the guild laws (and thus cannot be Mennonites).

4. That in all other villages on Danzig territory apart from the one retail shop, there shall be one farrier or general blacksmith, one harness maker and wheelwright, one tailor, and one shoemaker.

5. That the small shops that are to be removed, along with the grain dealers and other shops, and everything that has to do with trade, as well as all other illegal crafts, will not be tolerated after Easter 1750.[16]

This edict spelled ruin for a great number of Mennonites and would force them to move. In their distress they turned to the bishop on whose lands their fellow believers lived without difficulty. They showed him their business concessions, which each had purchased from the City Council for good money, and asked him to speak on their behalf. He looked at the concessions and said: "They could not be more worthless. You can use the paper they are printed on for whatever you want. Let your own authorities help you." But he did at least want to speak to the king for them, which, however, did not change anything.

According to another decision, the Mennonite traders were driven from the commodity exchanges (*Börse*), although they had been active there for fifty years "with the approval of all the Orders and many merchants."

Naturally the consequences of these harsh measures were soon visible. Many previously wealthy Mennonites became poor, some moved away as far as Königsberg and Amsterdam. Only the really wealthy business people in the city and the

---

[16]Archive of the Danzig Mennonite Church, LI, 65f.

manufacturers like Dirk Hekker[17] of *Lachs* as well as Mennonites living on the bishop's lands or in the delta could endure the bad times and thus preserve the congregation. The small craftsmen and merchants, who could no longer keep their shops, had to limit themselves severely in order to survive with their families, until after eight or ten years greater freedom was gradually extended to them.

Elder Hans von Steen from the City Territories
The main leader among the Danzig Mennonites during this difficult time was *Hans von Steen*. Elected as deacon in 1738 and already in 1743 as a preacher, he was soon the most influential person in the congregational leadership. The Elder Dirk Jantzen was old and tired (died January 25, 1750), and his successor Hans von Almonde (1751-53), a fine but sickly man, was not up to the demands of the time. Thus it happened that Hans von Steen had long been the spiritual leader of the church when he was elected elder in 1754.

He was born on March 9, 1705. His parents lived in Neugarten and belonged to the Frisian congregation. He was sent to Amsterdam at an early age, where he did an apprenticeship in business and was baptized in 1726. After his return he joined the Flemish congregation, married Sara Siemens in 1726 and owned a shop and distilled spirits in the city. He was a man of education and decisive in character, of deep and serious piety, honest and intelligent at the same time. For these reasons he enjoyed confidence and respect, not only in the congregation but also beyond that. His letters, which are saved in our archive, testify to a wide correspondence. They are almost all in Dutch.

---

[17]Of him it says in an old file that he "carried on like a nobleman and to the displeasure of the City Council, the citizenry and his congregation he had become a Royal Prussian Commerical Counsel." [Lachs was a well-known restuarant in Danzig where a famous liqueur, *Danziger Goldwasser,* was distilled. Lachs is the German word for salmon and today the restaurant goes by the Polish name with the same meaning, Pod Łososiem. Klassen, *Homeland for Strangers,* 70-1. Prussia was already trying to exert economic pressure on Danzig and thus association with Prussia would have been unpopular in business circles. Ed.]

He made many notes about the difficulties that beset him and his congregation from 1748 onward, and these are of value. Tirelessly he intervened on behalf of his congregation and the threatened trades in the city, and he had to undertake many a difficult and humbling visit. When the edict from all of the Orders was announced with "trumpets" and tacked up everywhere in order to "ridicule the Mennonites," he immediately went to the City Hall with his fellow church leader Arend Kauenhowen. "In order not to be seen by too many we went by a back gate, but it is beyond words how we were derided and laughed at by the agitated crowd. At the *Dielenmarkt*[18] we heard a song sung by the carpenters, in which we were derided, and everywhere we went we were a spectacle and reproach to all."

When in the fall of 1752 an inspection had revealed that a shopkeeper in the city had sold peas and another milled wheat, they were summoned to the City Hall on October 23 and reminded in strong language "that they should completely refrain from dealing in honey, craft goods, lace, and all such goods and not even a shilling's worth of business, indeed, not sell a single shoelace or string, on pain of heavy punishment and confiscation."

Hans von Steen and Arend Kauenhowen, along with the representatives of the shopkeepers and laborers from the city territory (including non-Mennonites), came forward and pleaded

that they might have pity on us and allow us to carry on these small dealings, since we did not know how we should feed ourselves and our wives and children in an honest fashion. But it was all for naught. One even said that we should be satisfied and not ask how we should support ourselves, or they would denounce us to be executed by axe on our necks. The Councilman Janzen seemed to be sympathetic to our fate and said: 'Children, you must comfort yourselves with the memory of the

---

[18]An open square in the area of the *Wiebenkaserne*. See Walther Stephan, *Die Strassennamen Danzigs* (Danzig: L. Saunier, 1911) 30.

first Christians, who also were persecuted!' I answered: 'Yes, that is true, but that was among heathen, and now we expect something better from you, who are Christians.'

But it was all of no avail, and the conclusion was: We cannot help you! And from the Third Order we heard many sarcastic words and had to leave in sorrow. Whereupon we each brought the sad tidings to our wives and children at home, causing many tears, since now everything seemed to be at an end for us. I too have to confess that I often said to my wife and to my friend Kauenhowen: 'What shall become of us, now that there is no future?' But some comforting words of the Savior came to mind: *Any yet your heavenly Father feeds them,*[19] and this was my sure hope as well."

The sterner application of these hated prohibitions was relaxed in the succeeding years, so that around 1760 the shops of the few who had remained were active again, especially since the peasants were not happy about the situation. They drove to the city in the morning "used their market baskets in order to take along their wares, and on the way home from the market filled up the same with vinegar, sugar, and the like" regardless of the prohibition against such trade.

The collection of the protection tax, which Hans von Steen had also taken on, created great difficulties for him. He did not want to depart from the congregational principle that all sums should be given voluntarily, but he occasionally had the unhappy experience of seeing that certain persons, not the poorest, were often very reticent to donate. He thought it unjust that the Frisian congregation, which had proportionately more wealthy members, only contributed 1,300 florins, basing this on their smaller overall number of members. Thus, as a result, for

---

[19]["Look at the birds of the air; they neither sow nor reap nor gather into barns, and yet your heavenly Father feeds them. Are you not of more value than they?" Matthew 6:26. Ed.]

example "the rich Dirk Hekker did not pay more than the old Cornelius Moor, a small silk dealer in the Sandgrube."

In light of the prevalent poverty of the settlements outside the city walls, it was not always possible to collect the 5,000 florins on time, and already in 1755 the city, responding to repeated requests, felt it necessary to reduce the protection tax to 3,000 florins.

The new city administration that had been created by the "Ordinance" of 1750[20] realized that the Mennonite congregations could not raise the protection tax in this amount, in addition to all the other burdens that their members had to share with citizens, often doubly or triply. And after the worst of the new Councilors, Wernick,[21] was out of the picture, the Council reduced the amount in 1759 to 2,000 florins.

That the congregation survived the difficult years from 1748 to 1760 is due in great part to its elder, Hans von Steen. He led the congregation with a calm hand through internal and external difficulties until better times arrived. In the 1760s and even more in the 1770s the congregation was again flourishing.

The number of baptisms in this period averaged twenty-six a year and the number of registered births forty. In 1779 there

---

[20][Royal intervention resulted in a revamping of Danzig's government, granting the Third Order some influence on the composition of the First and Second Orders. Cieślak and Czesław, *History of Gdańsk*, 251-4. Ed.]

[21]Hans von Steen in his simple fashion tells us about this infamous adventurer. "Gotthilf Wernick had come from Königsberg as a poor man, had married the daughter of a herring packer, and ran a small shop in the Röpergasse. He then came into the Third Order and soon was in charge. During his time as a representative to the royal court he had gathered a lot of money, and so, after he became a member of the City Council, he bought a fine house on the Langenmarkt/Długi Targ (the third house from the Junkerhof, where Gorley had previously lived, and where in 1678 the examination of the Mennonites had taken place), and had it beautifully restored and gilded. He was a spice wholesaler and built a fine cottage in Emaus, and flourished to all appearances. But in 1760 he acted as though he needed to travel to the court, and took residence in Warsaw, where he carried on his tricks at the royal court."

Wernick had committed serious frauds here and his bankrupcy amounted to two million fl. In Warsaw his role was also soon played out. He was delivered to the Danzig Council in 1762, which put him into strict confinement in the prison at Weichselmünde, where he died in 1773.

were thirty-eight baptismal candidates, and at the communion service on July 4, 569 members were present. The gifts for the poor in the church collection boxes were so great that from 1769 to 1775 no special collections were necessary. The times were not easy and the church had about a hundred poor to support. In the next chapter we will deal with the care of the poor in more detail.

The conditions for the Mennonites had improved in part because the citizenry no longer considered them enemies. A new time of greater tolerance and co-operation began. Guests from other religious backgrounds often came to the Dutch sermons of Hans von Steen, especially his solemn baptismal services.

In 1773 he suffered a stroke that affected his speech, but he stayed in his post until 1776. Then he had to be replaced by elders of other congregations who came to perform the special services. In 1775 he led a baptismal service with 28 candidates and on July 9 celebrated communion with 525 members. In 1776 and 1777 he could only lead the baptism but no longer the communion. After that he had to give up all duties due to weakness. In 1779 he resigned, precipitating the election of a new elder. The choice fell to the longest serving of the four preachers, Peter Epp from Neunhuben, who was ordained on January 30, 1780, and confirmed by the elder of the Heubuden congregation near Marienburg. It was the first time that a member of this rural branch had become elder in Danzig. However, he moved his residence to the city to be nearer to the church.

Hans von Steen died on September 21, 1781. He was married three times and had seventeen children, of whom only three outlived him. Death had often knocked on his door. Just in those hard years for the congregation when his own survival was also difficult, his first wife died (September 1749), and in July 1751, after a short marriage, his second wife, Elisabeth Tiessen, died immediately after the birth of a daughter. A year later he married Christina Loewen from Tiegenhof, who survived him. Of his seventeen children seven died in infancy, and the others in the happy time of childhood and youth. Even in 1780, a year before his death, he had to accompany two beautiful daughters of 18 and 28 years to their graves. But he remained unshaken in his manly faith, and at his grave the words so often misused could be spoken justly to the congregation: "Remember your leaders, those who spoke the word of God to you; consider the outcome of their way of life, and imitate their faith!" (Hebrews 13:7)

8

The Religious Life of the Danzig Mennonites to the Beginning of the Nineteenth Century

Church Buildings and Alms Houses

We have fairly accurate information about the church organization and practices of the Danzig Mennonites. Although at the beginning they had only been able to meet secretly in private homes, in the seventeenth century they were allowed to build places of worship.[1] These were very simple structures without any decoration that might attract attention. First, the Frisian congregation was successful in purchasing a lot at the Neugarten Gate, which was registered in the name of Hans van Beuningen on September 18, 1638.[2] Including a small building on the property, it cost 2,500 Polish florins. Here in the garden the church was built, which in its appearance could not be distinguished from other simple houses. This was in keeping with the Mennonites' principle of simplicity as well as with the rules of the authorities, since their worship was not allowed to have a public character. In a Charter of Privileges from King John Casimir of 1660 it states: "*their worship services are not public, but are of the kind allowed to them by the indulgence and tolerance of the clergy.*"

This house of worship remained the property of the heirs of Hans van Beuningen. By 1713 all the male heirs had died and the church property through marriage had come into the hands of strangers. A Mennonite by the name of Niklas Penner therefore repurchased it, this time for 3,000 Polish florins. His heirs in 1734 declared formally that the property, although registered in the name of their deceased father, properly belonged to the Neugarten Mennonite congregation. Because the congregation did not have legal standing, it could not be registered as the proprietor.

The Flemish congregation had its home at the Petershagen Gate. Since most of the members lived in Schottland, they built their house of worship in the nearest area of the city. They too

---

[1] [*Bethäuser*, a term still used today by some conservative German-speaking Mennonites to describe their church buildings. Ed.]

[2] A. Brons, *Mennoniten*, incorrectly gives the date of 1660, 244.

registered the deed in the name of one of their members, Hans Erich, whose "garden, house, and estate" they bought in 1648 for 7,300 florins. Judging by the price it must have been a fairly large piece of land, in keeping with the much larger Flemish membership. In 1686 the heirs of Hans Erich had the property transferred to the name of the current elder, Wilhelm Dunkel, and on December 9, 1732, it was registered in the name of the congregation.

Besides both churches there also arose an alms house, which no Mennonite congregation could do without, since they did not allow members to become homeless. The whole congregation was responsible to see that no one had to beg. Brotherly assistance from person to person, from house to house, from congregation to congregation, was among the first duties of the Mennonites. Their care for the poor was to be similar to that of the early Christians, and for that reason they had, besides the office of preacher, the office of deacon or caregiver to the poor. In addition the Flemish congregation almost always had a deaconess. The alms house only admitted members who were incapable of earning their living. The building manager under the supervision of the deacons kept a tight order, to which the inhabitants gladly submitted. The [Flemish] alms house in the city on average housed thirty people, and the one in Neugarten some ten to twelve persons. Orphans were not housed in the alms house but were rather placed in families, usually with their closest relatives.

Worship, Preaching, and Music
The office of *teaching and preaching* belonged to the elders and preachers, whose number varied according to the size of the congregation. The elder was the head of the congregation, and in spite of the equality of all members, he had considerable power. In the old records one occasionally finds the expression: "reigning elder." He alone could "serve" baptism and Communion, while the preachers were only "servants of the Word." The name "admonisher" (*Vermahner* or in Dutch *Vermaaner*), did not last long in Prussia, and was used more often by state officials than by the church. The elder and preachers were called collectively the "teaching council"

(*Lehrdienst*), or the "honorable council" (*Ehrsame Dienst*). All ministers were elected from the male membership by a majority of votes, and they served without pay while pursuing their secular occupations. It is still like that in our country congregations in West Prussia today.

The elders in Holland and elsewhere were also called bishops of the congregation, but the local clergy never allowed this title to be used here. Elders took office only when they had been installed by another elder and "confirmed" by the laying on of hands.

The Sunday worship service of the congregation proceeded in a simple manner. After a congregational song, led by the song leader (*Vorsänger*),[3] the sermon followed. There was no pulpit. A row of armchairs stood along one side of the house on a slightly raised platform. Here the teaching council took their places facing the congregation. The middle chair, known as the preacher's chair in Dutch (*preekstool*), was again raised somewhat and was used by the speaker of the day, who would deliver a sermon of considerable length in Dutch, *sitting and without a book or notes*. Not until the second half of the eighteenth century did High German gradually replace Dutch. Hans von Steen, who spoke and wrote a very good Dutch, opposed this change for a long time and held on to his mother tongue to the very end, but he too lived to see all his colleagues preaching in German.

The Transition from Dutch to German in the Pulpit and Catechism
On September 19, 1762, a German sermon was preached for the first time in the Flemish congregation in the city. Gerhard Wiebe of Elbing, who was here as a guest, only received permission with difficulty, and it was commented: "Since we were not used to this, there was no general affirmation." On April 20, 1767, another guest preacher, Cornelius Regier of Heubuden, held a German sermon and met with more

---

[3]There were no organs, since that was against the principle of simplicity. Music was banned from the church and home, apart from singing. In 1788 the [Frisian] congregation of Neugarten was the first Mennonite congregation in Prussia to build a small organ against the wishes of some members. In 1805 the [Flemish] church building in the city also received one.

affirmation. On January 1, 1771, one of the local preachers, Cornelius Moor, for the first time used High German, and then the others gradually followed, the last being the future elder, Peter Epp, who spoke German "mixed with Dutch words." At the same time the practice of standing to preach was introduced, as well as having some sermon notes, after a pulpit had been acquired and set up in front of the preacher's armchair. Hans von Steen regretted this novelty and commented: "that the beautiful simplicity of Menno's church was rapidly disappearing."

The Dutch language remained in use in the homes, but gradually changed into the comfortable Low German (*Plattdeutsch*) with Dutch expressions that was still used in Mennonite households in the first half of the nineteenth century. Nonetheless Hans von Steen acquired new *Confessions of Faith*, or catechisms in the German language, because he saw that the younger generation could no longer handle the involved Dutch of Georg Hansen's 1671 catechism. These new study booklets bore the title: *Confession or Brief and Simple Report of the Faith of the Old Flemish Anabaptist Congregations in Prussia, 1768.*[4] Henceforth all Flemish congregations in the area used this confession. In Danzig the [Flemish] Elder Jacob de Veer for his catechumens introduced a booklet of his own: *Catechism or Biblical Religious Teaching in Questions and Answers, Danzig, 1791.*[5]

In 1780 *a German hymnal* was also introduced with the title: *Spiritual Songbook for Public and Private Edification of the Mennonite Congregation in and around the City of Danzig.*[6] The preachers Peter

---

[4][*Confession oder kurtzer und einfältiger Glaubensbericht der Alten flämischen Tauff-Gesinnten Gemeinden in Preußen 1768.* Ed.]

[5][*Katechismus oder biblischer Religionsunterricht in Frage und Antwort* (Danzig, 1791). Ed.]

[6]It may be mentioned here that this songbook could not be printed in Danzig at that time, because the local printshops "had no freedom to print Mennonite materials." Thus it was printed at the Kanter printshop in Marienwerder. The 2,000 copies at 44 sheets cost 4,693 Danzig guilders. [Marienwerder was up the Vistula river from Danzig and part of Prussia. Danzig was part of the Kingdom of Poland until 1795. The German title of this hymnal is *Geistreiches Gesangbuch zur öffentlichen und besonderen Erbauung der Mennonitischen Gemeinde in und vor der Stadt Danzig.* Ed.]

Tiessen and Jacob de Veer had chosen the songs over many years with the help of the "richly talented brother Hans Momber (who later became a preacher also), some translated from the Dutch, some collected and some newly composed." Until then the congregation had used Dutch songbooks, the most recent being the Psalms, with the title: *Spiritual [Songs] of the New Harp of David* (Amsterdam, 1752).[7] The High German Psalms of Lobwasser were also used. The Dutch language had been abandoned earlier in the worship services in the Frisian congregation of Neugarten.

Baptism and Communion

Originally, *baptism* was given to individual persons when they requested it and when the elders approved. But as soon as congregations had been formed, the practice was adopted of baptizing once or twice a year, according to the size of the congregation. Here in Danzig baptism was celebrated once a year, as far as we know, usually in June or July. From 1814 to 1826 it was administered in the fall, and from 1827 to 1838 before Easter. From then until 1878 it was done in June, and since 1879 regularly on Palm Sunday.[8]

Baptismal candidates in the seventeenth century were always older than twenty; some were even over thirty. In the eighteenth century the average age was at first between twenty and thirty, but there were usually some older. In 1760 among nineteen candidates there were two who were nineteen years old and one was eighteen. In 1780 the majority were under twenty, but the average age was nineteen to twenty. In the nineteenth century the age of the baptismal candidates gradually went down. From 1825 onward it went to seventeen and sixteen years, and then remained at an average of sixteen years of age until today.

---

[7] [*Geestelyke ofte nieuwe Herpe Davidts.* The hymnal was also known by the title *Veelderhande Schriftuurlyke Liedekens*. Ed.]

[8] [One possible explanation for the shift to baptizing on Palm Sunday is the fact that Protestant churches in the nineteenth century tended to do confirmation on that Sunday. Karl-Heinrich Bieritz, *Das Kirchejahr: Feste, Gedenk- und Feiertage in Geschichte und Gegenwart*, 2d. ed. (Berlin: Union Verlag, 1988), 130. Ed.]

Baptismal instruction, which was held on Sunday afternoons in the eighteenth century, was preceded by a ceremony, namely, the reporting of the candidates to the church. In this ritual two or three active members as well as the "honorable council" introduced every applicant to the congregation. In this way the sponsoring members provided a surety for the worthy behavior of the newcomers until their baptism. After they were baptized, members were themselves responsible to carry out their Christian duties. Whoever was accepted into the "brotherhood" could vote at congregational meetings.[9]

Communion was celebrated twice a year, shortly after baptism and on a fall Sunday. The bread was broken and distributed, as it is today, and eaten by all at the same time. The wine was in a number of chalices and passed from hand to hand in the pews. With few exceptions all the members gathered for Communion. A good number took part in Communion in the summer as well as in the fall. The "announcers" (*Ansager*) or "requesters" (*Umbitter*), of whom there were one or two in each congregation, had to announce the coming celebration from house to house. The members of the leadership would enquire in each family if there were any conflicts (*Unfriede*) anywhere. In that case the antagonists should not come to Communion until they had been reconciled. Those who had been "separated" from the congregation were not admitted to the Communion, nor were any strangers admitted.

The Changing Form of Church Discipline

Church discipline had a prominent place in the order of the congregation. One could write a substantial book about this. The biblical basis for discipline in the congregation has already been discussed in chapters 1 and 2. Already in Menno's time there had been differences of opinion concerning this matter.

Here in Danzig a strict discipline was practiced by the leadership, according to the biblical precepts in Galatians 6:1, Matthew 18:16-17, I Corinthians 5:9-13, and 2 Thessalonians

---

[9][Women were allowed to vote following a reform of the congregational constitution in 1925, Göttner, "Hermann Gottlieb Mannhardt," 42. Ed.]

3:6-14. Accordingly, the *Cathecism* of 1778[10] states, in agreement with all the earlier confessions:

> When a brother or sister in the congregation is overtaken by a mistake, we should admonish them gently and help them see their error. But if the guilty one will not accept instruction, then two or three shall again admonish him or her. Whoever does not accept admonition or even lives in obvious sin *shall be separated from the congregation*, and members will have nothing to do with that individual, so that he or she will become red with shame. But if this party is converted away from sin, then it is enough that many punished this person. He or she must be forgiven all the more and comforted. 2 Corinthians 2:6-7.

Every Sunday, with the exception of Baptism and Communion Sundays, the leadership discussed the cases that might call for action. Since it was forbidden for one member to take another to court, all such cases had to be taken to the council. Such disputes resulted in much work, but most cases consisted of individual failings, mild or severe, that had to be punished.

The accused could either appear voluntarily or were summoned formally. In many cases, it was just a matter of verbal offenses or hasty errors, which were dealt with by an admonition. Often there were offenses against simplicity in dress and in outward appearance. Like all Puritans, the Mennonites earnestly struggled against the dictates of fashion. In this the leadership sometimes found itself gradually giving in. Sometimes they would defend a fashion that had been condemned a hundred years before. In the sixteenth century all the men wore beards. When the fashion of shaving arose in the seventeenth century it was considered unseemly, but the church

---

[10][*Katechismus, oder Kurze und einfältige Unterweisung aus der heiligen Schrift in Frage und Antwort, für die Kinder zum Gebrauch in den Schulen* (Elbing, 1778), 52. Ed.]

became so used to it that beards were later looked down upon. This repeated itself again in the eighteenth century, and even in the nineteenth century there was a time when beards were considered a "military symbol" in the Mennonite congregations, and certainly not tolerated.

In 1745 baptism was cancelled because a number of the young men who had applied gave offense by their fashionable dress. Since the elder did not wish to decide the matter, he called a meeting of the "brothers," concerning which was recorded:

> We were very worried about how to come to grips with this matter, since it concerned a number of youths from the most prominent families, namely: Cornelius von Almonde, Claus von Dyck, Isaac Ehlert, Jacob Dirksen, Carl Moor, and many who had already in the past year been passed over because of their fashionable dress. This consisted of shoes with buckles, three-cornered hats, neckties, and stiff tails on their jackets. One had even been to see a comedy.

Since the accused could give no sufficient answer it was decided unanimously to postpone the baptism. In the following year the candidates then were individually summoned and they laid aside their showy clothes. Of Jacob Dirksen it is said that since he had already made a number of trips to England and Holland he was "especially gaudy in his clothing."

In the following years there was great unrest in both congregations over the wearing of wigs. Their introduction, however, could not be halted after inquiries were made in Holland and it was discovered that there even the Mennonite preachers wore wigs to church.

Various moral failings made for more serious objects of church discipline. There were strict punishments for failing to pay the duties or sales tax, incurring debts, drunkenness, card playing and dancing, the beating of servants and especially the sin against the sixth commandment.[11]

Punishment usually was "separation" from the congregation until the person gave clear signs of betterment and asked for reinstatement. During the time of separation no one was allowed to have any dealings with the person, not even the family. Unrepentant sinners were expelled from the congregation.

It was inevitable that in the course of time church discipline became more lenient. The more the Mennonites moved from their relative isolation into public society, the harder it became to maintain by coercion the simplicity of their customs and of their outward appearance, which had been a symbol of their tradition. But into the nineteenth century we read of punishments for luxury, fashion, and the like. Discipline against moral failings of all kinds ceased as Mennonites, like everyone else, became more subject to the civil courts in matters of criminality and justice, something that had previously been forbidden them by the church even when they were cheated or robbed by strangers. Naturally church discipline, in spite of the best intentions of the congregation, often descended to loveless judgment, and actual penance and improvement gradually became an external show.

Marriage Customs

Marriage was a church ceremony and only valid in the eyes of the congregation when a preacher of the congregation performed it after proper announcement ahead of time. The state, however, required that the marriage had to be registered in the parish church books of the state church where the couple lived. This was later specially stated in Prussian law (Mennonite Edict), and included the registration of births and deaths. For each such entry a certain fee had to be paid to the relevant state church pastor.[12]

---

[11][Adultery. Ed.]

[12][The Edict referred to here was issued in 1789 and is discussed in detail in Jantzen, "At Home in Germany?" 81-6. An English translation is available there on pages 433-7. Ed.]

Mennonite *weddings* took place in their houses of worship, on Sunday morning following the sermon with the entire congregation present. The first marriage in a home took place in the Flemish congregation in 1769 and later such ceremonies were common in both congregations. In 1780 a marriage took place in a church *on a weekday* for the first time.

There was a courtship tradition that a proposal would not be made by the young man himself but through friends who would take this request to the parents of the bride. On May 5, 1765, the congregation was told that

> the old, respected custom was falling into disuse of using two men to make the proposal, and then, after allowing a one- or two-week period for consideration, to have the same men receive the decision. Some had even proposed on their own, others indeed had exchanged promises without the knowledge of the parents, and so on. All of this will be severely punished.

The elder himself was often the one who asked the bride, as Isaac Stobbe (1775-88) of the Neugarten congregation recounted many such cases.

When the proposal of marriage was favorably received, the groom was allowed to appear in person and the engagement was formalized in the presence of the parents, as Chodowiecki has depicted it. The engagement celebration in a larger family setting would follow a few days later, and the wedding itself after a short time. The cancellation of an engagement was only allowed for very serious reasons. Whoever broke off an engagement could not count on being able to marry anyone else in the congregation. Divorce was forbidden.

Oaths and Military Exemption

One of the religious principles of the Mennonites was *the refusal to swear oaths.* They had great difficulties concerning this, but in Poland and Danzig the situation was not as severe. Actually, only the oath required of witnesses applied to them, since earlier they had not taken any offices or court actions. In

Mennonite marriage proposal 1782 by Daniel Chodowiecki. [Scanned from 1919 edition. Ed.]

1572 a Mennonite, Tobias Ewerts, appeared in court as a witness in a case, and when he refused to swear to the veracity of his given testimony he was imprisoned. Once the parties in the case freed him from swearing an oath he was released.[13]

In a court case of May 17, 1601, I found the comment: "The usual oath which Mennonites swear in court is this: As he desires that God should deal with his soul, so true is all that he has said."[14] Since this formula is nearly a real oath it can only have been temporarily demanded of the Mennonites. In 1614 we find in the court records frequent references to the fact that

---

[13]Danzig City Archives, Mm. 10.
[14]Ibid., p. 159.

Mennonites do not have to lift their finger at the oath.[15] We will discuss the laws concerning the oath during the Prussian period below.

The *refusal to bear arms* did not cause any particular problems for the Mennonites in Danzig in the Polish period. In a decision of the City Council of April 3, 1613, we read: "Because the Mennonites are not available to stand guard nor to serve as soldiers, they may make a monthly donation for the support of soldiers."[16]

This decision was changed in 1624 as follows: "that the Mennonites living here, if they do not enlist personally, must provide a fit man in their place, and whoever has qualms about doing this must pay to the Quartermaster a guilder if he is well-to-do, and half as much if poor, which shall be used to support an able man. In times of war the Mennonites, who do not participate in the military, shall pay for their replacement by a monthly sum, so that their places may be filled by proven and reliable men."[17]

Later, in the war of 1656 they were required to pay for two substitutes.[18] That then remained the case in peacetime. Therefore the Mennonites on April 28, 1688, asked the Council to be satisfied with the replacement of one man, and referred to the above action of 1624.[19] Thereupon the Council decided: "that the Mennonites should either provide two men well provisioned in their place, or if they prefer pay the appropriate officer 6 *Reichstalers* one time for equipment and 2 *Reichstalers*

---

[15]Ibid., 43; 35, fol. 104; 37, fol. 239.

[16]Ibid., Mm. 4, p. 2. [Poland and Sweden had been at war since 1601, but since most of the fighting took place in modern-day Latvia, there seemed to be little immediate impact on Danzig. Cieślak and Biernat, *History of Gdańsk*, 154-5. Ed.]

[17][Danzig became a scene of fighting in the 1620s with the Swedish fleet appearing in the Bay of Danzig in 1622 and the Swedish army invading in 1626. A truce was finally reached in 1629. Ibid., 155-9. Ed.]

[18][The Polish-Swedish War of 1654-60, referred to as the "Swedish Deluge" by Polish historians, was tremendously damaging to the city of Danzig, which faced Swedish attacks early in 1656 and emerged from the war deeply in debt. Ibid., 212-218. Ed.]

[19]The information given in W. Mannhardt, *Wehrfreiheit*, 108, should be corrected accordingly.

monthly per man." In the "Revised Defense Order of the City of Danzig, 1733" it states: "The Mennonites shall provide for each one of them two fit substitutes who are not citizens and inhabitants but nonetheless eligible for conscription, who have already rendered the oath with the appointed military authorities." Such substitutes were easy to find at that time.

During the difficult siege of 1734 the Mennonites also had to serve in the hospitals and fire department "because they do not render military service," and they put out the fires caused by bombs so well, "that the enemy could not execute his desire to set the city on fire."[20]

Funerals

I was not able to discover much about the *funeral customs*. Since the Mennonite preachers were not allowed to speak at the cemeteries, funerals were held only in private homes. The church was never used for that purpose. I doubt whether funeral orations were used before the beginning of the nineteenth century, more likely only funeral songs were sung. Often a friend or acquaintance would compose a song for the particular individual that would be sung to a popular melody. We have a number of such songs from the eighteenth century, some in Dutch, some in German. Gergen Berentz for example, wrote: "A Song about the Death of the Beloved Elder Dirk Jantzen" to the melody: "O Gott, du frommer Gott." The twenty-eight stanzas probably took as long to sing as a funeral oration.[21]

---

[20]Löschin, *Geschichte Danzigs,*. 241. Mannhardt, *Wehrfreiheit*, 108. [The siege by Russian troops lasted from February to July 1734. The city of Danzig backed the duly-elected Stanisław Leszczyński for king, while the Russians backed a different and eventually victorious candidate, Augustus III. Cieślak and Biernat, *History of Gdańsk*, 241-7. Ed.]

[21][Mannhardt gave the Dutch title here. Jantzen was elder from 1733 to 1750. Penner, *Mennoniten*, 2:249. See also page 99 above. Ed.]

Hans von Steen Jr.[22] composed a funeral song for Elder Hans von Almonde (died 1753). The beginning letters of the fourteen stanzas reveal the name of the elder. A great number of Dutch songs by this young poet have survived. When he died his friend Jan Lambertz composed a song for him of sixteen stanzas. At the funeral of Elder Hans van Steen in 1781 a funeral song in German was sung, composed by Hans Momber and consisting of twenty-four stanzas.

The custom of funeral songs later took on a different form. When funeral orations came into use, songs from the hymnal were sung at funerals, but now *burial and memorial verses* were used, of which many have been preserved. Around 1800 Hans Momber, who was named above, composed many of these. During the first half of the nineteenth century they remained in use, and some examples can still be found in the 1860s.

In order to give a sample of this kind of epitaph I offer the following with their first lines:

Anthon Reimer
Born June 30, 1763
Died June 9, 1805
Buried June 14, 1805
   At the age of 41 years, 11 months and 10 days.

"Taken up to immeasurably better joys
than this earth can give to us,
this good man went, after sorrowful battles
to the eternal home above.
His wife and children stand at the graveside
and weep at his early death. —
But behind that sunset
shines a much brighter mirror.
For it is good – what God has ordained."

---

[22]This Hans von Steen was a son of the well-known elder. Highly talented and self-supporting from an early age, he was elected deacon in 1758 at 25 years of age, eight days after his marriage. To the great sorrow of his father he died already on July 9, 1759.

There follow twenty-eight rather sentimental stanzas without any numbered order.

For an old man, Johann Lambertz, who died on August 20, 1809 at age 79, a friend composed the following *burial and memorial verse*:

He died! – As when in its last rays
the sun gradually disappears
so he too was gently led
to the valley of death.
The rest of us – stand here at the grave
We often feel a heated brow
and still wipe the sweat of work
and our paths grow crooked
But he – by a higher grace
has reached his goal, the pious old man.

Two stanzas written in a different meter followed this epitaph. One stanza deals with general observations and the other with reference to this particular person.

The Danzig Mennonite Church had no burial grounds of its own. They buried their dead in the Protestant cemeteries, the Flemish congregation usually in the St. Salvator cemetery. Twelve members of the congregation would be chosen to carry the body. This practice (of carrying the body) fell out of use in the second half of the eighteenth century, as "almost all were conveyed in vehicles." But this was again reinstated in 1798 to its full complement. The congregation was admonished to use these persons at funerals, since they were also willing to carry the coffin to the wagon and from the wagon over the bridge to the cemetery "for the same wage as the grave diggers."

At weddings and especially funerals the previously mentioned "requesters" were active. They carried the invitations for the weddings and funerals to relatives and friends. The office of requester only disappeared around the middle of the nineteenth century, when the duties were transferred to the sextons and alms house officials.

Care for the Poor

We have already touched on the fact that *organized care of the poor* was a part of church life and that the Mennonite congregations never allowed their poor to become dependent on public welfare. This principle is stated in the various Confessions of Faith, in the "Old Flemish" as well as in the "united Flemish, Frisian and High German" article "On the Office of the Deacons." In order to look after the poor and needy, the deacons maintained an alms fund taken from collections, bequests, and sometimes from the interest on invested capital. Since the care of the poor, within and outside the alms house, was the major expense of the congregation, the congregational fund was simply called the alms fund.

Not until 1797 were regular contributions by individual members introduced and the accounting made more complete. The conditions leading to this development are important enough to be described here. In the 1760s the economic conditions of the congregation had improved to the point that the income for the alms fund rose gradually from 3,492 florins in 1757 to 6,751 florins in 1765. They remained at this level approximately until 1770. Then in the following years they rose again until 1773. In that year they reached their highest level, 8,087 florins. Then there was a gradual drop, a sign that the times were getting worse. In 1782 only 5,177 florins came in. During the 1780s the income was between 5,000 and 6,000 florins and then fell to 3,169 from 1790 to 1798.

Because the deacon or leader who was in charge of the alms fund had since 1776 advanced money from his own resources in order to pay all the expenses, it was necessary every year to have a special church and house collection in addition to the regular collections to recover these advances. In 1788 the deacon was Gerhard Bachdach, who administered the fund with great devotion and advanced 4,400 florins, which it was very hard to restore by a collection. In the next ten years this became even more difficult. And, when in 1797 Bachdach again had advanced 4,400 florins and declared that he could not carry out his office any more if the income from the congregation were not put on a firm foundation, the leadership decided to propose to the membership that they would commit themselves to fixed annual dues. Several turbulent membership meetings were required to formulate an appropriate decision. Some members who had been outvoted declared that they wished to stay with the old custom, only making their contributions according to the principle that in the Christian giving of alms the left hand should not know what the right hand is doing. But 128 members committed to make annual donations that totaled 6,910 florins. With this a better balance could be kept, especially since there were additional collections from Communion Sundays and also some interest from invested capital. The Communion collections in 1799 amounted to 3,171 florins, fell in the next year to 2,678 florins and then fell lower from year to year. On the occasion of this reform the administration of the congregation was also changed. Henceforth four deacons were elected who were commonly called the board members (*Vorsteher*), and six respected men from the congregation joined the church leadership as representatives. The whole administration was now called the church council (*Kirchenkollegium*).[23]

Regarding the care of the poor I would like to add here that beginning in 1781 a special fall collection was taken in order to butcher ten steers for the alms house. This collection was cancelled temporarily in 1797 but introduced again later and remained as the so-called meat collection until 1880.

The leader Johann Kauenhowen in his *Memorialbuch* (p. 131) says about this:

> Since we noticed that our incomes would be sufficient without it, we decided to omit the special collection. But the poor were supplied with meat just as well as in previous years, though there was a change. For many years ten steers had been slaughtered, but only small ones. Afterwards we saw that it was more advantageous for the poor to slaughter heavier ones, and so between 1788 and

---

[23][In cases where the original German contrasts the word *Vorsteher* with the word *Diakon*, we have translated *Vorsteher* as "board member." Elsewhere we have continued to translate both *Diakon* and *Vorsteher* as "deacon." Ed.]

1792 only eight, and then only six until 1800, and then only four, but always heavier ones. And since the number of poor, which had in 1795 been around a hundred, became fewer, the portions were not smaller, and the meat was better and the poor more satisfied and happier.

We have no precise information about the care of the poor in the Frisian congregation in Neugarten. But from an old account book used by a series of deacons we can see that the poor there were looked after in the same spirit. There were alms boxes (*Kastches*) in the church, and at Communion Sunday, for example in 1747, 426 florins were collected. The total income of freewill offerings in this church, which was so much smaller than the Flemish, was naturally proportionally less, but in 1750 was approximately 4,000 florins, in the 1760s around 5,000 florins and then sank here too to 3,000 florins in the 1780s.

The Partitions of Poland, 1772-1795

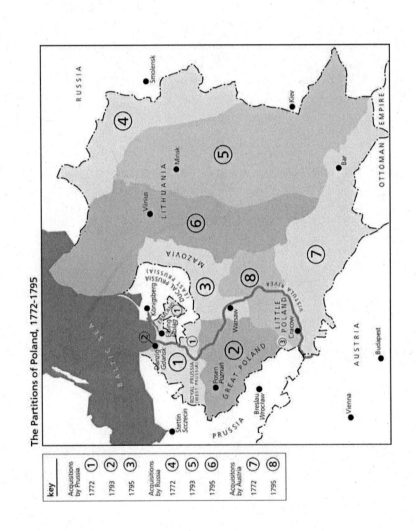

key

Acquisitions by Prussia
① 1772
② 1793
③ 1795

Acquisitions by Russia
④ 1772
⑤ 1793
⑥ 1795

Acquisitions by Austria
⑦ 1772
⑧ 1795

9

The Transition from the Eighteenth to the Nineteenth Century

The First Partition of Poland and Its Consequences
The first partition of Poland gave West Prussia to Frederick the Great, but Danzig and Thorn remained with Poland. A hard time began again for our city, and lasted until 1793. The King of Prussia circled the city with strict customs barriers, occupied Neufahrwasser/Gdańsk Nowy, and hindered trade both by sea and by land in every way.[1] Since the Danzig citizens, proud of their erstwhile rights and freedoms, did not want to become Prussian and sought to defend themselves, the city was blockaded in 1783 for many months. Frederick's successor continued the policy of force against Danzig. Powerless against the decisions of the great powers, the citizens had to recognize that their earlier autonomy was at an end. This fact alone was the grounds for their resistance, not a preference for Poland. But in time the voices in favor of a voluntary union with Prussia, namely those of the business class, grew stronger. In 1793 the decision finally was taken.[2] Very fittingly, Simson, in

---

[1] [Neufahrwasser was the mouth of the Vistula River just outside the city walls of Danzig, thus the Prussians were able to cut the city off from the sea. Ed.]

[2] [Mannhardt summarized here the impact of the Partitions of Poland in 1772, 1793, and 1795 during which Prussia, Russia, and Austria erased Poland from the map by dividing its territory amongst themselves. Especially Russia had involved itself in Polish politics during the eighteenth century on the side of Polish nobles who wished to guard their own privileges and limit the power of the elected Polish kings. Disagreements over the relative power of nobles and the king and the scope of religious toleration sparked a Polish civil war in 1768. Fighting along the Polish border with the Ottoman Empire soon brought that country into the conflict along with Russia. To mollify Austria and Prussia over Russian territorial gains at the expense of Poland and the Ottoman Empire, the three powers agreed each should take a section of Poland. The Prussian portion in 1772 included the Vistula Delta region, known as Royal Prussia and now renamed West Prussia, excepting the city of Danzig itself. Following revolutionary upheavals in what remained of Poland, Danzig was annexed to Prussia in 1793 and the Polish state disappeared entirely in 1795. For the attitudes of inhabitants in Danzig during these years see Friedrich, *The Other Prussia*, 189-216. The most complete assessment of the transition from Polish to Prussian rule is in

his little *History of the City of Danzig* says: "The period of Polish rule was over. If Danzig during this time reached its fullest inner and outer bloom, nevertheless it was still subjected to a totally foreign state. Although it had been almost independent, it had also been an important factor in the Polish state. Even though it had courageously defended its German culture (*Deutschtum*) and freedom of religion in a time of struggle, it was cut off from its national connection with its German counterparts, a constantly endangered outpost of German culture. That changed now as it entered the German state of the Hohenzollerns, which was called to be the leading state in Germany. Danzig now participated faithfully in the fortunes of this state, since it regained in 1793 its membership in a German state lost since 1454. Thus, the takeover by Prussia that it had at first resisted became a blessing. At that the terrible twenty-one year period of suffering also ceased, which had been such a heavy burden, and which let it see the dreaded union with Prussia as a salvation."[3]

Mennonites in Danzig and Prussia

The Danzig Mennonites in 1772 were divided into two groups, since a great number outside the city, in Schottland,

---

Hans-Jürgen Bömelburg, *Zwischen Polnischer Ständegesellschaft und Preussischem Obrigkeitsstaat: Vom Königlichen Preussen zu Westpreussen (1756-1806)* (Munich: R. Oldenbourg Verlag, 1995). For an English overview see Norman Davies, *God's Playground: A History of Poland* (New York: Columbia University Press, 1982), 1:511-546. Ed.]

[3]Paul Simson, *Geschichte der Stadt Danzig*, 116. [Interpretations of the Vistula Delta's history have changed over time. In the eighteenth century the primary emphasis was given to regional history and identity. By the time Mannhardt and the historian he quotes wrote in the early twentieth century the emphasis had shifted to competing national histories that pitted mutually exclusive Polish and German claims to the area against each other. This nationalistic historiography pressured Mennonites to take sides and, given their use of the German language and common ties to Protestants, Mennonites, as this quote demonstrates, clearly identified with German interests and perspectives in the region. For additional details see Jantzen "At Home in Germany?" 22-3. On the political agenda of German scholarship of the East see Michael Burleigh, *Germany Turns Eastwards: A Study of Ostforschung in the Third Reich* (New York: Cambridge University Press, 1988), 3-39. Ed]

Stoltzenberg, and in the countryside were now under Prussian rule. This resulted in many problems. When the preacher Peter Epp, who lived on Prussian territory, after his sermon on October 18, 1772, prayed for the King of Prussia instead of the King of Poland, the Danzig members complained to the Elder Hans von Steen, and when the matter became known in Danzig Peter Epp was advised not to appear in the city for a while. Indeed, the elder received a summons from the Mayor and had to bring Peter Epp with him. They were seriously admonished to offer prayers in their city church in the old manner.

The dispute became more serious in 1783. Johann Kauenhowen reports:

> In this year something happened which had a great influence on our congregation. The Prussian inhabitants of Altschottland, Langfuhr, etc., which include many of our members, had grain brought down to them on the Vistula River to Schellmühl. The Danzigers had allowed this to happen for a while, but this spring they began to prevent it and did not want any more to pass the customs house. The Prussian inhabitants complained about this to their government, and since their complaint was forwarded to the Danzig authorities, we found the names of our people among the petitioners, which caused very bad feelings. Since Danzig did not want to give in, the result was that the city was surrounded by Prussian troops for three months, October 17, 1783, to January 22, 1784. This circumstance caused great enmity against the Prussians in our congregation, so that they did not feel safe in the city. Ohm[4] Jacob de Veer therefore added an admonition to a sermon directed to the Prussian members, because they had complained to their king about the Danzig authorities. As lovingly as this was formulated, it caused our Prussian

---

[4]The term Ohm was used here, as in Holland, as a pleasant and patriarchal designation for Mennonite preachers.

members great unhappiness. They did not feel they had earned this punishment since they had not known, when they signed the document, that it would have such hard consequences for the city inhabitants.[5]

The New Legal Situation for West Prussian Mennonites and Frederick II

The transition to Prussia brought great relief to the West Prussian Mennonites (some 14,000), but also a new, serious problem. If on the one hand they had been freed from a condition of lawlessness and enjoyed the protection given to their religion as to all "tolerated religious societies," on the other hand they were threatened by a much greater danger to their nonresistance in the military Prussian state. And indeed, the next hundred years, from 1772 to 1868, were an almost uninterrupted struggle to maintain this article of faith.[6]

Frederick II actually was very willing to provide the Mennonites with generous protection in his lands. With his well-known words: "in my lands everyone can find salvation in his own way," he did not want to express indifference or ridicule of the religions of his subjects, but rather a political principle of great consequence, namely, that enjoyment of civil rights and freedoms did not depend on religious confession.[7] He was well disposed to the Mennonites of East Prussia and the Elbing area, who were under his rule, and proved this by granting rights of citizenship in the city to the Königsberg

---

[5]Memorialbuch fol. 16. Archive of the Danzig Mennonite Church. [Additional background on this incident is in Cieślak and Biernat, *History of Gdańsk*, 264-5. Ed.]

[6][The contemporary Mennonite records suggest neither relief nor dismay over these political developments. The main sentiment was rather to protect Mennonite privileges concerning freedom of worship and pursuit of their livelihoods. Given new Prussian regulations, an interest in obtaining freedom from military service was soon added as a concern as Mannhardt noted. In suggesting Mennonites felt "relief" at becoming Prussian subjects, Mannhardt was projecting early twentieth-century sentiments back into the late eighteenth century. See Jantzen, "At Home in Germany?" 35-110. Ed.]

[7]See my essay "Die Mennoniten unter den preußischen Königen" in *Christlicher Gemeindekalender*, 1902 (Jg. 11), 98-117.

Mennonites in 1744, as well as by intervening against the arbitrary behavior of General von Geßler, who in 1746 wanted to conscript the Elbing Mennonites into the army.[8]

After Frederick took possession of West Prussia on September 13, 1772, the representatives of the Mennonites already on September 27 presented a petition at the homage ceremony at Marienburg, requesting toleration. On October 6 of the same year the king informed them through the newly organized Prussian War and Domain Chambers[9] that "under his protection they would be free of all restrictions regarding their religious practice."[10] He even had special announcements made to the Mennonites remaining on Danzig territory inviting them to move to his lands as craftsmen or farmers.[11]

Military Exemption

A special tax of 5,000 talers was assessed in exchange for exemption from being registered for military service. The tax was to be paid collectively by all the congregations in East and West Prussia and used to support the Culm Cadet Academy.[12] In this connection it states:

"that His Majesty in His wisdom does not wish to interfere with anyone's conscience, and that the 5,000 talers are by no means a payment for their religious freedom, but rather recruiting fees for their exemption from registration for military service, in which they are being privileged above all other

---

[8]See Dr. W. Mannhardt, *Wehrfreiheit*, 102ff.

[9][The new provincial government headed by Joachim Friedrich von Domhardt. On governmental structures see Bär, *Behördenverfassung*, 88-92, and H. W. Koch, *A History of Prussia* (New York: Barnes and Noble Books, 1993), 90-2. Ed.]

[10][A copy of this document can be found in Berlin in the Secret Central Archives (*Geheimes Staatsarchiv Preußischer Kulturbesitz*) (GStA), Hauptabteilung (HA) II, Westpreußen, Materien. Titel 109 (Mennonistensachen), Nr. 1, vol. 1, 10. This document also immediately alerted Mennonites to the fact that they would have to pay a fee to be exempted from military service. Ed.]

[11]See Dr. W. Mannhardt, *Wehrfreiheit*, 122.

[12][This school was established as a pet project of the new provincial administrator von Domhardt as a primary-level officer training school in order to integrate the local Polish nobility's sons into the Prussian officer corps. Jantzen, "At Home in Germany?" 44-7. Ed.]

Christian subjects, so that instead of registration they may pay a moderate sum."[13]

From this we see how important it was to the king to bring to bear the principle of freedom of conscience, as long as no interest of the state would suffer.

Restrictions on the Right to Buy Real Estate

The provincial government in Marienwerder soon worried that state interests were indeed suffering. Frederick himself in 1774 had said that when permission was granted for buying land, the Mennonite cases should be treated cautiously and with limitations, so that "the cantons would not suffer too much."[14] The Chambers in Marienwerder established a policy that Mennonites would not be able to buy land from non-Mennonites, nor should they engage in new occupations. But here too the king intervened and relaxed this practice *by deciding that every individual case would have to be presented to him for a personal decision.*[15]

On March 29, 1780, the so-called Charter of Privileges was issued to the Mennonites, in which they were assured of freedom from military service for all time, as well as the enjoyment of freedom of religion and permission to practice their previous trades according to the relevant laws in the Kingdom of Prussia. One can sense that the last sentence contains a limitation, and one can understand that the Mennonites could not receive unlimited freedom to purchase land nor the full right to engage in business, as long as they held

---

[13][GStA, HA II, Westpreußen, Materien, Titel 109, Nr. 1, vol. 1, 153, 26 September 1777. This fee was actually imposed already back in 1773. This quote here is in reply to Mennonite complaints related to restrictions on buying real estate. Jantzen, "At Home in Germany?" 51-7. Ed.]

[14][GStA, HA II, Westpreußen, Materien, Titel 109, Nr. 1, vol. 1, 174, 11 May 1774. The cantons were military recruiting districts, each of which had to supply a set number of recruits. Here the term is shorthand for the lists of farmsteads that could supply sons or hired hands for military recruitment. Provincial officials feared that as the Mennonite population grew and bought more farms it would become more difficult to fill their quotas as they removed those exempted farmsteads from their recruitment rolls. Ed.]

[15][GStA, HA II, Westpreußen, Materien, Titel 109, Nr. 1, vol. 1, 175, 25 November 1777. Ed.]

to the principle of nonresistance. But in practice the king proved to be generous, for alone in the years 1781-83 Mennonites bought 296 new properties with his permission.[16]

The Edict of 1789

Under his successor, Friedrich Wilhelm II (1786-97), this changed. The state authorities drew attention to the fact that as real estate whose owners were obliged to serve in the military passed into the hands of the Mennonites, there might not be sufficient recruits for the army in West Prussia. The Lutheran congregations also became anxious about their economic survival. And so the king decided to issue a special law for the Mennonites. This was an "Edict Concerning the Future Establishment of the Mennonites in All Royal Prussian Provinces, Excluding the Duchy of Silesia, July 30, 1789."[17]

In this document, freedom of conscience, including freedom from military service, was granted anew, but the purchase of land in rural areas was significantly limited. Further, the duty of Mennonite landowners to contribute to the Lutheran churches was codified, and finally, rules were set up dealing with persons who converted to the Mennonites from other confessions. This last point had little practical application since the Mennonites did not approve of such conversions and some Mennonites rejected them in principle.

The other two restrictions, however, were significant, especially the first. What the Mennonites had hoped for under Prussian rule is contained in a petition that they presented to Governor von Stutterheim in Königsberg in 1773. They requested:

---

[16][Wilhelm Mannhardt first made this oft-repeated claim. *Wehrfreiheit*, 136. Other evidence suggests the statistics on which this claim was based were falsified. The amount of land actually owned by Mennonites in this time frame did not increase much and Mennonite petitions complaining about the difficulty of acquiring land continue unabated in the 1780s. Jantzen, "At Home in Germany?" 61-3. Ed.]

[17]Reprinted in Dr. W. Mannhardt, *Wehrfreiheit*, LXXVII. [Available in English translation in Jantzen, "At Home in Germany?" 433-7. Ed.]

1. Free practice of religion according to the Mennonite confession, freedom to conduct worship services wherever necessary, to preach, to baptize, to hold Communion and to practice church discipline.

2. To be able to maintain their present houses of worship and to build new ones as needed.

3. To have their children taught by their own teachers, or to be able to send them to other teachers.

4. Since, according to a Most Gracious Royal decree, the other religions are freed from paying support for each other's churches and clergy, the Catholics from the Lutherans and the Lutherans from the Catholics, we likewise should be free of such payments.

5. That our children and we be freed from all *impressment* into and *registration* for military service, now and in the future.

6. Not to be burdened with swearing an oath but to be free to say yes or no in good conscience.

7. To be allowed to carry on our businesses and trades in the cities and country like other honest subjects.

8. To be able to buy and sell our farms and property to and from other co-religionists as well as the freedom to own and use both newly purchased and previously owned land as we see fit.

9. To be able to bury our dead, both young and old, in the cemeteries.[18]

The "Mennonite Edict," as it was henceforth called, thus brought some disappointments. But since not much else had been expected after the death of Frederick II, the surplus of Mennonites no longer knew where to turn. Thus a new development appeared on the scene that must be described briefly, namely, *the emigration to Russia.*

---

[18][Reprinted from W. Mannhardt's *Wehrfreiheit,* 125-7. Ed.]

The Emigration to Russia Begins

Already before its promulgation, Mennonites had given up hope regarding the freedom to purchase property that they had at one time placed in the edict whose proclamation they anticipated. In February 1787, two representatives of the Mennonites from West Prussia, Elder Heinrich Donner for the Frisians and preacher Cornelius Warkentin for the Flemish, traveled to Berlin to bring their new requests to the government of the new king. They stayed in Berlin for ten weeks and did everything they could to accomplish their task, but regarding permission to purchase real estate they achieved nothing but the decision "that the Mennonites, who are freed from personal military service, may not expand their real estate holdings without special permits, since that would lower the amount of property on which the obligation for military service rests and may not purchase new farms."[19]

Just at this time, when the urgent need for more land was great, especially for the children of the Mennonite farmers, a call came from Russia offering help. Already on August 7, 1786, a text was read in both Danzig Mennonite churches, in which a Russian plenipotentiary in the name of the Empress Catherine II invited all free landholders, especially the Mennonites living in the Danzig area, to settle in Russia. Not far from the Turkish border there was a stretch of land that would be very suitable for their needs. Whoever was interested in moving there should report to the Russian consulate in Langgarten.[20]

When the Danzig Council heard of this, the mayor Pegelau summoned the Elders Peter Epp and Isaac Stobbe, and forbade any further communication with the Russians. The latter were not heard from again until December of 1787. But two Mennonites, Jakob Höppner of Bohnsack, of the city church,

---

[19]Archive of the Danzig Mennonite Church, A.M. I. 3. fol. 27. [Also available in GStA, HA I, Repositur (Rep.) 76 (Kulturministerium), III (Evangelisch-Geistliche Angelegenheiten), Sektion (Sekt.) 1 (Generalia), Abteilung (Abt.) XIIIa (Sekten- und Judensachen), no. 2 (Die Angelegenheiten der Mennoniten), vol. 1 (1812-1823), fol. 5v, Frederick William II to all Mennonites in Prussia, 24 April 1787. See also W. Mannhardt, *Wehrfreiheit*, 137. Ed.]

[20]Archive of the Danzig Mennonite Church, A.M. I. 3, fol. 25.

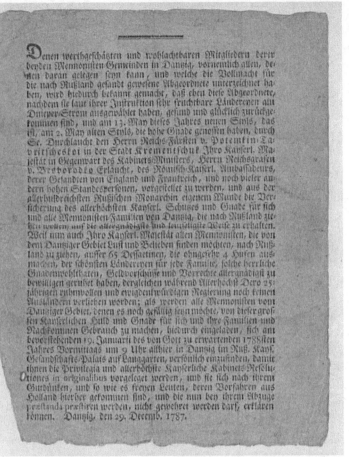

Flyer dated Dec. 29, 1787, distributed to Danzig Mennonites, offering them incentives to emigrate to Russia. It was saved over the centuries in a von Riesen/Friesen family Bible. [Mennonite Library and Archives, SA.II.55. Illustration added. Ed.]

and Johann Bartsch of the Neugarten congregation, without informing their leadership, had left for the province of Kherson in Russia at the expense of the Russian consulate, in order to look at the proposed lands. These two men returned in the fall of 1787 accompanied by a Russian commissioner named Trappe.[21] The latter had the authority from the Empress to

---

[21][Mannhardt spelled the name "Trapp" without a final "e" following the spelling used in an earlier account printed in the German Mennonite newspaper *Mennonitische Blätter.* For additional information on the Mennonite

recruit settlers and to transport them as far as Dubrovna without charge, where they would be given quarters and provided with one quarter ruble per diem expenses until they could travel onward. Höppner and Bartsch described the land to their neighbors and friends as suitable for settlement, and Trappe was able to persuade many to emigrate. He also went to the elders and asked for permission to be able to read the announcement from the Empress in the churches. He even insisted that Peter Epp take a beautiful fur and a hat, as well as a case of Russian candles.[22] But when Epp, obedient to the direction of the authorities, refused to allow the reading in the church, Trappe had the announcement printed and distributed after the church service by two unknown men. The church leadership could defend itself by insisting that they had known nothing of this distribution and that it was not in a position to prevent it, since it had happened outside the church.

After Trappe had gone to the mayor and declared that he took all the efforts of the City Council to hinder his plans as insults against the Russian Empress, the prohibitions on the part of the authorities ceased. On Sunday, February 3, Trappe himself appeared at the worship service in the city Mennonite church, embraced and kissed the elder and gave him ten talers for the poor.

With the permission of the City Council, which was given after some delay, the first four families, Neufeld, Claassen, Sawatzki, and Reimer, left for Russia on February 23, 1788. In the course of the year another 18 families from the Danzig congregation followed, and from the Prussian areas also the emigration began, although the authorities there withheld permission for a time. The Mennonites who were leaving Danzig were mainly not the wealthy but workers who "earned a difficult living by

---

migration to Russia see Lawrence Klippenstein, "The Mennonite Migration to Russia, 1786-1806," in *Mennonites in Russia, 1788-1988: Essays in Honor of Gerhard Lohrenz*, edited by John Friesen (Winnipeg: CMBC Publications, 1989):13-42 and Peter Hildebrand, *From Danzig to Russia: The First Emigration of Mennonites from the Danzig Region to Southern Russia* (Winnipeg: CMBC Publications, 2000). Ed.]

[22][*russische Lichte*. The translation of this expression is very uncertain. Ed.]

delivering milk, carpentry, and other crafts. Only one is supposed to have taken some 4,000 florins Danzig currency with him." The emigrants were concerned that only decent people join them. "Jacob Wilms and Arend Fast, who had also been ready to leave, were left behind because they were more attached to drink than to work."[23]

The emigration to Russia marked a new chapter in the history of the Mennonites. That is why I did not want to omit the beginnings of this movement. It seems peculiar that the authorities, who did not want to allow young people access to highly-sought farmland, still denied permission for emigration, so that the majority at least of the first wave to leave had to leave the country secretly. At the end of 1788, 152 families from the West Prussian congregations, more than 900 persons, had arrived in South Russia. How they made the bare but wonderfully fruitful steppe arable, how they at first lived in dugouts until those blooming, beautiful villages arose which in the nineteenth century testified to their industry and wealth, how they multiplied and founded ever more colonies so that their number before the war [World War I] was estimated at 80,000, what was the nature of their experience and how terrible their situation may be today—describing all that is not part of my present task.

Peter Epp

I only wish to report that these emigrants wrote in many letters to us that they were still without a preacher in Russia. They requested urgently that an elder would come to them and establish order in the congregation and administer an election for preachers and elders. And in fact the Danzig elder, Peter Epp, in spite of his 65 years, decided to make the arduous journey. All the preparations had already been made, the wagon in which he, together with four emigrant families, wanted to make the trip, was built and provisioned. On August 2, 1789, he took his farewell in a moving service in the church and wanted

---

[23]Memorialbuch of Joh. Kauenhowen, fol. 38, Danzig Menn. Church Archive.

to leave on August 4. But then he fell seriously ill and was bedridden until death released him on November 12.

It was not until 1794 that in his place Elder Cornelius Regier of Heubuden near Marienburg and preacher Cornelius Warkentin of the Rosenort district of the Greater Delta congregation undertook the journey. There in the province of Jekaterinoslav they found eight newly founded Mennonite villages on the Dnieper river at Chortitza. In the time from the middle of April to the end of July they straightened out the affairs of the churches very well. Unfortunately, Regier died during this time, quite prematurely.[24]

The Rural Danzig Congregation

The Mennonite inhabitants of the Danzig Delta had long belonged to the Danzig Mennonite congregation. They were only a minority of the congregation numbering some 120 baptized members and often had a difficult time getting to the city for church. In 1768 they asked whether it might be possible for services to be held in a private house from time to time, which was easily accomplished since two of the preachers lived in the country. Then in 1791, the rural congregation became somewhat independent. It was made into a district of the city church and subsequently elected two preachers and a deacon from their own midst, had their own alms fund, and was only connected with the city church by a common elder, who administered baptism there and held Communion services twice a year.

After Peter Epp's death, the Danzig congregation elected as elder the energetic and gifted Jacob de Veer (1790-1807), a man 51 years old who had been a preacher since 1774 and who had won great affection for his preaching and teaching. He was the author of a new catechism, which was used in the congregation until 1825.

---

[24]See Johannes van der Smissen, "Zur Geschichte der ersten Gemeindebildung in den Mennoniten-Colonien Süd-Rußlands," *Mennonitische Blätter*, 3, no. 2 (March 1856):18-21, 3, no. 3 (May 1856):34-37, 3, no. 4 (July 1856):19-51.

[The Second Partition of Poland in] 1793 and Rights of Citizenship in the City

On April 4, 1793, Danzig became a Prussian city, and on May 7 the ceremonial homage was made in the presence of the royal commissioners to whom the elders of both Mennonite congregations, Jacob de Veer and Heinrich Roths, had been summoned. They were allowed to give their homage oath of loyalty with a simple "Yes" and a handshake, right after the Protestant clergy.

The laws that in the meantime had been passed for the Mennonites in West Prussia were now also valid for the whole Danzig congregation. The oppressive protection tax that they had had to pay to the city — lowered since 1774 to 1,200 florins per year — was now dropped. In its place 600 talers had to be paid to the Prussian treasury in the same sense as the 5,000 talers the other congregations had to raise for the Culm Cadet Academy.

After being integrated into the Prussian state, the Danzig Mennonites put their efforts into gaining civil rights that the Danzig City Council had so stubbornly denied them. Although the city authorities opposed them vigorously now, too, in 1800 they were finally given by royal decree the possibility of obtaining these rights in Danzig. Berend Momber and Johann Busenitz were the first to obtain them, and the others followed gradually. But the special regulation remained that required Mennonites to pay a purchase fee of 6 percent to the city treasurer when acquiring real estate, while others only had to pay one percent. Not until January 1847 was this injustice done away with on the motion of several Mennonite representatives on the Council.

The Turn of the Century

The general decline in commerce and the whole economy between 1772 and 1793 affected both the Danzig Mennonites and their congregational finances. The number of members had decreased due to departures for Prussian localities elsewhere and the emigration to Russia. Toward the end of the century beginning in 1793 there was some improvement, but there were many negative consequences. The firm sense of cohesion among church members had become lax. Many daughters of respected families married outside the church. While this was possible in the Neugarten congregation, the Flemish church excommunicated such members without hesitation. Apart from this, too, there were many other unfavorable indications. On April 22, 1794, Elder Jacob de Veer on the occasion of announcing baptismal candidates held a very serious talk, in which he lamented the decline of the old moral simplicity, the desire for amusement and the growing indifference regarding the congregation, which came to the fore especially at important consultations of the brotherhood meetings. Also, what had never occurred before was happening now, that at the election of deacons those chosen refused the office, a grave offense against the congregational order and a sign of decay.

The sermon preached by Hans Momber, "known for his excellent talents," at the close of the century on December 28 in the city church, was fairly resigned. Looking back at the past and with a view to the future, he used the text of Col. 4:5 "making the most of the time." He asked: How shall we behave as we take our leave of the last century and try to deal with its events? And he answered: 1. In view of the good and the useful that we have experienced we must be heartily thankful for all physical and spiritual blessings from God, for all religious and moral improvement. 2. For the evil things that have come about, especially in the terrible conditions of the last decades, and the harm that has been done to religion and morality we must seek for improvement.

10
The Time from 1801 to 1820

Hope and Grief at the Advent of a New Century – New Year's Day 1801

At the turn of centuries, people always hope that things will finally improve in the world. "The world is old and become young again, but mankind always hopes for improvement."[1] Unfortunately, no century has ever fulfilled these expectations, held in such confidence.

The preacher from the city territory, Peter Tiessen Jr. who preached the New Year's sermon in the Mennonite church there on January 1, 1801, adopted a more hopeful tone than his colleague Hans Momber when he said farewell to the old century. Tiessen preached on 2 Corinthians 5:17, "Everything old has passed away; see, everything has become new." His topic was: What we can learn about the future by looking into the past? What we can expect? In the first part he reminded his congregation about the past century and the most remarkable happenings in the fatherland, and particularly in this locale [Danzig]. These were, first, the considerable progress in the whole of Europe and especially in our German fatherland of the Enlightenment, of science, the arts and inventions; second, raising the House of Hohenzollern to the title of king;[2] and third, the strange, partly pleasant and partly sad events of our native city. In the second part he considered what the prospects of the new century might be: first, more enlightenment and right thinking among all classes; second, more progress in the practical sciences and the appropriate application of the same; and third, more tranquility and *peace and less war!*

---

[1] ["Die Welt wird alt und wird wieder jung, doch der Mensch hofft immer Verbesserung." – the last sentence of the first stanza of a poem entitled "Hope" (*Hoffnung*) from 1797 by Friedrich von Schiller (1759-1805), Ludwig Kellermann, *Schillers Werke* (Leipzig: Bibliographisches Institut, 1895), 1:219. Ed.]

[2] By royal decree the celebration of the hundredth anniversary of this event had been combined with the New Year's church service. [The Hohenzollerns had been Electors of Brandenburg, Dukes of Prussia, et al. until the Elector Frederick III in 1701 was crowned Frederick I, King in Prussia. Koch, *History of Prussia*, 65-77. Ed.]

Peter Tiessen was thus no pessimist, and that was in keeping with his youthful manliness. Only 36 years old, he was elected preacher on August 17, 1800, and he dedicated himself to that office with zeal, along with his father, who had been a teacher in the congregation since 1774, and since 1807 Jacob de Veer's successor as elder.

Johann Kauenhowen, who attended that New Year's service, no doubt shared the preacher's hopes for the future, but he candidly remarked:

> Our church leadership council marked the beginning of this century with grief. Our dear, respected Elder Jacob de Veer, who had led the congregation with such great care, was weakened in body and spirit since the spring. The first deacon, Gerdt Bachdach, was forced to resign. The second deacon, Cornelius Focking, was terminally ill and departed this life January 9. I had to take over both positions. The newly elected chairman Abraham Reimer wanted to come to my aid, but no sooner had our friend Focking passed into eternity than he [Reimer] had to resign due to poor health.[3] The only comfort was that the long vacant position of preacher was again filled so well, and we hoped that with the help of God we would soon have capable leadership.

Nonetheless Kauenhowen wanted to acknowledge the changes wrought by time. In connection with the New Year's celebration he noted,

> Through the years customs, fashions, traditions, and languages change. Things that were proper in our younger years seem astonishing in our middle years and laughable in our old age, even though we have not lived through an entire century. In the past I have written in good German, but what may

---

[3] He also died a few months later.

be called a uniquely Mennonite language. My current and succeeding colleagues will not consider it pride or contempt if I, at the beginning of this new century, use a somewhat different language in my chronicle; if I leave out the old traditional titles, like Uncle [*Ohm*] or Honorable [*Ehrbare*] and refer to preacher [*Prediger*] instead of teacher [*Lehrer*] and board member [*Vorsteher*] instead of deacon [*Diakon*] and so on.[4] Changes in fashion and customs are inevitable and should be followed to some extent to maintain our respectability. If my successors find any way to improve on this, my ashes will bless them for it."

Although this upright man in his progressive zeal turned his attention to even such minor details, he did not lose sight of important events in the broader society. And in this he had to realize, along with all those who shared his views, that the hopes for peace, which were so important to the Mennonites, did not have any chance of success.

Certainly, some members of the Mennonite congregation were reminded of Schiller's poem, "The Arrival of the New Century,"[5] which begins:

> Noble friend! Where is there a place of refuge for peace or freedom? The last century passed in a storm, and the new one has begun with murder.[6] The bond between nations is loosed and the old molds are crumbling. The primordial sea cannot restrain war's raging, neither can the Nile god or the old Rhine. Two powerful nations struggle for sole possession of the world; to devour the

---

[4] [Kauenhowen is updating traditional Mennonite titles to more modern German usage. As noted earlier, this translation will continue to use the English terms preacher and deacon in most instances. Ed.]

[5] ["Der Antritt des neuen Jahrhunderts." Ed.]

[6] Tsar Paul of Russia was murdered on March 23, 1801.

freedom of all nations they swing the trident and the lightning bolt.

No, peace between nations (this ideal of Mennonite faith) had faded into the misty distance: "Alas, you look in vain on the maps of all the countries, for the blessed area where the evergreen garden of freedom and the beautiful youth of mankind blooms."

The Mennonites were all the more determined to hold fast to their nonresistance and at least in their small circles to create a peaceable kingdom. Where the bonds of fellowship had threatened to loosen, and where old differences from the past were still present, as between the Flemish and the Frisian congregations, the common struggle for their peace principles brought them together again in the new century.

The poet's final admonition — "You must flee to the quiet, holy rooms in your heart from the storms of life!" — they took to mean that, since they were incapable of influencing the larger world and its actions, they could nonetheless still build and preserve a quiet holy place in their houses and families, and finally also in their congregations.

It was from this deeply felt longing that everything that the Danzig Mennonites accomplished in the following decades proceeded.

The Frisian congregation in Neugarten also began the new century with a celebration. Elder Jacob Kliewer preached on Luke 12:56[7] to a large congregation. His theme was "Principles for Testing the Times." He did not leave notes of his sermon, or if he did they are no longer available to us. One may conclude from his choice of text that the tone of his sermon was more serious than celebratory.

New Restrictions

In the course of time, the two congregations had grown closer and the worsening conditions for the Mennonites prepared the ground for the union of the Flemish and Frisian congregations. In order to limit the land ownership of the

---

[7] ["You hypocrites! You know how to interpret the appearance of earth and sky, but why do you not know how to interpret the present time?" Ed.]

Mennonites even more, a "Declaration concerning the Edict of July 30, 1789" appeared at the end of 1801, according to which they could only possess inherited land and were not allowed to purchase any real estate, not even from their co-religionists. Naturally this caused the greatest consternation, and the congregations tried by petitions to the king and sending representatives to Berlin to achieve a modification. At the same time a new wave of emigration to Russia set in, and since that meant that the state lost both people and money, a new arrangement was achieved. From now on the amount of land owned by Mennonites could not exceed what they owned as of November 24, 1803. Mennonites could inherit, buy, or trade each other's land, but they could not buy new properties from the king's Lutheran or Catholic subjects. No further exceptions were allowed. This did not really affect the city inhabitants but only those in rural areas. But since both Danzig congregations had rural members, it was indeed relevant, and all members participated in brotherly fashion in these dealings and the related expenses of this matter.[8]

The times would soon become even worse, and trials of incredible severity would come over Prussia, of which the severely tested city of Danzig would receive a full measure. In the years 1804 and 1805 there was no hint of what was to come. The Mennonite congregation in the city had two new leaders since 1801, Jakob Mahl and Gerhard Zimmermann, who, together with the experienced Johann Kauenhowen took up the leadership with zeal. But Elder Jakob de Veer found it necessary to resign his position due to increasing weakness. His successor was Peter Tiessen the elder, who was supported by his son and Hans Momber.

Renovation of the City Church Building and Guests of the Neugarten Congregation

In 1805 there was still such a feeling of security that a substantial renovation of the church including the acquisition of an organ was decided upon. The construction cost 11,420

---

[8] For a detailed description as well as the documents concerning this matter, see W. Mannhardt, *Wehrfreiheit*, 150.

Title page of 1806 organ chorale accompaniment book. Now at Mennonite Church USA Archives, Bethel College, North Newton, Kansas, Bd. Ms. 183. [Illustration added. Ed.]

Danzig florins in total. Of that 9,747 florins were gathered in freewill offerings, and the rest covered by later collections. The church now had a very attractive appearance. It had been raised five feet, had a plaster ceiling, arched windows, and a new balcony on the garden side. Unfortunately, we do not possess a picture of either this or of the Neugarten church.

During the renovation, which took place in the months of July, August, and September, both congregations joined in common worship services in the church in Neugarten, where their preachers alternated preaching. The new organ was not ready until July 20, 1806. This innovation caused much offense in the rural congregations, and in the city church there was a minority who did not agree with it. But the beautiful dedication service and the vastly improved congregational singing reconciled the opponents. Peter Tiessen Jr. touched people's hearts with a sermon on Col. 3:16. Elder Kliewer and Deacon Claassen of the Frisian congregation attended as special guests.

1806-1807: Destruction of the Neugarten Church Building
Thus everything seemed to be in order for the future. But storm clouds were gathering over Prussia. The old Holy Roman Empire had been buried and Napoleon had formed the Confederation of the Rhine. Prussia declared war [on

Napoleon] on October 8 and lost the battle of Jena on the 14th. The forts on the Elbe and Oder rivers capitulated. Napoleon's army moved eastward and within a few weeks appeared outside Danzig. On November 16 the Governor von Mannstein ordered the inhabitants of the suburbs to take their most prized possessions into the city, since all the houses up to 800 paces from the walls would have to be destroyed if the enemy approached. Since no news of Napoleon's advance was received, people felt a false security. But on December 25 Elder Jakob Kliewer wrote:

> Up to the present we have been able to have our services in Neugarten, but on December 21, the fourth Sunday of Advent, *Erdmann Stobbe preached for the last time there.* For, as I was preparing to preach this morning and came there with my wife and Heinrich von Steen, the soldiers were already busy dismantling the buildings of Neugarten on order of the governor, including our alms house. I immediately ordered the organists to remove the organ and the deacons took care of the rest. They also found quarters for our poor in the city and saved as much as possible. In a few days our beautiful church along with all the other buildings was transformed into a pile of stones and debris and we had been driven out of our house of worship, which is very hard for the congregation! Nonetheless, God, may your will be done!

That was a sad Christmas celebration and a bad close to the year. What would the year 1807 bring?

First, it brought the concern about where the congregation would have its worship services. The Flemish congregation had immediately offered its church on city territory through the preacher Hans Momber, but there was hesitation to accept this offer, since it would only be for a short time, as the French armies were gradually approaching. So Kliewer turned to the leadership of the English chapel on Heilige Geistgasse/Św. Ducha and was met with willing acceptance. On January 18 he was able to preach there, on Luke 12:6-7. They were going to have Communion in the Flemish church building on March 8, but it had to be cancelled due to the advancing enemy.

The Siege and Its Consequences — The Free State of Danzig

On March 11 the siege began. For more than two months the Mennonites in the city were cut off from their church. The inhabitants of the congregational alms house had been given three months' advances, so that they could manage, if barely. Both congregations held their worship services in the English chapel until the bombardment of the city after April 24 made this impossible. After the capitulation on May 25 one could see that indeed many houses of members had been destroyed, including that of Elder Peter Tiessen senior in Schlapke. But the church and alms house were undamaged. Johann Jantzen of St. Albrecht/Św. Wojciech had supplied the poor weekly with money and foodstuffs. On June 21 it was possible to preach in the city again. The congregation rebuilt the elder's house and sought to repair the damages of the siege to its members.

This was made more difficult by the levies which the Mennonites in the so-called *"Free State of Danzig,"*[9] cut off from Prussia, had to pay, once together with other citizens and then separately as Mennonites, on orders of the French commander. In April 1808 the Mennonites of the suburbs were forced to provide a loan of 40,000 talers as an exceptional war tax, under the threat of military confiscation of the total. In the city the Mennonites had to raise their share of the forced contribution levied on the general population. In the years 1807 and 1808 this amounted to more than seven million talers.

The Two Congregations Unite 1808

Brought ever closer together by the distress of war and because there could be no thought of rebuilding the Neugarten church building, the two congregations in 1808 joined to form

---

[9] [As part of the Treaty of Tilsit, which ended the war between France and Prussia, the Free City of Danzig was created as an autonomous political entity. Real political control of the city was vested in the French governor. Cieślak and Biernat, *History of Gdańsk*, 317-8. Ed.]

the "United Frisian and Flemish Mennonite Congregation." The former Frisian congregation with its 166 baptized members joined the city church, and on May 22 there was a celebration of the union.

The leadership of the united church now provisionally consisted of a good number of capable, respected men. First of all, there were the two elders, Peter Tiessen Sr., 68 years of age, and Jakob Kliewer, 65; in addition the four preachers, Hans Momber, 66; Erdmann Stobbe, 67; Peter Tiessen Jr., 43; and Jakob von Dühren, 41. Then the deacons, Johann Kauenhowen, 56; Gerhard Claassen, 61; Jakob Mahl, 42; Heinrich von Dühren, 42; Abraham de Veer, 38; Johann von Steen, 39; and Johann Penner, 35.

The *Frisian congregation* has only been referred to occasionally due to the sparse sources available. I may comment here that their elders after Jan Gerrits van Embden (see p. 51) in the seventeenth century are not known. Not until 1676 do we find Heinrich von Dühren I as elder, who had been a teacher in the congregation since 1664. His sons followed him, Albrecht von Dühren (1694-96), and Heinrich von Dühren II (1701-1746). Then Jacob Kliewer I (1742-1775), Isaak Stobbe (1775-1788), Heinrich Roths (1788-1797), and Jakob Kliewer II, since 1798.

In this union the Frisian congregation had to give up certain practices that had been used earlier, especially *allowing mixed marriages*. It had been open-minded in this respect and had allowed those who had married Lutheran or Reformed spouses to remain members. But because this practice included the danger that children of such marriages would not be granted freedom from military service, the Flemish congregation had long since excommunicated all those who married outside the congregation, and they continued this practice. For the same reason no members were accepted from other denominations.[10]

---

[10] [Prussian law since the 1720s — that is, even before Prussia ruled over the Mennonites of the Vistula River — made it illegal in the eastern provinces of the kingdom, including the former Duchy of Prussia (East Prussia), for children from such religiously mixed marriages to win military exemption. The Mennonite Edict of 1789 extended this ruling to the Mennonites of the Vistula area. Since Mennonites would not accept men who were liable for military service into their congregations, the law de facto

Both of these practices had the effect of lessening the number of Mennonites. Those existing "blended" members continued as members of the congregation. There were thirty-eight of them, of whom thirty-six were women.

Jacob Kliewer II, elder 1798-1826. [Scanned from 1919 German edition. Ed.]

A New Terrible Siege in 1813 and Foreign Occupation to 1814

The "seven-years suffering" of the unhappy citizenry of the "Free State of Danzig" is too well known to be described again here.[11] From January 21, 1813, to January 2, 1814, it reached its zenith in a siege of unheard of length and horror.

---

prevented such children from becoming Mennonites. Jantzen, "At Home in Germany?" 75-80. Ed.]

[11] There is abundant material for such a description in our archives.

Danzig was a ruined city. Almost 6,000 persons had died during the siege. Wealth and livelihood had vanished. Huge sums had had to be raised for the French. The debt load of the individual and of the city was immense. The era of the Free State cost the city over 14 million talers and about 12 million remained to be paid. All joy of life, enthusiasm, and happiness had disappeared, and it took years before the general depression of spirit could be lifted somewhat, and before the deep wounds began to heal.[12]

We must keep this in mind when we return to the Mennonite congregation and consider their fate and their actions in the following years. They had suffered terribly. The church on the city territory was a pile of rubble, and for a half mile around the city everything lay in awful ruins. The number of dead in 1813 was five times more than usual.

I will now let Dr. Wilhelm Mannhardt speak, who, in his essay "Building Our Church Fifty Years Ago,"[13] reported the following based on our church archives:

Not until January 2, 1814, did the hour of our salvation strike. The reconquered Danzig paid homage again to the Prussian royal house. The Mennonites had been affected most severely, a high proportion of them had lost all they owned when the suburbs were razed. The city dwellers, too, and many others who had fled into the city had suffered in turn through the long siege, through the extortion of the defenders, the inflation of food prices (for example, a bushel of grain for 40 to 46 talers, potatoes for 42 talers, a pound of coffee for 7 talers, a pound of meat for one taler, a pound of butter for 7 talers). All were seriously weakened financially, and the poor condition of trade as well

---

[12] Simson, *Geschichte der Stadt Danzig*, 152.
[13] *Mennonitische Blätter*, Vol. 16, No. 7 (September 1869), 54-7.

as the devaluation of money and property did not bode well for improvement in the future.

Cut off from their own church during the siege, the Mennonite congregation had once again rented the English chapel for its services, while the poor of the alms house were housed and fed at various locations. The whole routine of the church was disorganized, since many of the leaders had taken refuge in places far from Danzig. Order returned only gradually. In April 1814 we see the congregation gathering in great numbers for Communion with feelings of inexpressible thanksgiving. But since the English chapel was too small to hold all the members at once, Communion had to be held on two consecutive Sundays. This served as a warning to think about the acquisition of an adequate church building as soon as possible. But it took all the courage and love of hearts filled with zeal for God to move to the building of a new church that would be adequate for future needs during a time when most people had to struggle for their own survival. The painful experiences of the past decade advised against building a new structure outside the gates. Apart from that, no houses could be built within 1,300 paces of the outer walls due to requirements of the city's fortifications, and thus the re-use of the old properties became impossible. For the same reason many from the razed suburbs now took their permanent residence in the city, and since now the majority of the members lived in the city this had to be taken into consideration. Accordingly, various projects were proposed. One could postpone building the church until times improved if there were a more suitable building that they could rent for a longer time, or if it were less suitable and small to furnish it with what was necessary for their immediate needs. For both of these options there were offers. The leaders of Church of St. Jacob on the Schüsseldamm/Lagiewniki proposed their building, which had been used of late as a warehouse. At the same time a house in the Sandgrube was suggested, which at little cost could be remodeled as a house of worship. It should be recognized that the leaders did not allow their thinking to be influenced by the hardship of the period. The two members of the leadership who had been asked to view both localities, Heinrich von Steen and Abraham de Veer, on June 22 declared that the modest villa (*Gartenhaus*) would be too small and insufficient, while the St. Jacob's Church presented too many difficulties and questions. It was therefore decided that the English chapel would be kept until things improved. But when on October 20 the whole church leadership thoroughly inspected the St. Jacob's Church in all its parts and found it to be in better condition than had been thought, they responded favorably, and the representatives were called for further discussions. Among these, however, a decided opposition arose, especially from Berend Momber, and the whole matter was adjourned for the time being.

Napoleon's return from Elba and the new dangers of the year 1815 pushed construction ideas to the background. But when peace finally seemed to have been assured, the desire for one's own place of worship became more pressing and the members looked for a suitable place within the fortifications. Church board member Johann Busenitz found a piece of land that was for sale in the *Schwarzes Meer* area near the Salvator cemetery. The congregation buried its dead there and so at that time that cemetery was already called the Mennonite cemetery. It had been taken over by the city from the heirs of the wholesaler Simon Spieß. The lot measured 2,264 square meters[14] and included a large

---

[14] ["1 Morgen, 165 Ruten, 55 Fuss" in the original text. The lot was

garden and a very decrepit old house with a balcony. The location of the place seemed very suitable. Not too far for the inhabitants of the inner city, it was also suitable for those members living in either direction, in the suburbs and the villages of Oliva, Langfuhr, St. Albrecht, and Ohra. Separated from the highway by the Radaune canal, it had a clear view and was not in danger of being closed in by new construction in the surrounding streets and lanes. On the other side of the highway one could see the green inner walls and above them the wonderful facade of the St. Trinitatis Church and the church building of the Reformed congregation (St. Peter and Paul) which was so closely related to the Mennonites. These buildings greeted one's view like friendly neighbors. The decision in favor of this location was soon made. Johann Busenitz purchased the property on May 6, 1816, in the name of the congregation for 1,000 talers, with a 50 taler yearly tax. On the third day of Pentecost, June 4, the purchase contract was announced to the membership and the first discussion about a new building begun. There was unanimity about the need, but concerning the building plan and raising the necessary funds there were very different opinions. The aftermath of the war was still in evidence. And so the appeal to pledge for contributions did not meet the need.

Only a few persons pledged, and the amount collected, some 2,000 Danzig florins, was not even enough to pay for a fence around the newly acquired property. Since nothing much had changed by September, the leadership supported by the church board members decided to take the next step in God's name, and, if another appeal to the congregation did not increase the original sum, to take the necessary money from the capital fund. To

---

roughly two-thirds of an acre. Ed.]

replace the lost interest everyone would be approached to increase the semi-annual membership dues. Since this last measure could be carried out in the next weeks without opposition, and the self-imposed regular increase amounted to about 1,000 florins, the leadership on October 3 named Heinrich von Steen to oversee construction and authorized him to proceed, not only with the fence but also with the alms house. On October 17 the city granted the building permit and on November 27 the enclosure of the property was completed. The same year a shed was built, which was used at first as a tool shed during construction but later as a carriage shed for those who came in from the country. The bank of the Radaune was protected by a strong wooden retaining wall, and a forty-foot staircase was installed down to the river along with a dock, a drainage pipe, and two catchment barrels. A fence separated the larger, southern portion of the property that was to be the garden from the church grounds. The master carpenter Fuchs carried out these projects for the sum of 4,992 florins. Winter interrupted further construction. During 1817 the alms house was erected in half-timbering, 136 feet long, 18 feet deep, and two stories high.[15] It contained eight apartments on each floor, and between each two apartments was a common room and kitchen. A pent roof with clay roofing tiles covered the whole building. The master mason Bretschneider and the master carpenter Fuchs had accepted the project for 22,500 florins and were able to deliver it so far ahead of schedule that on October 24 the final inspection was passed, despite several alterations.

---

[15] [The Prussian foot at 314 mm or 12.35 inches is slightly longer than the American foot measure. August Blind, *Maß-, Münz-, und Gewichtswesen* (Leipzig: G. J. Göschen'sche Verlagshandlung, 1906), 42. Ed.]

The construction costs were immediately covered by the capital of the alms fund.

At Easter 1818 the leader of the English congregation, Mr. Atkinson, gave notice that the rental contract of the chapel in the Heilige Geistgasse would run out at Michaelmas [September 29], because the owner wanted to use it for their own church services. Now there was no choice. The construction of the church could not be postponed any longer. But since it did not seem advisable to dip into the capital of the congregation again, the time had come to make an extraordinary sacrifice to keep the work going. The leadership was not mistaken when it assumed that the congregation was eager to participate. In a meeting of the church leaders with the council on the Thursday after Easter, March 26, the deacon Heinrich von Dühren, who with his family came from the Neugarten church, made a preliminary estimate of the amount that the members would have to raise. On March 30 then, since the infirm Elder P. Tiessen Sr. felt too weak, the preacher P. Tiessen Jr. presented this need in warm and eloquent words to the brotherhood assembled in the English Chapel and asked for their response. The brethren immediately showed themselves willing to take a one-time collection dedicated to the need, and one after the other they approached the table to sign up. Many offered to increase their amount if necessary. Even the pennies of the poor amounted to 25 florins, while the well-to-do signed for amounts of 500 to 1,200 florins according to their means, for example, Johann Busenitz, Peter Stobbe in Tiegenhof, Johann Schreder, Dirck de Veer, Jacob Tiessen, Arend v. Niessen, Gerhard Ludwichsen, widow A. Reimer, widow Fluge, and widow W. Zimmermann. As the collection continued, no financially independent member abstained. For most of them it was not easy to part with the gift they had freely given, and they had to do without many of their simple and innocent pleasures to cover the deficit, for their contributions were all very generous in comparison to their financial standing, and for some it was almost too much. Those of us born much later are filled with respect when we consider the moral strength which reveals itself in such sacrifice, whose extent we only can truly honor when we consider the extent of the general economic ruin after the war, especially in the area of Danzig. Although the members had given the most, they did not lack for help and encouragement through gifts of love from their sister congregations. From Königsberg they received 1,836 florins, from Orloff/Orłowo 233 florins, from Tiegenhagen 314 florins, from Fürstenwerder 233 florins, and from Elbing 780 florins. Including these contributions, the sum of voluntary pledges for church construction from about 140 members came to 34,523 Danzig florins.

The means were at hand and construction could begin. In June a contract was concluded with the master mason Bretschneider and master carpenter Fuchs, according to which they were obliged by July 1, 1819, to complete the construction of the church for 46,000 Danzig florins including the pews and chancel and three coats of oil paint, but not including the organ. For every further month delay 1,000 florins would be deducted. The board members Johann Busenitz and K.H. Focking served as project supervisors. Heinrich Wegner, a church member, offered to build an organ for 6,000 florins. At first, it seemed he would have the contract, but the church then opted for Arend, an experienced organ builder.

The construction plans were submitted to the inspectors and a permit was granted on July 3, 1818. A few days later, on July 9, in the presence of all the elders,[16] preachers,[17] deacons,[18] and church council members,[19] the cornerstone of the church was laid. A large portion of the congregation was present at the celebration, which Elder P. Tiessen Sr. opened with a moving prayer. After a wistful look back at the wounds caused by the past, he overflowed with praise and thanks "a thousand times over" to the "exalted Helper above" and with the "humble confession 'You, our God, are kind and true, yes, you lover of our souls, you rule in grace.'" The prayer concluded with a plea for the blessing of the Most High to bring about the successful conclusion of the work in this holy place. At this, the stone was placed and a memorial statement and a number of coins were laid inside it. Master · mason Bretschneider gave a solemn talk that had been written by his friend, the widely admired junior police official (*Polizeiassessor*) Kühnel. In concluding, he gave the church chairman Abraham de Veer a trowel and hammer, and de Veer said a few words in rhyme. A speech of praise and thanks and a prayer by Erdmann Stobbe concluded the ceremony.

Soon the building arose over the foundations. It was 75 feet long, 45 feet wide and 28 feet high above ground level in brickwork. The old place of worship on city territory had been taken as a model, but numerous improvements were incorporated. The new church has its long back wall along the river, while the front faces the courtyard and is across from the alms house. Here we find the main entrance, to which leads a hallway in a low annex. The sacristy is attached on the left side, while on the

---

[16] Peter Tiessen Sr. and Jacob Kliewer.
[17] Erdmann Stobbe, Peter Tiessen Jr., and Jacob von Dühren.
[18] Abr. de Veer, Heinrich von Dühren, and Johann von Steen.
[19] Johann Busenitz, K.H. Focking, Wilh. Jantzen, Arend von Niessen, and J.H. Focking.

right there is a coatroom for the women. On both the front and back sides two large and two smaller windows crowned with rounded arches let a bright light into the friendly interior. Across from the entrance door the pulpit rises under a star of white glass, on both sides of which the chairs for the preachers and deacons stand along the wall. On both of the narrow sides there is a balcony; the one on the right has the melodious organ with a double keyboard, while the one on the left is arranged for seating. There are comfortable stairs that lead to both of these balconies from foyers that have side doors leading into the building. Below the pulpit is the Communion table (the current one is a gift from a later time). The seating for the congregation is arranged symmetrically on both sides of the pulpit, those nearest the main entrance being intended for the female audience. The unadorned walls are whitewashed, and all wooden trim soberly painted gray. An arched ceiling crowns the whole building, which makes for a harmonious impression and is full of dignity in its simplicity. The contractor found a good solution to the architectural assignment to create an image of Mennonite thought and sensibility in wood and stone.

The work of the builders was already done when the whole project was once again threatened by a not inconsiderable danger. According to the requirements of the fortification regulations it was necessary to obtain permission from military officials for building the church. Since the local authorities in Danzig had given this permission, the work had proceeded. When the building was all but finished, apart from its furnishing, an order came on July 19, 1819, from the Ministry of War, stating that the building could be erected, though in the case of military necessity it would be demolished. In any case it should be turned with its narrow side against the main city wall so as to be placed in the most favorable alignment for the fortification and the peak of the roof should remain several feet lower than the city wall. The military commander's office wanted to persuade the Mennonites to build massively, so that if part of the outer defenses were lost the building could serve as a blockhouse in the gap. But the considerate engineer of the district, von Bartsch, deflected the danger by deciding on July 28 that all the legal requirements had been fulfilled, and the wishes of the War Ministry could not be accommodated since the building was already finished.

The work could now reach its conclusion without disturbance. The organ was installed, the upholstering of the benches and the other interior furnishings were completed. Now, too, the costs for all these expenditures could be seen.

1. To the contractors Fuchs and Bretschneider
   - a) for contracted construction   46,000 florins
   - b) for other work   4,300 florins
2. Related construction costs   6,101 florins
3. For the yard, pavement, and other buildings on the church lot during 1818 and 1819 (if not included in 2)   3,256 florins
4. For the organ   1,443 Prussian Reichstalers

These expenses were covered in part by the freewill contributions mentioned earlier, and in part by a loan.

On September 5, 1819, Peter Tiessen Jr. gave the farewell sermon in the English Chapel, whose further use had in the meantime been reserved for one more year. He spoke on Psalm 27:4. The dedication of the new church building in the so-called Schwarzen Meer area of Danzig followed on September 12. A week earlier the printed invitations to this celebration had been sent to the leading citizens of the city. The church was decorated with flowers and could barely hold the many visitors. In addition to the good turnout of members, the guests included Prince Hermann von Hohenzollern, Commander von Kamke and his wife, Chief of Police (*Polizeipräsident*) von Vegesack, police official Kühnel, and senior church administrator[20] and Pastor of St. Mary's Dr. Bertling. Also noticed among those present were Dr. Böckel, deacon of St. John's, and the then teacher at St. Barbara, Dr. G. Löschin, along with many other friends of the Lutheran and Reformed confessions.

Surrounded by a half-circle of the congregational leadership, which the preacher von Riesen from Elbing had joined, the eighty-year-old Elder P.Tiessen Sr. prayed a solemn prayer from behind the Communion table. Then the organ joined in and the congregation united to sing the songs "Auf meine Seele, singe," "Auf, jauchzet Gott! Auf alle Welt!", "Wir glauben an den einigen Gott" (No. 494, 493, 628).[21] After that P. Tiessen Jr. went to the pulpit and delivered the dedicatory sermon on 1 Kings 9:3 "The Lord said to him, 'I have heard your prayer and your plea, which you made before me; I have consecrated this house that you have built, and put my name there forever; my eyes and my heart will be there for all time.'"

Following this text, the speaker preached on the theme: "What must we consider and hope for upon completing this house of God and the related buildings." He expounded on this place as a holy place. Not the place itself, but the holy purpose of the same awakens respect in us. God's nearness is

---

[20] [*Konsistorialrat*, a government official with regulatory responsibilities for the Protestant churches. Ed.]

[21] [In 1819 the congregation would have been using the hymnal *Geistreiches Gesangbuch, zur öffentlichen und besondern Erbauung der mennonitischen Gemeine in und vor der Stadt Danzig* (Marienwerder, 1780), see chapter 8. Hymns 493, 494, and 628 are as listed above in this hymnal, the latter however is in an appendix that was published at an unknown later date. Ed.]

not limited to any place or time. But forgetful humanity with its limited perception needs a place where it can be challenged to pause in serious reflection on occasion. Here the soul may commune with God and Jesus, its exalted benefactor, undisturbed by the turbulence of the outer world. Here we can make holy decisions and be inspired to active love of neighbor. It is not accidental that our predecessors have long combined an alms house with their churches, to remind the congregation constantly that the mark of a true Christian is not merely feeling but action. We are to recognize the tree by its fruits. Therefore we have cause to be happy and thankful to God and to all those who directly or indirectly helped, so that after the painful loss of two houses of God we now have a new temple and a home for our poor. We hope that God will fulfill his promise: "I have consecrated this house that you have built, and put my name there forever." May He take this building into His care, may He answer the prayers that arise in it, and may He bless the holy rites enacted here with rich fruit. May He never let this place lack in faithful, pious and gifted preachers and leaders, and may He awaken in us and our descendants love and respect toward His house and its ways and tenets."[22]

So concludes Dr. Wilhelm Mannhardt's description.

---

[22] [H. G. Mannhardt here only reprints a portion of Wilhelm Mannhardt's longer essay on the history of Mennonite church buildings in Danzig. Here H. G. Mannhardt omits the last two paragraphs regarding the 1819 dedication church service and a page on the fiftieth-anniversary celebration. Ed.]

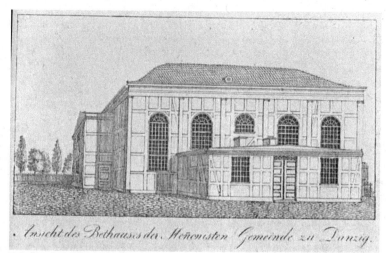

Ansicht des Bethauses der Mennonisten Gemeinde zu Danzig.

Exterior view of the 1819 Danzig church building. [This illustration was used in the 1919 German edition, but comes originally from Reiswitz, *Beiträge zur Kenntnis der taufgesinnten Gemeinden . . .* (1829). Ed.]

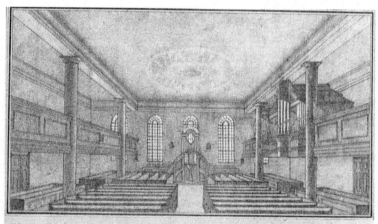

Innere Ansicht des Bethauses der Mennonisten Gemeinde zu Danzig.

Interior view of the 1819 church building. [This illustration did not appear in the 1919 German edition. It also comes from Reiswitz, 1829. Ed.]

11
From 1820 to 1869

Reverberations from the Building Project
The construction of the new church was an accomplished fact. In a time of general impoverishment, a small congregation of eight to nine hundred souls erected a new house of worship, while almost all its members struggled to make ends meet. It is true that several sister congregations of the Danzig Mennonites had come to their aid and had donated at least 3,000 florins. They also received, albeit after completion of the church, 1,188 talers from the Royal Prussian "Reestablishment Commission," 550 florins for the destroyed Neugarten church and 638 for the church and alms house on city territory. Since the total costs, including the alms house and the organ, came to some 88,000 Danzig guilders,[1] the congregation, after subtracting the above sums of 8,138 florins, had raised almost 80,000 Danzig florins, or, in today's [1919] currency, 51,200 marks.

Honor and thanks to our forefathers, who a hundred years ago created a center for the religious life of the community with such sacrificial love. With satisfaction the grandchildren and great-grandchildren of today will read what Professor Friedrich Wadzeck[2] wrote in the *Berlin Weekly Journal* of November 28, 1818, after the dedication ceremony:

> In this current time of pettiness where most people are concerned only with themselves and their affairs, and even those who judge things

---

[1]A Danzig guilder had the approximate worth of 6.4 silver Groschen Prussian, the equivalent today [1919] of 64 pfennigs.

[2][Friedrich Wadzeck (1762-1823) was a member of the Moravian Brethren congregation in Berlin and presumably learned about Mennonites through those connections. From 1788 to 1819 he taught at the Royal Cadet Academy for officers' training in Berlin. The Culm Cadet Academy that Mennonites supported in lieu of military service was a feeder school to this Berlin school (see chapter 9). The *Berlin Weekly Journal* (*Berliner Wochenblatt*) was Wadzeck's own paper, begun in 1809. In 1821 together with Baron George Leopold von Reiswitz (1764-1828) he published *Beiträge zur Kenntnis der Mennoniten-Gemeinden in Europa und Amerika, statistischen, historischen und religiösen Inhalts*. Christian Hege and Harold S. Bender, "Wadzeck, Friedrich," *Mennonite Encyclopedia* (Scottdale, PA: Herald Press, 1955-1959), 867. Ed.]

coolly can seldom distinguish between the essence
and the circumstantial, it is rare indeed to see
institutions rising from ashes and ruins. Such an
event confirms the authentic essence of a
beneficent religious doctrine, and expresses the
true meaning of honoring God and loving one's
brother. This feeling is alive in Danzig, even if not
much is written about it — and more than
elsewhere. This is shown by the good attendance at
all the churches. In spite of the indescribable
suffering of wartime and the destruction of trade
and the crafts, this is shown also by the
maintenance of benevolent and generous
institutions for the sick, the poor, and for
education. What our predecessors founded out of
piety the heirs honored by preservation.

The Mennonite congregation, too, has given a
good example in this respect. The Mennonites lost
two beautiful houses of worship and two alms
houses for infirm, needy members in the sieges of
1807 and 1813. They have held their services in a
building in which the English congregation had
their worship, because it was not only at a suitable
location, but also because in those poor times they
lacked the means to establish a house of worship
of their own.

With this in mind, and with great care, the
leaders of the congregation were able to buy a
beautiful, roomy garden outside the Hohes Tor
and to obtain permission for the construction
project they had planned. Already in 1817 a
welcoming building was erected on this place for
the care of more than thirty needy congregational
members, who in addition to a free dwelling and
fuel received a certain weekly supplement of
money, meat, and bread. On July 8 this year the
cornerstone for a house of worship was also laid.

The oldest preacher prayed a moving and
heartfelt prayer. Then the cornerstone was put in

place, and the following words were spoken by the much respected and experienced master mason, Bretschneider:

Solemn and serious is the purpose which has called us to this place, and may it be granted to me, the general contractor, to speak an earnest word. Man in his madness destroys what is holiest, but only man is able to rise to that divine power which teaches him to recognize the holy and to honor and preserve it. He is led to this power and this will by pious faith, pure love, and by that most beautiful daughter of heaven, hope! Who does not recognize that friendly companion of heaven in this project that the members of an honored Christian congregation now intend to carry out. The raging of war was able to destroy the work of humanity but not their *faith*. The faithful *love* of the congregation rebuilds the divine temple. Whoever is persecuted by fate, tired of life, or forsaken by friends, finds comfort, care, and protection in the *love* of the congregation, and all, united in love, find joy in the hope of a better world. We entrust to the earth the first stone for this house of God, that it will faithfully protect it, so that it will remain firm and unmoved like this faith and our trust in Him to whose praise and honor this building is erected! It is a great honor for my friend, the master carpenter and engineer Mr. Friedrich Gotthilf Fuchs, and I, to have been given the contract for the construction of this building. For me personally it is a particular joy for my heart. May the work of our hands be pleasing to heaven, may the Master builder of the worlds protect it with His almighty hand and keep it from danger! For the leaders and all the members of this congregation may this house be a house of comfort and a source of rejoicing for one's soul, a point of common striving toward the highest human dignity, to eternal salvation! And when we have all been

returned to the dust, may future generations still
lift their hearts here to their Creator and Preserver.
May they remember those who founded this house,
and with the joy of the Psalmist call out: "O Lord,
I love the house in which you dwell, and the place
where your glory abides. (Psalm 26:8)

The article in the *Berlin Weekly Journal*[3] then concludes with
the words: "Already this house, conceived in a simple, beautiful
style, is rising. The spirit of order and the quiet but energetic
activity which is embodied in most of the members is truly a
good spirit."

As so often happens, that which had been a serious threat to
the predecessors becomes a blessing to their successors, a saying
that came true also in our congregation. The former first
suffered and then built for us. If the church had remained on
city territory where it had been closest for most members, it
would not have remained a central locale for them in the course
of the nineteenth century. For after the limitations had been
removed which made residence inside city walls difficult for
Mennonites, more and more moved and settled in the city
proper and especially in the old city. The suburbs too often had
experienced the horrors of war, and were no longer a desirable
location. The "united towns of Stoltzenberg," created by
Friedrich II and including Old Schottland, had almost
completely disappeared after 1813. In 1805, 36 Mennonite
families had still lived here, but by 1820 none seems to have
remained. From the immediate suburbs, too, most of them had
moved to the inner city. So the new church was much more
suitably located, especially since those who lived outside mostly
came to church with their own carriages.

Innovations in Selecting Preachers

Around 1825 there was a significant change in the way
preachers were selected. Both elders who had led the church since
the union of 1808, Peter Tiessen Sr. and Jacob Kliewer, were
old and requested the election of a younger preacher as a co-

---

[3] *Berliner Wochenblatt.*

Peter Tiessen Jr., elder. Died 1826. [Scanned
from 1919 German edition. Ed.]

elder. Tiessen did not live to see this election. He died on March
17, 1825, at the age of 86 and was buried with a large funeral.[4]
The aged Elder Kliewer now really insisted that the
congregation provide a younger elder, so on May 24 there was
an election between the two preachers of the congregation,
Peter Tiessen Jr. and Jacob von Dühren. Tiessen was elected
with 119 votes and confirmed in his office by the 83-year-old
Jacob Kliewer. The new elder was 61 years of age and enjoyed
the highest confidence in the congregation, which he had served
as a preacher since 1800. Nonetheless, the future did not look
very bright, for he, too, was not a young man, and besides him
and the old Elder Kliewer, there was only the preacher Jacob
von Dühren, who was already 58 years old.[5] The election of a

---

[4]In the death register his name is followed by the words: "This honored
old man lived in a happy and blessed marriage of 63 years with his wife, who
had died a few months earlier."

[5]The other preacher, Erdmann Stobbe, had died on September 22, 1824,
at the age of 83.

new preacher had not come about, since no one was willing to accept the office. Then an unexpected solution presented itself.

In October 1824 the leadership received a letter from a Mennonite preacher, *Jacob van der Smissen* of Friedrichstadt an der Eider. He was asking whether here in Prussia, perhaps in Königsberg, Elbing, or Danzig, there would be a Mennonite congregation that would be willing to appoint him with a fixed salary. In his present church, due to the small size of the congregation, he was unable to fully exercise his gifts and at forty years of age he desired to serve a larger congregation. The answer from here was at first negative, since the congregation was not in need of more preachers and was not used to paying a salary. Until then only one preacher had received something to supplement his income.[6]

On July 8, 1825, van der Smissen nonetheless appeared in Danzig as a visitor and guest after visiting the Elbing and Heubuden congregations. He preached on July 10. "His sermon on Romans 1:16-17, was received positively. His expressions were so heartfelt and penetrating and his decorum so appropriate that one had to admit that we had not heard anything similar. His delivery without notes added to this impression." After his departure many members desired to win this man for the congregation. Following some initial resistance from the leadership, negotiations with van der Smissen began. Since there were 96 members who were willing to raise 500 talers collectively every year for the salary for the next ten years, a contract was drawn up, according to which he would be appointed for these ten years at 500 talers per year. He was not, however, to have the authority of an elder at first, although he had long since been ordained as such. A face-saving measure to

---

[6] In the year 1765 during a time of general prosperity, some members of the congregation had expressed the wish that a preachers' fund be set up, and "that well-off and philanthropic brothers or sisters might be mindful of the needy preachers, who sacrificed so much time and energy that they often could not look after their own businesses." Arend Kauenhowen, the father of the deacon Johann Kauenhowen, had donated a starting capital of 2,000 florins. In his will he added 3,000 florins, which his son paid out in 1792. Through these and other grants this fund in 1801 had some 12,000 florins. The support named above was taken from the interest.

justify this aspect of the contract was sought and found by naming him elder of the rural branch of the Danzig congregation. But the members there were not in agreement with this arrangement and clung to the old ways more strongly than the city church, which is always the case. This church then took the novelty of a paid preacher as grounds to separate from the Danzig congregation and to join the Fürstenwerder congregation. In 1844 they built a small church building of their own in Neunhuben/Dziewięć Włók and the congregation has since been called by the name of this village.

Jacob van der Smissen Arrives in Danzig from Friedrichstadt

On June 30, 1826, after a very difficult 28-day journey by land with his wife and five children, the preacher Jacob van der Smissen arrived here. His possessions had preceded him by boat, and it required a lot of effort to retrieve them from customs and to bring them to his dwelling, which the leadership had rented for his family in the Fleischergasse. Many generous women of the congregation had brought supplies of meat, butter, cheese, coffee, sugar, and rice into the apartment, so that the new arrivals would find it stocked with these necessities.

On July 9 van der Smissen gave his inaugural sermon. The deacon [Anton] Schreder comments about it in his congregational chronicle "The new preacher was used to appearing in his home church in clerical collar and preaching bands, robed in a silk gown. We convinced him to take off the robe and to appear in a simple jacket, while keeping the collar and preaching bands.[7] He had chosen Romans 15:29 as his text: 'and I know that when I come to you, I will come in the fullness of the blessing of Christ.' The numerous listeners included the senior church administrator Gerhard,[8] who after the sermon found his way into the preachers' room and had a friendly

---

[7][Hence van der Smissen was dressed in the style of German Protestant clergy. The long, black robe he was asked to lay aside derived from academic regalia and looked much like an undergraduate graduation robe. The preaching bands were two small rectangular bands of white cloth that hung down from the collar. Ed.]

[8][*Oberconsistorialrat.* Ed.]

discussion with the leadership. The acceptance and appreciation of this new pastor were shown in the following time by the many meaningful gifts he received, often from anonymous donors, including a gift of 50 Reichstalers from the elderly Madam Fluge."

The Acquisition of a Parsonage through a Gift

This lady was at that time the oldest member of the congregation and in spite of her 88 years, she took an active interest in the well-being of the church. She had long wished that the Mennonites of Danzig would elect a preacher who would not be bound by other employment, but could dedicate himself completely to preaching, pastoral work, and teaching. In her joy at seeing this wish now realized, she gave the church leadership a house at the Hohes Tor (Heumarkt/Targ Sienny 5), on the condition that two preacher apartments would be arranged there. When she died on December 1, 1823, at almost 90 years of age, 1,000 florins from her estate were distributed to 44 needy persons in the congregation. After a small but necessary alteration, the preacher's family moved into the right side of the house, which included a pleasant garden, while the left side was rented out.

Illness and Death of Both Elders Tiessen and Kliewer in 1826

If at first it had appeared that van der Smissen, as a third elder, would be very limited in his activity, that perception changed in a short time. He had only been here for two months when Peter Tiessen fell seriously ill, so that he was not able to baptize the youth whom he had prepared for baptism. The elderly Kliewer was not able to do that either. So, without having to take the initiative, the young preacher was given the task of administering baptism. Even before that took place on October 8, Peter Tiessen died, at age 62 on October 1. And on October 5 the aged Jacob Kliewer, who was almost 84 years old, followed him. Still under the impression of these two deaths, the baptism of October 8 was carried out by van der Smissen, and a week later the celebration of Communion.

Now van der Smissen was alone with only one remaining preacher, Jacob von Dühren, who preached every third week.

By appointing a paid minister with a theological education, the congregation had taken a step that appeared to be a break with tradition. In fact, they followed the path of the Dutch and Northwest German Mennonite city congregations. Here, as there, this change was not introduced without much hesitation and not without lively opposition by a minority who wanted to be faithful to the old ways. Admittedly the traditional custom had a worthy basis in the idea of the priesthood of all believers. If the congregation chooses men out of its own midst who are to be its servants of the Word, and if every young man at his baptism takes on the responsibility not to refuse the call of the congregation should he be elected to a spiritual leadership role, then we have before us a higher stage of Christian congregational life than when the congregation is supplied with preachers appointed by the state from above or chooses one from a number of applicants who are strangers and who must first gain their confidence, a process not necessary when the character and walk of the individual is well known because the preacher is called out of the congregation.

It would be unjust to claim that the traditional usage had outlived its purpose. The men who were active in the Danzig Mennonite congregation as elders and preachers, these honored craftsmen, merchants, and business people, were energetic and capable — for example, Hans Momber.[9] Many were intellectually gifted and had some education, often self-acquired. They were shepherds of the church. This was especially true of the last elders of the old style, who together with the outstanding deacons Kauenhowen, Bachdach, Focking, Abraham de Veer, and Anton Schreder, had so faithfully led the congregation through the worst time of their history and had planned and carried out the building of the new church. They should be remembered in high honor.

---

[9]He had earned much respect in the matter of the union of the two congregations in 1808. He was a writer of many poems for special occasions, both public and in families (died 1815).

The Deacons

Here a word must be said about the deacons of the congregation. At first, the deacons, according to Acts 6:1-6, cared for the poor, but they were also responsible for seeing that church services were conducted properly and they helped at baptisms and Communion. Gradually their tasks grew. They became administrators of the common property. Other funds were added to the alms fund, and keeping the books became a large task, which was shared among the deacons. In 1801 a "main account book" was set up and all accounting was centralized. The name "deacon" receded behind the name "board member" (*Vorsteher*), although the church responsibilities remained the same. Since then the deacons have divided the various responsibilities among themselves, the most important being the bookkeeping and the administration of the buildings. These arrangements have remained to the present.

van der Smissen's Departure

Jacob van der Smissen soon had great influence in the congregation.[10] He introduced some needed changes, expanding the teaching of the youth and even, with the permission of the deacons, arranged for Dutch sermons in the afternoon. This had been requested of him by local Dutch business people and people of various confessions who were involved in shipping. In 1829 he and his wife made their first trip to his old home in

---

[10][Jacob van der Smissen came from an influential and wealthy Mennonite family with roots near Hamburg. His family had long-standing ties to the Pietist movement that placed a premium on individual salvation and a crisis conversion experience as well as a socially active Christianity, while at the same time down playing denominational loyalties. Jacob, for example, had married a poor Lutheran pastor's daughter, Wilhemine Wiehe, in 1805 at a time when marriages outside of Mennonite circles were strictly forbidden in Danzig. He had no specific theological schooling, but had been tutored as a child by the family's private tutor, Johann Wilhelm Mannhardt. His son Carl Justus (1811-1890) was the founding director in 1869 of the Wadsworth Institute, Wadsworth, Ohio, the first Mennonite institution of higher learning in the Americas. Matthias H. Rauert and Annelie Kümpers-Greve, *van der Smissen. Eine mennonitische Familie vor dem Hintergrund der Geschichte Altonas und Schleswig-Holstein* (Hamburg: Nord Magazin, 1992), 83-8, 98-103. Ed.]

Altona, where his father had just died; on his return the entire leadership and many members welcomed him in Dirschau/Tczew, so that he arrived at his home in the accompaniment of seven carriages.

But in the course of time, tension arose between him and a part of the congregation because in some matters he made his own decisions and ignored the deacons. At the beginning of 1835, he suddenly sent a message to the church leadership in which he made a number of demands and offered his resignation for July 1 should they not be granted. Although the leadership met as many of his demands as possible, he answered brusquely that they must all be met and were not open to negotiation. He later moderated his tone under the influence of some friends, and was more forthcoming when a number of members tried to keep him here, but a congregational meeting decided with a large majority to accept his resignation. Even his earlier supporters in part voted against him, since his vehemence suggested more strife to come. But he was asked to remain until the end of September.

That is what then happened. In September he administered baptism and Communion and on the 27th preached his farewell sermon. Only the preacher Jacob von Dühren and two deacons were present from the leadership, from whom he took his formal leave. He then left on September 30. Anton Schreder, who earlier had been his closest friend, remarked on his leaving: "During his nine and a half years he did much good in the church, especially by his excellent sermons and his instruction of the youth, but unfortunately, he also caused an unhappy disruption whose consequences will undoubtedly be felt for some time to come."

Jacob Mannhardt's Election and Installation
Already during the discussions with van der Smissen, some members urged a return to the old order. They proposed electing two new preachers from the congregation while electing the aged von Dühren as elder, but the great majority rejected this idea. The church council then contacted the preacher *Jacob Mannhardt* in Friedrichstadt, invited him to come for a visit and, following a brotherhood meeting, agreed to have him and his

Jacob Mannhardt, elder and pastor 1836-1885.
[Scanned from 1919 German edition. Ed.]

family come to Danzig in the spring of 1836. He was hired with a salary of 600 talers and free lodging. He was given 300 talers to cover moving expenses and asked to take on the office of elder and preacher in the congregation.

On Saturday, May 14, preacher Mannhardt arrived in Neufahrwasser after a difficult journey by sea with his wife and three small children. He stayed on board ship overnight and on the following day was greeted by many men and taken by carriage to the preacher's house, where all the deacons with their wives and other church council members greeted him. They then led him to the Hotel de Thorn, where the Mannhardt family stayed for a few days. On May 17 they could move into the preacher's house, which had in the meantime been well stocked with supplies.

On a beautiful Pentecost, May 22, 1836, Mannhardt preached his inaugural sermon on I John 1:1-4 following warm words of welcome and installation by Peter Regier, the elder of the Tiegenhagen congregation. He now shared the preaching duties with Jacob von Dühren, who had faithfully done all the preaching the last eight months. Now Mannhardt preached twice for every sermon of Dühren's, until the latter died at the age of 72 on April 13, 1839. The congregational chronicle says about his death: "Today the congregation suffered a severe blow in that a gentle death ended the life of our honored second preacher, Jacob von Dühren. He administered his office with love and faithfulness for 39 years. On the 19th of this month his body was returned to mother earth. Preacher Mannhardt made a profound speech at his grave. The few words on his tombstone describe who and what he was: 'He was an influence by teaching and example.'"

Participation in Society

Jacob Mannhardt's[11] installation as pastor here in 1836 marked the beginning of a time of peaceful inner development for the congregation, as well as growing influence in the community. It is true that the size of the congregation had diminished since 1800, and in 1836 counted only 467 baptized members, but there were among these a number of respected citizens. Since the limitations on citizenship had fallen away, it soon could be seen what interests and abilities for participation in society were hidden in these so-called "quiet in the land." Since 1815 they were elected in great numbers as representatives of city district councils and members of the poor commission, and since 1817 they were also always represented on the city council itself. And from 1851 to the present they have almost always had one or more seats in the city administration. There was a significant change, too, in their forms of employment. Earlier they had been forced by legal limitations to engage only in small retail enterprises such as taverns or shops dealing in yarn and lace. Over the decades these businesses disappeared until at the end of the nineteenth century no taverns at all were

---

[11]He was born on October 4, 1801 in Hanerau, Holstein, as the son of the estate owner J.W. Mannhardt and his wife Anna, nee van der Smissen, and through his mother was distantly related to his predecessor. He studied theology in Tübingen and Bonn and became a minister of the Mennonite church in Friedrichstadt on April 20, 1828, where he married Margarete Adriane Thomsen on June 13, 1830.

[Jacob Mannhardt's mother Anna was in fact a second cousin of Jacob van der Smissen. Heinz-Jürgen Mannhardt, ed., *Die Mennonitenfamilie van der Smissen und ihre Nachkommenschaft*, 2nd ed. (Darmstadt: Mannhardt, 1999), 62-4, 69-70. Ed.]

in Mennonite hands anymore. Instead, the younger entrepreneurs turned to wholesale trade in grain, wood, and groceries, or they established large-scale shops in the best parts of the city. We also find the Mennonites well represented in the administrations of charitable organizations since 1820. The Deaconess Home was founded with the active participation of several respected members of the Mennonite congregation. The same was true of the Protestant Johannesstift,[12] and in both institutions Mennonites have always been among the leadership. The same applies to the Reinickestift, the Infant and Toddler Protection Society, the Chamber of Commerce, the Society for Support of the Poor, as well as various charities sponsored by local businesses.

Church Leadership and Constitution
Naturally, the congregation was not short of men willing to provide leadership. When the preacher Jacob Mannhardt took over his position in Danzig in 1836 — a position he held for almost 50 years with quiet dignity, both mild and firm at once — he was joined by a leadership with which he was able to work together for many years in happy harmony. He himself was 35 years old, and he found two younger men in the

---

[12][The deaconess movement had its roots in a conservative revival movement in nineteenth-century Germany that led many Protestants to take direct personal action to address the problems of poverty, urbanization, and industrialization. Deaconesses committed themselves to lives of poverty, chastity, and service and were organized in homes that served both as residences for the sisters and service institutions for the poor, elderly, or sick. The establishment of these institutions took Dutch Mennonite deaconesses as one of several models. The first such home was founded in 1836 in Kaiserswerth along the Rhine River; the Danzig Deaconess Home was founded in 1862.

Johann Hinrich Wichern (1808-1881) was the most important leader of the movement among nineteenth-century German Protestants to take up social service and home mission work. As part of these efforts he founded the *Johannesstift* in Berlin in 1858 as a male counterpart to the deaconess movement. The *Johannesstift* placed special emphasis on training men to do the work of deacons and established various branches for this purpose around Germany. Martin Jung, *Der Protestantismus in Deutschland vom 1815 bis 1870* (Leipzig: Evangelische Verlagsanstalt, 2000), 124-5, 138-140. Ed.]

leadership, Heinrich Wilhelm Conwentz, 34, and Johann Jacob van Kampen, 33, who joined him in friendship. In his first year the old, honored deacon Anton Schreder died, and the aged Isaac Mahl resigned his post. To replace them, Carl Friedrich Jantzen, 44, and Friedrich Gustav Kliewer, 33, were elected by the congregation. And this leadership council remained in place until 1862, except that in 1860 van Kampen was elected to be a second preacher, causing a new deacon to be elected.

This closely united leadership, supported by insightful church council members, led the congregation through the next decades with intelligence and energy. H.W. Conwentz introduced new procedures to the administration of church funds. J. J. van Kampen organized the archive and collected books for the church library. He also conscientiously continued the congregational chronicle begun by Anton Schreder. Apart from that, after J. von Dühren died he also declared himself willing to preach when the regular pastor could not. In the years 1840 to 1860 he preached thirty times as a deacon before his election as preacher. The leadership in 1841 set about putting the traditional church order into a written constitution. In 1845 this document was used, albeit after long and difficult negotiations, to achieve *limited incorporation* through a special royal decree. After this, church capital funds could be used to cover mortgages in the name of the congregation, something that the register of deeds had previously accepted or rejected arbitrarily.

New Songbook

The "Spiritual Songbook" (*Geistreiches Gesangbuch* see page 118) which had been used since 1780, proved to be too ponderous and out of date. Thus, in 185'1 a committee of eight members, including a young theology student from the congregation, H.A. Neufeld,[13] put together the new hymnal, which was introduced on the first Sunday of Advent, 1854, with the title: "Songbook for edification in church and home for

---

[13][Heinrich August Neufeld (1826-1900). See Christian Neff, "Neufeld, Heinrich August," *Mennonite Encyclopedia* 3:849. Ed.]

Mennonite congregations, edited by the leadership of the Mennonite congregation in Danzig, 1854."[14]

Economic Situation

The 1840s and 1850s were eventful in other ways as well. The economic condition of the congregation was still fairly bad. Some individuals gained wealth, but the majority of the membership could only make ends meet. And so the income of the church funds was also limited, and they had to be thrifty with necessary construction expenses. A larger improvement of the church in 1837 had cost 1,400 talers, and it had been quite difficult to raise this amount through a special collection. Now the preacher's house at Heumarkt 5 needed 100 talers every year and more for maintenance and repair. So when the deacon Wilhelm Conwentz proposed to buy the house from the church for 5,000 talers, the leadership gladly accepted, with the condition that Conwentz would maintain the right half of the house as a preacher's residence as long as the current preacher was in office. For this the congregation paid 150 talers a year rent. Due to the reasons mentioned above, the usual congregational income, apart from the interest on some invested capital, only amounted to 1,621 talers in 1846. This came from church collections (118), members' contributions (660), military exemption self-tax (290), contributions for the preacher's salary (315), and pew rental (238). Of these the 290 talers military exemption tax had to be paid to the state, since this was part of the sum paid by the congregation for freedom from military service.

The wonderful custom of donating a special sum of 50 to 100 talers for the poor when a wealthy member died made it easier for the leadership to maintain care of the poor. This custom was faithfully maintained, and on certain special occasions like silver or golden weddings such gifts often were

---

[14][*Gesangbuch zur kirchlichen und häuslichen Erbauung für Mennoniten-Gemeinden* (Danzig: Church Council of the Danzig Mennonite Church, 1854). For analysis of the hymnology of this hymnal, see Walter Jost, "The Hymn Tune Tradition of the General Conference Mennonite Church" (PhD diss., University of Southern California, 1966), 93-6. Ed.]

given. Even today this good tradition has not died out, though it could be practiced more actively.

1848 and Armed Mennonites[15]

The year 1848 naturally brought a great deal of unrest. Politics, formerly foreign territory for the Mennonites, invaded their offices and shops and then also the families. The principle of nonresistance was in danger when local civil militias were to be organized. A large meeting of all the West Prussian Mennonite congregations in Heubuden agreed to permit participation in such militias, *but they were not to bear deadly weapons or wear military insignias.* Of course that actually meant forbidding participation. A fairly stormy brotherhood meeting in Danzig decided, 65 votes to 36, that whoever wanted to join the militia could do so, and would then naturally have to bear arms. J.J. van Kampen commented: "We are going to see something that has not occurred since the founding of the Mennonites, namely, armed and marching Mennonites. But it must be said in honor of our fellow believers, that only a few hotheads took part, for whom this game soon became tiresome." I must comment here that the deep pangs of conscience that the Mennonites in Prussia had experienced earlier during the Napoleonic time had bypassed the Danzig congregation insofar as the Free State of Danzig did not have to call up soldiers. Otherwise there would certainly have been some young men who marched off into the

---

[15][1848 saw numerous revolutions from southern Italy to France to Prussia and Austria in favor of constitutional and parliamentary limitations on monarchs' power. Since most kings, including Prussia's Frederick William IV, eventually used their armies to quash these rebellions, citizen militias were commonly formed both to check the power of the royal army and to provide for law and order on behalf of the middle-class supporters of the revolutions. The constitutional projects of the revolutionaries inevitably included a call for conscription in part because a mass citizen army was seen to be less susceptible to being turned against civilians than the existing royal armies sworn to loyalty to the king. Mennonites' responses to these events were indeed quite mixed; in the western city of Krefeld they joined the local militia in great numbers while rural Mennonites near Danzig petitioned the revolutionary German National Assembly meeting in Frankfurt to preserve the Mennonite exemption, Jantzen. "At Home in Germany?" 199-200, 226-240. Ed.]

War of Liberation, even at the risk of being excommunicated from their home congregation.[16]

Ernst von Wildenbruch as we know has dealt with such a case in his drama *Der Mennonit*.[17] This led to an exchange of letters between the leadership of the Mennonite church in Danzig and the author, which can be found in the November 1888 issue of the *Mennonite Journal (Mennonitische Blätter)*.[18] After

---

[16][As part of the anti-Napoleonic wars in the early 1800s, Prussia instituted the draft in 1813. This new law did not affect Mennonites in Danzig because the city was a Free State under French control from 1807 to 1813 (see chapter 10). The other Mennonites of the area negotiated an exemption to this new draft law and did indeed excommunicate the few members who joined the Prussian army. Mark Jantzen, "Vistula Delta Mennonites Encounter German Nationalism, 1813-1820," *Mennonite Quarterly Review* 73, no. 2 (April 2004), 185-212. Ed.]

[17][Ernst von Wildenbruch was a popular playwright of the late nineteenth century who specialized in nationalistic historical dramas. The play Mannhardt refers to here was first written in 1877 and staged in Berlin at the Royal Theater in 1888. It portrayed Mennonites in the Napoleonic era as gutless traitors to a glorious Prussian rebellion against French oppression. H. G. Mannhardt was heavily involved in efforts to ban the play outright — efforts that eventually brought the controversy to the attention of the Emperor Frederick III. The original title was *Der Menonit*, misspelled with only one "n." Mannhardt here has at least corrected the spelling even though his efforts to change the content of the play were largely unsuccessful. See Jantzen, "At Home in Germany?" 384-395. When Mannhardt first became aware of Wildenbruch's play in the early 1880s, he thought the drama was based on the case of Heinrich Jantzen, a Danzig church member who was indeed banned for volunteering for the Prussian army in 1813. "Der Bischof Eylert und die Mennoniten. Zur Abwehr falscher Urtheile," *Mennonitische Blätter* 31, no. 3 (March 1884): 17-20. Relatively soon, however, it became clear the drama was based on the case of David van Riesen of the Elbing-Ellerwald congregation. Ed.]

[18][The letter written by the leadership of the Danzig Mennonite Church to Wildenbruch and his reply are actually in "Noch einmal der 'Menonit:' Correspondenz zwischen dem Vorstand der Gemeinde zu Danzig und Ernst von Wildenbruch," *Mennonitische Blätter*, 35, no. 11 (June 1, 1888): 61-4. The Mennonites complain that Wildenbruch's portrayal of them was completely unhistorical while Wildenbruch responded that he meant to illuminate a general problem with a lack of patriotism on the part of some, not a specific problem with Mennonites. Additional correspondence, including reprinted commentary on the controversy, are available in *Mennonitische Blätter* 35, no. 12 (June 15,1888): 70; 35, no. 13 (July 1, 1888): 74-5; 35, no. 17 (Sept. 1, 1888): 97-8; 35, no. 19 (Oct. 1, 1888): 110-1; and 35, no. 20 (Oct. 17, 1888):

1848 the question of military exemption would not rest. The next twenty years were an unceasing struggle by the congregations to uphold their old religious principle.[19]

Related to that question was the matter of mixed marriages, which especially in 1852 and 1853 provoked a lively exchange of diverse views because a number of respected members of the congregation got married.[20]

In all these struggles Elder Jacob Mannhardt knew how to lead his congregation peacefully through those troubled times. He no doubt realized that nonresistance as well as the rejection of mixed marriages could not be maintained, since the church would decline in numbers as a result, but he did not want to adopt a one-sided position, or push forward harshly, injure the fearful, and confuse tender consciences. The change would have to take place gradually and the view of what was in the congregation's best interest would have to be clarified. This clarification was furthered by the *Mennonite Journal*, which appeared beginning in 1854, founded and edited by Mannhardt. This newspaper was soon eagerly read in all the German Mennonite congregations, fostering discussion about crucial questions from congregation to congregation.

The preacher's household had at this time found itself in informal spiritual and social contact with many families within and outside the congregation. This was due especially to the loving and hospitable manner of Mrs. Mannhardt and the

---

119-20. Ed.]

[19]These struggles are described in detail by Dr. W. Mannhardt in the book already mentioned, *Die Wehrfreiheit der Altpreußischen Mennoniten*. The further development of this matter from 1861 to 1868 can be found in my article "Zur Entstehung und Geschichte der Konigl. Kabinettsordre vom 3. Marz 1868," in *Christlicher Gemeindekalender*, vol. 28 (1919): 97-107.

[20][Both older Prussian laws and Mennonite tradition forbade Mennonites from marrying non-Mennonites, or in some cases the law required non-Mennonite husbands to serve in the army even if they wished to convert. In effect that meant neither those men nor their Mennonite wives could remain members in the congregation since refusal to serve in the military was a condition of membership. Relaxing this ban on mixed marriages was therefore reflective both of the state's less conservative approach to these questions after 1848 and the Danzig Mennonite congregation's decision that military service need not preclude one's good standing. Ed.]

intellectual liveliness of the growing children. When the preacher couple celebrated their silver wedding anniversary on June 13, 1855, the love of the congregational members was shown in many ways through friendly gifts of love.

Van Kampen's Election as Preacher
Through the election of the deacon van Kampen as second preacher, the congregation once again returned to the old form of the office of a non-salaried preacher. This election had the purpose of providing relief for the elder. In the years between 1849 and 1856 the theology students Heinrich Neufeld and Johannes van der Smissen[21] had been in Danzig and often preached here. Both were elected as preachers elsewhere in 1856. Thus, Mannhardt was dependent on van Kampen alone when he was out of town. Then in 1859 he was asked by the Elbing congregation[22] to help them because the preacher Carl Harder, who had served them from Königsberg, had left that city and gone to Neuwied.[23]

With the permission of the leadership, Mannhardt agreed to preach in Elbing every three weeks, and was then replaced by van Kampen. After the Elbing congregation had formally joined the Danzig church, it was expected that this connection would last. And so the Danzig congregation decided to elect van Kampen as a preacher, so that he could alternate with Mannhardt in Elbing. This happened on September 23, 1860. Shortly before, on July 23, he had celebrated the twenty-fifth anniversary of being a deacon together with H.W. Conwentz,

---

[21][Johannes (I) van der Smissen (1808-1879), a first cousin of Jacob Mannhardt. See Heinz-Jürgen Mannhardt, *Die Mennonitenfamilie van der Smissen*, 66. Ed.]

[22]This congregation had separated from the Elbing-Ellerwalder congregation, because a number of the city families desired better instruction for their youth.

[23][Harder's departure was the result of heavy pressure from both the rural Mennonite leadership, who suspected Harder of heretical liberal theology, and the provincial government, which suspected Harder of dangerously liberal politics. Thus for Jacob Mannhardt to accept this post was also to take a mediating position between conservative, mostly rural, and liberal Mennonite factions. Jantzen, "At Home in Germany?" 285-91. Ed.]

on which occasion these very deserving men were presented with a beautiful memorial plaque.

For seven years this excellent, well-rounded man served as a preacher beside his elder, and had a great influence on the congregation, and especially on the family circles close to him as relatives or friends. He was a stimulating presence in these circles, and always prepared to enliven family celebrations with serious or less serious speeches, sometimes in rhyme. It was a time of family get-togethers, "conversation evenings," and the like, in short, a warm, familial atmosphere, which was cultivated within the home in winter and in summer in the church garden, where the women gathered for coffee with their children, and where their husbands would meet them in the evenings. The families of van Kampen, von Dühren, Zimmermann, Kliewer, von Steen, and Loewens had various connections of this kind, and at a time when excursions to the sea shore at Zoppot/Sopot or other places were not yet common, the friendly church garden on many an afternoon was filled with happy people.

The Year of Decision 1867
The year 1867 was a year of decision for the congregation in more than one respect. First, Carl Friedrich Jantzen, who looked after the building, died. Together with his colleague Friedrich Gustav Kliewer, he had been able to celebrate his 25th anniversary as deacon on July 31, 1861, amid signs of respect from the thankful congregation, as had the two other deacons in previous years.

Van Kampen's Death and Funeral
Then preacher van Kampen died on November 8 at the age of 65 years, after several weeks of illness. Although already ill, he had ascended the pulpit on October 13, and also conscientiously had attended a large Mennonite gathering in Warnau/Kościeleczki near Marienburg on October 23, which was called to discuss the ominous decision of the North German Reichstag of October 18 to revoke Mennonites' exemption from military service.

On November 11 in the evening the coffin was brought to our church,[24] and on the 12th it was taken to the nearby Salvator cemetery and buried there. The large attendance testified to the great love and esteem that the faithful man had enjoyed in the congregation and far beyond that. The whole congregation had assembled, and among the many guests were several members of the city offices, the Protestant clergy and the leadership of charitable institutions. The distinguished technical high school director,[25] Dr. Löschin, also was present; the deceased had been one of his earliest pupils.

Van Kampen had been born in Altschottland in 1803, where his parents (Jakob van Kampen and Anna Löwens) and his grandparents (Heinrich van Kampen and Magdalene Siemens) lived. His great grandfather, married to Susanna von Dyck in 1719, lived outside the Hohes Tor and was born in Elbing between 1690 and 1696.

Johann Jakob van Kampen himself, married in 1832 to Katherina Zimmermann, had purchased a lot in the inner city on Kalkgasse 6, and carried on a retail business there. The needy population of the old city found in him a loving and untiring caregiver, and he was elected a city district chairman in 1843. For some years he was a city representative, and then he returned to his beloved work as a member and later chair of the poor commission. He became the head of a city home for children and orphans outside the Oliva Gate, and was energetically active in all his offices. His desire to help those in distress made him for a number of years the most active and zealous member in the leadership of the *Johannesstift*, a rescue mission for neglected boys. Out of his love for his native city and its history, he volunteered for the city archivists, Professor Dr. Hirsch and Professor Böszörmeny, sorting and identifying the valuable documents of a great past according to his knowledge and strength, for which already on September 29,

---

[24]Not until 1864 was it common practice for the funeral service to take place in the church.

[25][*Realschuldirektor*. This type of high school was not designed to prepare students for university, but rather for an apprenticeship, typically in a white-collar trade as a clerk or in similar occupations. Ed.]

1854, the city authorities thanked him with a certificate of gratitude. Since that time he devoted as much time as he could spare to this beloved work, to his last days. He made use of the experience acquired in the city archive to order and organize the archive of the Mennonite congregation.

In the chronicle of our congregation Dr. Wilhelm Mannhardt says of him: "Contented cheerfulness was the basic mood of his soul. Sunny humor added spice to his speech and his small literary creations. An unlimited humility and mildness were characteristics that marked him, and registered even with those who did not have the opportunity to test the pure gold of his pious, lovable, and steadfast nature. His wife, who was similar to him in character, had preceded him in death some years before."

He left two sons, the older of which carried on his father's business. The younger died as a classical high school (*Gymnasium*) professor in Gotha in 1891. Several of his children again live here in Danzig as members of the Mennonite congregation.

The death of this last congregational preacher of the old order left a painful gap. It was unthinkable to elect a successor out of the midst of the congregation, and so preacher Mannhardt, who was now 66 years of age, had to take over the preaching in Danzig and Elbing by himself. When he preached in Elbing one of the leaders of the city church would read a printed sermon. In the course of 1868 the connection with the Elbing congregation was dropped out of necessity. In 1869 that church become independent and elected Carl Harder as minister, who had been in Neuwied for ten years. This congregation existed parallel to the older Mennonite congregation of Elbing-Ellerwald. Harder dedicated his excellent energies to this church from that time on.[26]

On April 18, 1869, he was installed into his office in Elbing by preacher Mannhardt. At the same time the leadership of the Danzig church gave the son of their minister, Dr. phil. Wilhelm Mannhardt, who was living in his father's house as a private

[26]Cf. Carl Harder, *Kurzgefasste Geschichte der Elbinger Mennonitengemeinde*, (Elbing, 1884).

scholar and city librarian, the task of substituting for his father by reading sermons, and also to look after the archive and church library, as well as writing the congregation's chronicle from 1862 on. Up to that time van Kampen had done that. Dr. Mannhardt not only took on this task as a chronicler, but wrote rather as a participant and observer in the spirit of the new times. The period from 1862 to 1874 with its struggle over exemption from military service is described in such a lively fashion and in such detail in volume three of the congregational chronicles that a general history of our Prussian Mennonite congregations cannot afford to overlook this source.

The End of Military Exemption

As in all Mennonite congregations, the threat of losing our freedom from military service provoked difficult internal conflicts that cannot be described here in detail. Against the whole of Mennonite tradition, politics also entered the congregational meetings and threatened to sow discord. But the wise guidance of the leadership was able to avoid the danger of a split.

On *November 9, 1867,* a new conscription law was signed and declared that all male inhabitants in the territory of the North German Confederation were subject to military service and all charters of privileges suspended. In order to make military service easier for the Mennonites to accept, the King of Prussia as Commander-in-Chief on March 3, 1868, issued a Cabinet Order, according to which they could enlist as drivers, medics, clerks, or as craftsmen[27] in the army.[28]

---

[27][The army proposed accepting only trained tailors, cobblers, and saddlers for this type of exemption. We do not know how this actually worked out in practice. GStA, HA I, Rep. 77 (Innenministerium), Tit. 332t (Militärpflicht), no. 5 (Militarpflichtigkeit der Mennoniten), vol. 1, (1819-1868), n. p., 16 Dec., 1867, Minister of War Roon. Ed.]

[28][Following Prussia's victory over Austria in 1866, Prussia annexed some north German states and convinced others to join in creating a North German Confederation that was dominated by Prussia. This Confederation received a constitution, a new government, and new military laws in 1867. The German Empire, which was created in 1871 after Prussia defeated France in yet another war, replaced this Confederation but kept the basic

Whoever could not accept even this form of service had to emigrate. And in fact from our congregation a number of families went to America, among them the much honored and respected deacon, Ludwig Eduard Zimmermann (1860-69).[29] The beginning of the next chapter will report on the final decision of the Danzig congregation regarding its reaction to the military question.

Anniversary of the Church's Construction in 1869 and the Four Deacons

The year 1869 also brought the memorial service for the church building of 50 years earlier, celebrated on Sunday, September 12. A good number met in the beautifully decorated church. A mixed choir accompanied by the organ sang some songs in four-part harmony. The sermon had the text Psalm 26:8, "O Lord, I love the house in which you dwell, and the place where your glory abides." After the service the deacons and the representatives, as well as the small choir, met in the preacher's house at Heumarkt 5 for a breakfast of warm fellowship.

The leadership that successfully led the congregation through this difficult time in 1869 consisted, apart from the elder and preacher Jacob Mannhardt, of the four deacons, Commercial Councilor (*Kommerzienrat*)[30] *Heinrich Wilhelm Conwentz* (born 1802) starting in 1835, who looked after the finances with steady intelligence and faithfulness, *Carl Heinrich Zimmermann*

---

constitutional and military frameworks from 1867. For additional background on the crisis in the Mennonite community provoked by the imposition of the draft see John D. Thiesen, "First Duty of the Citizen: Mennonite Identity and Military Exemption in Prussia, 1848-1877," *Mennonite Quarterly Review* 72 (April 1998): 161-187; Jantzen, "At Home in Germany?" 317-83 and Peter Brock, *Freedom from Violence: Sectarian Nonresistance from the Middle Ages to the Great War* (Toronto: University of Toronto Press, 1991), 131-8. Ed.]

[29][The Mennonite Church USA Archives–North Newton (Mennonite Library and Archives, Bethel College) has an extensive collection of Ludwig Zimmermann's diaries, running from 1852 to 1892 in 19 volumes, a uniquely valuable source for Vistula Mennonite history in the nineteenth century. Ed.]

[30][An honorary title given by the government to businessmen for notable achievements or business success. Ed.]

(born 1818), who had been elected to the place of the much-honored deacon Kliewer, *Johann Carl von Steen*, building administrator and Kliewer's brother-in-law (born 1799), elected as successor to Carl Friedrich Jantzen in 1867, and *August Momber* (born 1807), who had just been elected to replace Ludwig Eduard Zimmermann who resigned. All of these were businessmen living in Danzig.

Heinrich Wilhelm Conwentz. [Scanned from 1919 German edition. Ed.]

Carl Heinrich Zimmermann. [Scanned from 1919 German edition. Ed.]

Johann Carl von Steen. [Scanned from 1919 German edition. Ed.]

August Momber. [Scanned from 1919 German edition. Ed.]

Church and alms house in 1869

Church and parsonage ca. 1890. Board members Ferdinand Stobbe (died 1892) and Eduard Loewens (died 1899). [Scanned from 1919 German edition. Ed.]

12
From 1870 to 1900

1870 and the First Mennonite Soldiers

The great year of 1870, which brought our German fatherland its long desired unification, was for the Danzig Mennonite congregation the year of complete integration into the new times and into the new laws of the great German nation.[1]

For the last three years an interim status had existed concerning military service. The group of those who were unmoved and firm adherents of the old position of absolute nonresistance was small, but there were in it men of high respect and moral honor. One must recognize that they were willing to suffer for the sake of their faith. They did not decide lightly to emigrate. Another group felt, together with the majority of the Mennonite rural congregations, that one should

---

[1][In 1870 Prussia led the North German Confederation and the remaining sovereign south German states into war against France. At the successful conclusion of this war, the German Empire was declared with King William I of Prussia serving also now as the German Emperor. Mannhardt's claim that Mennonites had now joined the German nation (*Volksgemeinschaft*) underlined his own personal desire to unite his Mennonite and German national commitments. Ed.]

"give to the emperor (*Kaiser*) what is the emperor's and to God
what is God's." They therefore argued that the [non-combatant
status afforded by the] Royal Cabinet Order of March 3, 1868,
should be the new required Mennonite practice. Finally, a third
party, which grew steadily,[2] was decidedly in favor of the new
conditions and wanted every individual to decide for himself in
which form he would conform to the military obligation. The
congregational meetings in 1868 and 1869 that discussed these
matters were wise enough not to decide the issues with an
arbitrary majority vote, and tabled the decision time after time.
In this way division was avoided during the transition period,
when the waves of feeling were highest.

The young men who were inducted into the military after
1868 at first all presumably served under that Cabinet order. We
can hardly imagine today the shock of seeing young Mennonites
appearing in church in Prussian military uniforms.

The Final Decisions

Thus when in 1870 the German people were united in a
patriotic enthusiasm that engulfed old and young, the first
defenders of the Fatherland marched off to France from our
congregation as well.

On October 2, a month after the Battle of Sedan,[3] the
decisive meeting was held in our church, in which almost the
entire brotherhood unanimously passed the following
resolution:[4]

---

[2]Dr. W. Mannhardt reports on these three parties in very just, enlightened
commentary in "Der Reichstagbeschluß vom 9. Nov. 1867," *Mennonitische
Blätter Beilage* 15, no. 7 (August 1868): 58-60.
[3][The Battle of Sedan, fought on Sept. 1, 1870, was the decisive battle of
the war. At its conclusion the French Emperor Napoleon III and his army
were Prussian captives. The day became an important holiday in the German
Empire. Ed.]
[4]Deacon Carl Heinrich Zimmermann and church council member
Heinrich von Dühren presented these proposals. They were the two most
influential members of the church leadership and were also the leaders of the
progressive majority.

1. Although we, together with our fathers, recognize every war as a great evil resulting from sin and consider it to be our calling to present the love and the peace of the gospel of Jesus Christ through our Constitution and through every aspect of the life of our congregation, it does appear very difficult, on the other hand, to prove from scripture the absolute inadmissibility of the obligation to military service required of every citizen of the state.

Accordingly, we will cease from setting up a binding and compulsory congregational requirement and in changing our traditional confession *on this point*, we will unite in saying that it is up to each brother to decide in which manner and to what degree he considers himself permitted in his conscience before God to follow the demands of the authorities. At the same time we declare that we consider it to be most in keeping with the nature of our fellowship if our members only participate as drivers, medics, clerks, or craftsmen.

With the revocation of the military exemption the rationale for prohibiting mixed marriages and refusing to accept persons from other denominations into membership also disappeared and so the other motions were as follows:

2. Although we hold that for a truly Christian marriage — a tender and intimate relationship — it is highly important that both partners be united *in one faith and confession* and belong to *one* congregation, we cannot find in the Word of God any reason to forbid a marriage covenant entered into by members of two different Christian denominations. For this reason we will, following the removal of state prohibitions, not deny membership to members of our congregation who marry members of another Christian community.

3. Since with the loss of military exemption the difficulties are removed concerning the acceptance of members from other denominations, we will no longer forbid those who wish to join our church in future from doing so.

4. In all other matters we hold fast to the doctrine and order of our fellowship, as it has been valid in the past, and as we have expressed it in our congregational constitution.

Finally, in connection with these decisions the Communion celebration was also opened up and the following decided about it: "Members of other Christian churches who have married members of our church shall not be denied participation in our celebration of Communion on their request. In special cases other members of other churches shall be allowed this participation by the elder."

The New Position of the Congregation
With these resolutions our congregation entered a new position in the circle of its fellow citizens. From being a separated fragment of the nation, a strictly separated sect, we became an independent religious society, founded on the gospel and closely related to the Protestant church, yet having the advantage of being independent of the state.

Equal duties meant equal rights. Thus the Mennonites strove to put their legal rights on a new foundation. They applied to the government to cancel the so-called Mennonite Edict of 1789 and for the passage of a new law in which the earlier limitations would fall away and the payments Mennonites had been forced to make to other churches would be eliminated.

After 1868 the so-called exemption payment (also called Cadet money), which amounted to 5,000 talers for the other West Prussian Mennonite congregations and 300 talers for the Danzig congregation, was not collected. A proposal by the Danzig congregation to continue collecting it in order to set up a common fund did not meet with the approval of the rural congregations. But from 1873 onward there were again fairly regular annual meetings of the leadership of all the West

Prussian congregations. Here issues of general concern were discussed and brotherly fellowship was cultivated. The differences that had arisen between our congregation and those in the rural area between 1868 and 1870 gradually slipped into the background, and the alienation was overcome by the brotherly exchange of ideas. In the course of time, the practice was adopted that in the week after Pentecost a meeting would be held in all the congregations in rotation with the local elder presiding. In addition a common general fund and a fund for home missions were established. The Heubuden-Marienburg congregation currently administers the former fund, the Danzig congregation the latter.

The Mennonite Law of June 12, 1874
The promised new law finally appeared with the title: *Law of June 12, 1874, Concerning the Situation of the Mennonites.*[5] The law reads as follows:

§1 Mennonite congregations can be legally incorporated by the joint proclamation of the Ministries of Justice, the Interior, and Religious Affairs.
§2 The *rights of incorporation* may only be granted and may not be denied if
1. geographic congregational boundaries are clearly drawn,
2. the members' number and wealth indicate that the congregation can ensure that the necessary means required to provide church services according to their customs will be available for the long term,
3. their by-laws do not contain any provisions that are contrary to the general laws of the land.
§3 The regulations that require Mennonites to pay personal taxes or fees to Protestant or Catholic parishes, especially the Edict Concerning the

---

[5] *Preussische Gesetzsammlung* (Berlin, 1874), 238.

Future Establishment of the Mennonites in all Royal Provinces Excluding the Duchy of Silesia of July 30, 1789, are repealed.

Taxes and fees of a non-personal nature due to Protestant or Catholic parishes are not affected by this law, especially such taxes and fees which are based on legal agreements tied to individual pieces of property or to all the property in a district or to all the property of a certain type in a district.

On the basis of this law almost all the Mennonite congregations acquired the right to incorporate as a legal body in the course of the next twenty years, including our own in 1887. This law brought one additional advantage for our members, namely that from then on cemetery fees only had to be paid to the parish whose cemetery was actually used. Before this, on the basis of the Edict of 1789, they were counted as members of the Protestant parish in which they lived and had to pay all the burial fees to that church without necessarily receiving any services.

Another law passed by the Imperial parliament in 1874 required all marriages to be conducted before a civil marriage official, which caused much unrest and opposition in church circles. Mennonite congregations were not upset, since their views on the separation of church and state were in keeping with this law.[6]

---

[6][This law was part of a broader social conflict in German society in the 1870s given the title of *Kulturkampf*, literally the struggle for culture. In the newly unified German Empire, the population on the western, southern, and eastern borders were predominately Catholic. The Protestant liberal politicians who dominated the Prussian parliament were suspicious of Catholics in general and especially of the political influence of the Catholic church hierarchy. Bismarck, who served as both the Prussian and the Imperial Chancellor and was the chief political architect of German unity, proposed anti-Catholic laws beginning in 1873 as a way of reconciling Protestant liberals to some of his other illiberal policies. The law Mannhardt refers to here, the *Zivilstandgesetz*, was intended among other things to make it easier for Catholics to get married without necessarily having to obey the teachings of the Catholic church and thereby wean lay Catholics from clerical influence. In the face of this discrimination, however, most German

Gustav de Veer, assistant pastor, 1870-1876

Since preacher Mannhardt, who turned 70 on October 4, 1871, had served alone after the death of van Kampen [in 1867], a search for an assistant was initiated. It just so happened that the earlier preacher of the Mennonite congregation in Neuwied on the Rhine, Gustav de Veer, who had been born in Danzig, had had to give up his position in 1855 due to a lung disease. He had moved to Madeira for several years and for some time had been living in his native city as a private tutor. In 1870 he agreed to preach from time to time, and in 1871 he was appointed assistant preacher, with the duty of preaching every fourth week. He had been born in 1815 as a son of the Deacon Abraham de Veer and was thus a grandson of Elder Jacob de Veer. This arrangement lasted until the sudden death of de Veer, who succumbed to his lung illness.

Various attempts to find another assistant preacher met with no success. And so Mannhardt remained the sole preacher of the congregation. That would not have been so bad, since in such a small congregation the work could naturally be done by one man assuming he were healthy and active. But here was an old man who had passed his mid-seventies and, in spite of good physical health, was no longer mentally alert enough to satisfy the needs of a demanding congregation. He stayed at his post faithfully, and shared his concern with the leadership about finding a successor if he became ill or died.

His fiftieth anniversary of service was on April 20, 1878. All the signs of love and respect[7] given to this faithful shepherd of the congregation, which cannot be recounted here in detail, could not banish the concern that moved the hearts of the congregation when thinking of the future. At that time it was rare for young men to decide to study theology. Theology departments at the state universities had few students. And our congregation in the last thirty years had not produced a single pastor. Mennonite theology students from elsewhere had

---

Catholics actually rallied to their church. Ed.]

[7]Cf. the detailed description of the celebration from April 20 - 22, 1878, in C.H. Zimmermann, *Gedenkbuch der Danziger Mennoniten Gemeinde*, Vol. 3, 325-33.

appeared from time to time as visiting preachers, but had then been appointed in other congregations.

The Theology Student Hermann Gottlieb Mannhardt

Then it happened that in the same year, in the fall of 1878, a nephew of Mannhardt who had completed a degree in Protestant theology returned to Danzig. He was no stranger in the parsonage or in the congregation, since he had lived in that house for four years, from 1871-75, while attending the local classical high school (*Gymnasium*). He was simply considered a member of this lively and affectionate pastor's family. He was especially influenced by the intellect and piety of his cousin, Dr. Wilhelm Mannhardt, with whom he had shared a study for many years. They had carried on correspondence during his university years in Strasbourg, Berlin, and Kiel, and Wilhelm, who was 24 years older, gave the younger student much worthwhile advice, especially in the areas of German language studies, history, and philosophy, subjects he studied in addition to theology. It was Dr. Wilhelm Mannhardt, too, who during a visit in Berlin in the spring of 1878 urged his cousin to return to Danzig after completing his examinations, in order to renew old relationships and to find a firmer connection with the Mennonite congregation. This advice met my interests — for it is the writer of these lines who is referred to here. I felt that I could never be a "man of the [state Protestant] church," and already at the university when studying the history of the Reformation I had become a strong opponent of the idea of an established church.

Like some other theologians, I did not feel a call to serve in the state Protestant church and therefore I decided to switch to teaching the subject of Protestant religion in school.[8] At the conclusion of my theological studies, I did take the first round of exams at the University in Kiel, but then did not sit for the

---

[8][Both Catholic and Protestant theology were taught as regular subjects in the public schools. These teachers had to be certified by the state, thus Mannhardt took those certification exams as described below. Being a teacher instead of a Protestant pastor would have also meant accepting a lower salary. Ed.]

second and final round of theological exams. Instead I took the teacher certification exams at the University in Königsberg on June 19, 1880, in German and history. There in April 1879 I also passed the exams in German culture, required at that time for Protestant pastors.[9]

In the meantime I had returned to Danzig in October 1878, and, due to a shortage of teachers, I quickly found opportunity to teach my subjects at a number of higher schools for girls. At the same time, due to the great dearth of Protestant pastors, I had opportunity to preach several times in a number of Danzig Protestant churches such as St. Mary's, St. John's, St. Peter's, and Corpus Christi. Very gladly I accepted the invitation of my uncle to fill in for him as preacher on occasion. Here I preached for the first time on November 3, 1878, and I felt all the more at home, since I had spent many a Sunday and holiday among the congregational members, and now saw almost only familiar faces before me.

In the old parsonage I found the same spirit of love as before, although the quiet and faithful housewife had died in 1873. I did not live there, but had rented a room on Heilige Geistgasse and came to the parsonage for the noon meal every day. I was also invited into the homes of many members — I will name only some: Conwentz, Claassen, Loewens, von Niessen, Stobbe, Zimmermann, Momber, Dr. Wiebe — and found the same hearty hospitality everywhere.

In the summer of 1879 I formally joined the Mennonite congregation and thereby made myself ineligible to preach in the state Protestant church. Soon thereafter, in response to a friendly request by the church leadership, I declared myself willing to stand for election as a preacher. I was in fact elected at a brotherhood meeting on October 19, and dedicated to the

---

[9][The first theological exams were taken upon completion of the course of study. A second set of exams followed after several years of serving in what amounted to an extensive independent internship along with some additional education. Both sets of exams had to be passed before one could be ordained and installed as a pastor. The culture exams were required of Catholic priests as well and as a feature of the anti-Catholic *Kulturkampf* were aimed primarily at keeping foreign priests out of Germany. Ed.]

work of this office by my uncle, the respected elder and pastor, Jacob Mannhardt.

I trust that I will be excused for these personal recollections, but the nearer the history of our congregation approaches the present, the greater the temptation to focus on personal matters. In order to avoid the danger of writing a family history or an autobiography instead of a congregational history or getting too detailed, I will limit myself to reporting on events in the manner of a chronicle, and referring to sources where more detailed information may be found.

The Deacons J. C. von Steen and H. W. Conwentz

In 1876 the much-respected deacon and building trustee Johann Carl von Steen had died, and in his place the congregation elected Ludwig Ferdinand Stobbe, a man of private means. He took over the tasks of his predecessor very knowledgeably and conscientiously, and in addition started a new family registration book and looked after the rest of the church record books, a labor of some years, which can only be appreciated by someone who has examined their fine quality and great accuracy for himself.

The oldest deacon, Commercial Counselor (*Kommerzienrat*) H.W. Conwentz, retired in 1878 due to his advanced age. He had managed the investments of the congregation with wisdom and faithfulness (see Luke 12:42) for forty-three years. *Carl Heinrich Zimmermann* now brought the same spirit to this task. The businessman Eduard Loewens was elected as the fourth deacon.

The grateful congregation named Conwentz a Deacon Emeritus. He had a very dignified appearance. On his good days he rode his beautiful, grey Arabian stallion Alamansor, and otherwise, too, he cut a figure of a fine, simple Danzig businessman of the mid-nineteenth century. He was also a man of unlimited charity, spending much of his wealth quietly for the needy. On the day of his golden wedding, August 12, 1878, he made a series of gifts, together with his wife, among them 6,000 marks for the Mennonite church. His will increased this fund, which is administered by the church in his name, to 20,000 marks after his death, and to 30,000 after the death of his wife.

Donations and Baptismal Vessels

Since we are talking of estate gifts here, we should mention that a similar donation for the poor of the congregation, although smaller, had been made by the church council member Arend von Niessen already in 1865, when he left the sum of 1,200 talers on the condition that the interest should be donated annually on August 6, the date of death of his wife, to twelve particularly poor persons of the congregation. In the same year, 1865, the widow Magdalena Geertzen, nee Foth, who had been ill for years and then at the age of 80 had become well again, in thankfulness gave the congregation new silver *baptismal vessels*. The leadership asked the well-known sculptor Rudolf Freitag to create a wax model of a baptismal pitcher and basin. The goldsmith Carl Heinrich Momber then made the vessels.

Since Freitag had spent a long time in Italy, including eight years with Zahn in Pompeii, and four years in Rome with Thorvaldsen, he was inclined to choose a classical model.[10] He succeeded in uniting the Pompeian form of the vessels with their sacral use in the church — the wide rim of the baptismal bowl is surrounded by a wreath of stylized arabesques, while the inner side has the text in raised lettering — "The one who believes and is baptized will be saved" (Mark 16:16). The bottom of the basin depicts in relief the baptism of Jesus. Above, a dove hovers in the rays of the sun. John the Baptist holds a banner with the words *Agnus Dei* [The Lamb of God].

Finally, it should be mentioned that preacher Jacob Mannhardt, at the celebration of the three-hundred-year anniversary of Menno Simons' death, established a *Menno Fund* for the purpose of helping needy congregations of our confession. Also, some years before, a stipend fund had been established to help young people both male and female in their studies.

---

[10][Bertel Thorvaldsen (1770-1844), a Dane, in the first half of the nineteenth century was central Europe's most prominent sculptor. He lived and worked in Rome from 1797-1838. H. W. Janson, *19th-Century Sculpture* (New York: Harry N. Abrams, Inc., 1985), 57, 71-5. Ed.]

The Deaths of August Momber and Heinrich von Dühren

In 1880 the congregation again lost one of their experienced deacons, the businessman August Momber, the founder of the firm of that name, who became blind and had to give up his position. He, too, was a man of charity and dedicated participation in many good causes. His successor as deacon was his son, Julius Momber, who together with his younger brother had taken over his father's firm many years earlier.

In the same year the church council member *Heinrich von Dühren*, who has been mentioned earlier, died. He was the head of a large family and one of the most influential men of the congregation. He always favored every reasonable progress while strictly protecting traditional Mennonite simplicity.

Co-Elder Hermann Gottlieb Mannhardt and the Death of Wilhelm Mannhardt

In the same year the congregation decided to install the assistant preacher, Hermann Gottlieb Mannhardt, in full service. He was ordained as an elder on September 12, in the presence of many leaders from the West Prussian congregations and immediately took over the instruction of the youth and baptism.

The family of the old pastor Mannhardt suffered a painful blow in the death of their oldest son, the often-mentioned Dr. Wilhelm Mannhardt. He died of heart disease on December 25, 1880, surrounded by his family in the apartment of the young preacher couple, at almost 50 years of age. For the congregation and a larger circle of scholarly friends the death of this man so gifted in mind and heart was a very painful event.

On December 30 his body was buried beside that of his beloved mother in the St. Salvator cemetery, in the presence of many people drawn from all circles of Danzig's officials and citizenry.[11]

---

[11]Cf. *Gedichte* by Wilhelm Mannhardt, including a short biography of the poet, (Danzig, 1881) and H.G. Mannhardt, *Predigten und Reden*, 2nd ed. (Danzig, 1913), 289.

A New Cemetery and Legal Questions

The 1880s were replete with important and meaningful events for the congregation.

First of all, the old Salvator cemetery, which had been used for centuries, was supposed to be closed in the foreseeable future, and the congregation would have to look for a new cemetery. Discussions that lasted through 1881 and 1882 led to the decision on August 27, 1882, to join with the Reformed St. Peter and Paul church in the use of the so-called "United Cemeteries" in the Halb Allee. The negotiations had been led mainly by the Deacon C.F. Stobbe, and after being approved by the congregation, resulted in the well-known contract of March 16, 1883. After this, the bodies of Mennonite church members were accepted there under the same conditions as for Reformed members, and for as long as that cemetery would exist.

In 1882 the congregation was shaken by a strange edict of the Provincial Governor, which forbade registry offices to accept certificates from Mennonite church records, and claimed that all marriages performed before 1874 by Mennonite preachers were invalid. A young civil servant who obviously did not know the terms of the General State Law Code had made this discovery.[12] Concerning this whole matter and its conclusion, which was favorable for us, I refer the reader to my *Yearbook of the Mennonite Congregations in West and East Prussia*, Danzig, 1883, 54-73, as well as to the *Congregational Chronicle*, vol. 3, 391ff.

---

[12][The law code referred to here, the *Allgemeines Landrecht*, had been promulgated in 1794 and provided the first legal tolerance of Mennonites in the general laws of Prussia as opposed to the more easily modified charters of privileges. In most cases, however, it did not override existing provincial law. The specific case here dealt with the issue of providing the birth certificates that were necessary for acquiring marriage licenses under the 1874 civil marriage act. Initially the local government refused to accept birth certificates issued by the Mennonite elders on the basis of Mennonite church books while Mennonites argued such documents had always been accepted as legal documents. Eventually the government agreed to accept these documents but only as private and not as legal documents. Ed.]

The Construction of a Parsonage

An important new building was first proposed in 1882 and then constructed in the following two years, a *residence for the preacher*. The house at Heumarkt 5, which the widow Fluge had given to the church in 1826 as a residence for ministers, had been sold to J.W. Conwentz in 1844 during the difficult times. He rebuilt it according to his own taste, and lived in the south part, while the north half remained a preacher's residence as long as Jacob Mannhardt was in office. It seemed very desirable for the future to arrange a house near the church for the preacher, especially since the leadership had always had the plan since 1844 of building or buying a house with the money obtained by the sale of the house in the Heumarkt.

This plan now took shape. The hope was to end the situation where the preacher would have to move from one rented house to another, and after detailed discussions, and when a suitable lot adjacent to the church could not be purchased, the leadership presented the proposal to the membership to build a parsonage next to the church in the roomy garden. After a detailed explanation of the reasons by C.H. Zimmermann, and a description of the planned building, a great majority accepted the motion on July 1, 1883.

That same summer the building arose under the guidance of the architect Hermann Wiens and the construction supervisor Krüger. On September 8 the topping-out ceremony was celebrated.[13] In the following weeks the building was completed in the rough and roofed, and then stayed that way to dry out during the winter. At the end of March, work resumed and on September 1 the attractive building was finished.

On Sunday, August 24, there was a small dedication after the church service. Benches had been set up in the yard across from the door of the new house for the many participants, and the contractor Wiens presented the oldest deacon, Zimmermann, with a set of decorated keys, along with a short speech in which he described the story of the construction. He then unlocked

---

[13][*Richtfest*, a ceremony typically held for construction projects where an evergreen tree is attached to the rafters before the roof is finished. Ed.]

the door for the first inhabitant and gave him the keys with the words:

> May the blessing of God always rest on this building, which has been built with love. May not only the first inhabitant whom we accompany to this doorway, but all who will follow him as spiritual leader of our dear congregation, have the importance of this office in mind and carry it out accordingly. May our new preacher's house be and remain what our old one was and is: a place of inner peace and of noble Christian morals and piety. May it be for all who come here with spiritual needs, the poor and the wealthy, a pleasant refuge in the trials and pains of this life and may it offer to them in sorrow and suffering a word of comfort and exaltation. May God grant that this will be the enduring spirit of this new house!

Hereupon Hermann Gottlieb Mannhardt spoke the following words:

> The house that was built before us all in the last fourteen months, and which generated such interest, is now complete. Friendly and attractive inside and out, it testifies to the skill, the diligence, and the care of its builders.
>
> Our Deacon Zimmermann has just expressed the memories and hopes that the congregation attaches to this building. It is my obligation to give words to the thanks I feel at receiving the key at this threshold.
>
> I say a heartfelt thanks to the congregation, to whom this house belongs, for providing it for my use. A hearty thanks to the leadership, who began the building and had it completed so that it meets all requirements of health and comfort. A special thanks to the building committee, whose leader, Mister Stobbe, is prevented from attending due to

illness. We are all the sadder, since he was particularly dedicated to this work. May he and all those who dedicated time and effort to the leadership of this building project be rewarded for their efforts, and may they long enjoy the fruit of their labors!

I have nothing to add to the warm words of our first deacon about the purpose of this house, namely, that it is to be a minister's house in this congregation, and what the congregation expects from its inhabitants. Those words speak to the longing of my soul as well. But for these expectations to be fulfilled, that this house will be a place where every member of the congregation may always hear a friendly word in joy and sorrow, and where necessary, help through advice or deed, this requires not only good will from the one side, but also sincere trust from the other, and this I ask of the dear congregational members for the more distant future. May no one be reluctant to approach this house if they have a concern for themselves or their family for which one could use the advice of a sympathetic friend. Only then can the preacher's house be a *part of the congregation* and truly belong to all its members.

As for the rest, this house, as a human habitation, will not be a stranger to human events. Here, too, as in other houses, work and rest will alternate, in this house too there will be sorrow and hope and prayer. These walls will hear the voices of joy and of complaint. Here too joy and sorrow will enter according to God's will. In this house in the course of time human eyes will open for the first time and also close for the last sleep. The house indeed will last many years, God willing, but its inhabitants will change. How often and how soon that will occur, how long or how short our time here is measured, that rests in God's hand.

Beside our church, which is such a telling witness of the unity and sacrifice of our fathers in hard and threatening times, now stands this preacher's residence, together with the church and alms house a common possession of the Danzig Mennonite congregation. As common property unites people, so may this also bind our fellowship together for now and for coming generations! May God grant this wish!

The old pastor Jacob Mannhardt then spoke a heartfelt prayer, after which the door of the new house opened and those present toured the friendly rooms from the cellar to the attic. On Monday and Tuesday, September 8 and 9, the move was made by the young preacher couple from their previous home, Sandgrube 23, and soon the rooms of the new house were comfortably furnished.

Dr. Samuel Cramer from Holland

The relationship of our congregation *with the Dutch Mennonites*, which had been interrupted for many years, was picked up again in 1883, and at the same time the foundation was laid for a firmer connection to the scattered German Mennonite congregations.

Dr. *Samuel Cramer*, at that time pastor of the Mennonite congregation in Enschede, later in Zwolle and finally professor of theology at the University of Amsterdam,[14] was a man enthusiastic about the closer union of all Mennonites. Already in 1883 he visited the congregations of the Palatinate and had met our Deacon Zimmermann at the German Protestant Church Assembly in Neustadt a.d.H. Zimmermann had invited him to visit the Danzig congregation.

Cramer had a strong desire to get to know the scattered German co-religionists, of whom he had previously only known the East Frisian ones who were closely connected with Holland. Should it not be possible, he asked himself, to gather these

---

[14]The theological faculty there always consists of two Lutheran, two Reformed, and two Mennonite professors.

scattered branches, to preserve existing life and to give new life to what seemed to have died? Should not also a new connection between the Dutch and German Mennonites be possible?

In the summer of 1884 he visited us in Danzig, and from here he traveled to the Vistula delta and into Poland. He arrived in Danzig on July 24 and lived with the young preacher (the old pastor Mannhardt was traveling) and had discussions with the church leadership, with the aim of arranging a meeting of representatives from all the German Mennonite congregations as soon as possible. From here he traveled to Hamburg and Krefeld and back to Holland.

Following the suggestion of pastor Cramer, the leadership of the Mennonite congregations in Krefeld, Danzig, and Hamburg-Altona invited representatives of the German Mennonite congregations to a first meeting in Berlin, which took place there on October 2. This was the beginning of the Alliance of Mennonite Congregations in the German Empire (*Vereinigung der Mennonitengemeinden im Deutschen Reich*), which was founded in 1886. I have given a detailed description of the history of this founding in my *Yearbook of the Old Evangelical Baptism-Minded or Mennonite Congregations* (Danzig, 1888). Our congregation had a substantial part in the preparation and realization of the "Alliance" and has always been represented in its administration.

The founding principle of this Alliance is to insure the independent nature of every single congregation by emphasizing what is held in common and combining the congregations that have joined in the co-operative work in the preservation and animation of German Mennonitism.

Today the Alliance, after more than thirty years of existence, is in a position, due to its growth in funding, its preacher fund, and its fund for preachers' widows, to apply considerable means to its projects, which in the constitution are designated as follows:

A. The preservation and support of the preaching of the Gospel in the German Mennonite congregations.

B. The animation and strengthening of Christian and Mennonite common purpose by means of literary publications.

The headquarters of the Alliance, which was registered in 1902, is Hamburg, and its current chair is Pastor H. van der Smissen, in Altona.

Jacob Mannhardt's Illness and Death

In the fall of 1884 the aged Elder Jacob Mannhardt began to complain about pain in his tongue. But he continued to serve in his office as leader of the church, and until the middle of March 1885, he continued to preach every three or four weeks. Then his doctor forbade him to speak at length. To that point this localized suffering had not influenced his otherwise vigorous health, but since this was a cancerous tumor, the sad development was foreseeable. With his usual decisiveness the 83-year old opted for an operation, which led to his death on May 12, 1885.

The funeral took place on Saturday, May 16 at 4:30 in the afternoon in our church, with the whole congregation in attendance, along with a number of Mennonite preachers from the Thiensdorf, Elbing, Heubuden, Ladekopp, and other congregations, as well as the Protestant clergy of Danzig. Mannhardt junior preached the memorial sermon on Hebrews 13:9 for his honored and loved uncle, predecessor, and colleague. At the grave, the Protestant District Pastor Kahle, a friend of the deceased, spoke a prayer. Then preacher Harder from Elbing gave a farewell address, and all the preachers present threw earth on the coffin accompanied by a word of Scripture.[15]

A few months later on October 3, 1885, his 84th birthday, the grateful congregation dedicated a memorial stone at the Salvator cemetery for their elder and for his wife, who had predeceased him, and their son, Dr. Wilhelm Mannhardt. The

---

[15]Cf. "Rede am Grabe von Jakob Mannhardt," *Mennonitische Blätter*, 32, no. 9 (August 1885), 75-7 and "Jakob Mannhardt," *Christlicher Gemeindekalender*, 1 (1893), 80-91.

day happened to fall on Thanksgiving, and the congregation after the service went to the cemetery near by.[16] The words that Deacon C. H. Zimmermann spoke to the surviving daughters at the dedication of this stone were such a good witness of the high estimation in which even those leaders who disagreed with him on doctrinal matters held him, that I will repeat them here. He said:

> Honored guests, the friends of the old preacher's house used to gather there on every fourth of October to honor the esteemed head of the family. Today, we gather around this grave, which is furnished with a worthy monument that includes his wife and son along with the much-loved long-serving pastor.
>
> Immediately after the death of this aged friend, whose imposing personality ensured him of the admiration and love of young and old, the wish arose to honor his memory and his family with a memorial stone. The leadership, which recognized this wish as its own, gladly took the task upon itself, especially since the means came together from all sides. And so we are today in a position to give this memorial stone decorated with flowers to the bereaved family on the birthday of the beloved patriarch. This stone according to the inscription is dedicated to father, mother, and son, a noble trinity of human figures, of whom we — far from all idolization of humans — will preserve the feeling that their lives testified to the edifying revelation of God. Happy are they, the honored daughters of the preacher's house, that they may follow such excellent examples with honoring love. Happy the congregation such as ours that for over a generation has benefited from the quiet but

---

[16][German Protestants typically celebrate a harvest festival or Thanksgiving on the first Sunday of October. Ed.]

eloquent influence of this house, whose family life was itself an exemplary sermon.

For the church leadership not much changed with the death of the elder, since his fellow elder had worked together with him in perfect harmony. But he declined to chair the church council, for one thing because he was by far the youngest of this respected circle, and besides, he defended the principle that in the leadership of the Mennonite church the elder should not be above other members. Instead, they should all have equal rights, and only he should lead who had the confidence of all the others and was elected. This principle was enshrined in the new Constitution of 1887. For the time being the oldest deacon, C.H. Zimmermann, was elected leader.

Right of Incorporation

In the course of time it had become clear that the limited incorporation rights which the congregation had received in 1844 by a royal edict were no longer sufficient.[17] In the case of estate transfers and other register of deeds entries there were often difficulties that made it desirable for the congregation to obtain the full rights of incorporation on the basis of the law of June 12, 1874.[18]

How this was done after two years of preparatory work along with a complete rewriting of the congregational constitution cannot be told here in detail. One may consult the congregational minutes and chronicle. Sufficient to say that on November 14, 1886, the new constitution was adopted unanimously, and that as a consequence on January 31, 1887, the Ministries of the Interior, of Culture, and of Justice granted incorporation to our congregation. The congregational chronicle says about this:

> In the course of the year 1887 the new regulations were introduced into our congregational life and will hopefully prove

---

[17]See page 189.
[18]See page 207 and H.G. Mannhardt, *Jahrbuch 1888*, 154-61.

themselves in the future. The leadership may note with satisfaction and thanksgiving that the occasion of the introduction of this new constitution, in which both our Christian principles and the regulations concerning administration and governance are established, there was not the least conflict. In a spirit of true unity and genuine brotherly understanding the work of the leadership was begun, continued with the representatives and finally accepted by the membership after serious examination. And in carrying out the new regulations, too, there were no difficulties or misunderstandings noticed.

Congregational Growth and the Death of our Deacons

The eighties were a time of peaceful and steady growth. The number of baptized members, which in 1882 had been only 448, grew to 570 at the end of 1890, and in addition there were 210 children. The participation of the congregation in its own affairs and especially in the worship services was active. The church council, a happy combination, remained unchanged and worked together in untroubled harmony for the good of the congregation. This harmony was expressed most clearly during the 25th anniversary celebration of Deacon C.H. Zimmermann on March 2, 1887.[19]

Just as the internal bonds of the congregation were strengthened, so, too, were our ties outside the congregation. This was evident in 1888 when a terrible flood came to the Vistula lowlands. Thanks to the new Alliance of Mennonite Congregations in the German Empire, as well as to the new relationship with the Dutch congregations stimulated by Pastor Dr. Cramer, a generous relief program for the victims was begun. In our own collection center in Danzig 33,202 marks were donated to preacher Mannhardt, mostly from Holland. Our congregational members also participated in this relief effort, which was not limited to our fellow Mennonites.

---

[19]*Gedenkbuch*, vol. 4, 82ff.

In the decade from 1891 to 1900 the congregation continued to grow, and on December 31, 1900, it had reached 735 baptized members. But these years took all four of our deacons from us.

First our building trustee, Ludwig Ferdinand Stobbe, who had carried out his duties for fifteen years with exemplary dedication, had to retire in 1891 due to illness. He died a year later on October 18, 1892, at the age of 70. His successor was the church council member and brewery owner Wilhelm Penner from St. Albrecht. At this election the regulation of the new constitution came into force, according to which the deacon was not elected for life but rather only for a twelve-year term.

In 1897 Carl Heinrich Zimmermann died, who since 1885 had been re-elected annually as chair of the church council. On January 11, 1897, he still felt mentally and physically well enough to accept this post for another year. In addition he had also for many years served as treasurer. A few days later he suffered a stroke, which led to his death after two months on April 9. It would be a worthwhile task to write a biography of this many-sided man, but we must refrain from that here. Suffice it to refer to earlier comments about Zimmermann and to his obituary (congregational chronicle vol. 4, p. 256-60) and his memorial sermon.[20]

In his will he had included the congregation as an heir, and in a separate document he had instructed the leadership how to use the interest. In this document Zimmermann's generous and deeply pious nature found beautiful expression, along with his love of the congregation and his faith in its future.[21] Almost unanimously the congregation elected as a new deacon for a term of twelve years Zimmermann's brother-in-law, the alderman and businessman, Adolph Claassen, already long since a member of the church council.

Our dear Deacon Eduard Loewens would also not live to see the end of the century. He died after a short illness on February 7, 1899, at 72 years of age. He had not held any particular post

[20]H.G. Mannhardt, *Predigten und Reden*, 2nd ed. (Danzig: Verlag von John & Rosenberg, 1913), 295-301.

[21]Cf. *Protokolbuch*, 1897, 387ff.

in the leadership, to which he belonged since 1878, but his personal qualities made him beloved to us all and to the congregation. He was a genuine Mennonite through and through, full of the love of peace and patience, and of a pure, noble nature. He was greatly attached to everything connected with our church, because he saw in it the realization of his deepest principles. Like Zimmermann, he belonged to one of the old Mennonite families who have been resident in Danzig for 300 years. Loewens' successor was the Danzig retailer Eduard Lepp, who is still a member of the leadership today.

Zimmermann and Loewens had died in old age, but shortly before the end of the nineteenth century a man was taken from us who was still at the height of his powers. *Julius Momber,* whom we have mentioned earlier, emerged as a key leader soon after his election in 1880, and took a leading role beside Zimmermann and hand in hand with him. He was one of the most zealous advocates of the Alliance of Mennonite Congregations in the German Empire, and at its founding was elected into its board of trustees and then as its secretary, an office that involved much work and annual travel. In our church council as well he served as secretary, as temporary building

Julius Momber. [Scanned from 1919 German edition. Ed.]

trustee after Stobbe's death, and finally as treasurer after C.H. Zimmermann's death, excelling in all these tasks. It was only natural that he would replace Zimmermann as chair.

Carl Julius Momber was born in Danzig on December 25, 1839, thus he died not yet 61 years of age. He had studied business in Hildesheim and Berlin and then joined his father's firm here, first as an assistant, then as head clerk and finally as a partner. But he did not devote his considerable energy only to his business and his large family, but also to public duties and the civic administration, and above all, the congregation. His last project, together with the other leaders and representatives, was the new construction of our congregational alms house, whose completion he did not live to see.

If I have reported on these men in greater detail, it was in the first instance because of their unforgettable merit on behalf of our congregation. But it also was due to a feeling of deep gratitude. For they were the ones who supported the young preacher in the first twenty years of his service, in all things advising and accompanying him with their faithful personal friendship, and influencing him with their inner values. One does not forget such men, who, even if unconsciously, enrich and improve us by their lives and experience. And I am happy to present them to the future world, which will reap the fruit of what they have sown.

13
Conclusion: In the Twentieth Century

Addenda from the Menno Anniversary of 1892
From the last decade of the nineteenth century the following
should be noted: Our church on March 8, 1892, had made a
request to the Alliance of Mennonite Congregations in the
German Empire to celebrate the 400th birthday of Menno
Simons in this year everywhere in a simple ceremony. Since the
day of his birth is not known, we suggested November 6, the
day of the Reformation celebration. There would be enough
time until then to make arrangements for the individual church
groups and congregations. The board of trustees of the Alliance
agreed with us and sent a letter to all Mennonite congregations
to stimulate interest in such an event.[1] From all sides, especially
in Germany, Russia, and Holland, there was happy agreement.
The West Prussian congregations at their meeting on June 9
decided unanimously to have a simple but dignified celebration
in all churches, and to make this memorial day a demonstration
of the unity of all Mennonite churches in the spirit of their
erstwhile leaders, without thereby descending to thoughtless
glorification of men. At the same time it was decided to prepare
a book for circulation in the congregations to be written by
H.G. Mannhardt. This book was prepared on time and 4,500
copies were distributed in the congregations.[2] The details of the
celebration in our congregation, which drew an unusually large
crowd, are reported in detail in our congregational chronicle.[3]

The Menno Anniversary was on the one hand an expression
of the reawakened historical memory of a meaningful past, and
on the other a sign of the growing feeling of belonging together
with other Mennonite congregations in spite of many seeming
differences.

The awakening of a historical sense among us is the
achievement of women and men inside and outside our

---

[1]"Zur Gedächtnisfeier Mennos," *Mennonitische Blätter*, 39, no. 10 (May 16,
1892), 73.
[2][H. G. Mannhardt, *Festschrift zu Menno Simons' 400jähriger Geburtstagsfeier,
den 6. November 1892* (Danzig: Selbstverlag der westpreussischen Mennoniten-
Gemeinden, 1892). Ed.]
[3]Cf. also H.G. Mannhardt, *Predigten und Reden*, 2nd ed., 253-62.

fellowship. Dr. Ludwig Keller, a state archivist in Münster, belongs to the latter. He rediscovered the most important Anabaptist leader, Hans Denk, in his book *An Apostle of the Anabaptists*. Anna Brons, nee Cremer ten Doornkaat, of Emden, belongs to the former group with her book *Origin, Development, and Fate of the Anabaptists or Mennonites*.[4]

The founding of the Alliance in the years from 1884 to 1886 also was driven by this newly awakened interest in their historical development and the desire to gather together again what had been scattered.

These developments characterized the last twenty years of the nineteenth century. In the newly created German Empire we had given up our separate status and felt ourselves to be members of this land, our fatherland. But we had second thoughts about our one-sided principle of non-resistance and about the real meaning of the spirit of Anabaptism in the past and present. We noticed that our task in the present world was not strict separation but rather joyous participation in everything that contributes to permeating humanity with the spirit of living Christianity.

Our Danzig congregation likewise followed this path of both practicing faithfulness to the good that our predecessors possessed and being open to all the good possessed by others. Therefore: *unity* with one another first of all, and then with all others who want to build the Kingdom of Christ as a realm of truth, of justice, of love and peace.

Comenius Anniversary

For this reason our congregation had also had an active part in the memorial celebration for Johann Amos Comenius on March 27, 1892, and it was not by chance, nor a personal choice, that the memorial address was given by our preacher.[5] Rather, this was recognition that there was a deep, inner relationship between Comenius — this fighter for the

---

[4] [Ludwig Keller *Ein Apostel der Wiedertäufer* (Leipzig: Verlag von G. Hirzel, 1882). For Keller's impact on Anabapist historiography see page 7. On Brons' book see page xxxi. Ed.]

[5] H.G. Mannhardt, *Predigten und Reden*, 2nd ed., 314-25.

The old alms house 1817-1901. [Scanned from 1919 German edition. Ed.]

ennoblement of humanity on the basis of a pure, evangelical Christianity, this martyr and last bishop of the old Bohemian Brotherhood — and the Mennonites.[6]

New Alms House and New Hymnal
The *important events since 1900* will be noted here only briefly. First, the completion of our new alms house that, unfortunately, due to the arbitrary actions of the contractor, received a quite unlovely outward appearance. The building was completed in August 1901, and occupied at the beginning of September. A very important new facility was the roomy classroom, in which our archive and congregational library finally found a dignified home.

---

[6][Mannhardt is here following the academic lead of historian and archivist Ludwig Keller, who argued that a continuous line of influence ran from the Waldensians via the Bohemian or Czech Brethren to the early Anabaptists. On this basis Keller in the 1880s agitated for establishing ecumenical contacts between these groups, a call that is echoed in a different form in the preceding paragraph. In 1892, on the 300th anniversary of Comenius's birth, Keller launched a new organization, *Comenius Gesellschaft*, with its own journal, *Monatshefte*, to promote this vision. Comenius was the last bishop of the Bohemian Brethren. H. G. Mannhardt was one of Keller's most enthusiastic Mennonite supporters in this new endeavor. Friesen, *History and Renewal*, 41-112. Ed.]

Deacons and church board members of the Danzig Mennonite Church 1904. Standing: 1. businessman Max van Dühren, bd. memb.; 2. businessman Johannes Foth, bd. memb.; 3. businessman Otto Momber, bd. memb.; 4. businessman Max Loewens, bd. memb. (died 1916). Seated: 1. businessman Eduard Lepp, deacon; 2. city councilor (*Stadtverordneter*) Wilhelm Penner, since 1900 chair of the church board; 3. city administrator (*Stadtrat*) Wilhelm Siemens (retired), bd. memb. (died 1905); 4. city administrator Adolph Claassen, deacon (died 1915); 6. Prof. Albert Momber, director of the Society for the Study of Nature, deacon (died 1909); 6. city administrator and foundry owner August Zimmermann, bd. memb., (died 1919). [Scanned from 1919 German edition. Ed.]

On September 23 a meeting of the church leadership took place in this room for the first time. The leadership at that time consisted of city councilman Wilhelm Penner as chairman; H.G. Mannhardt, vice-chair and secretary; city councilman Adolph Claassen, building trustee; businessman Eduard Lepp; and professor Albert Momber; lay church council members were Alexander von Dühren, retired (died 1904); Wilhelm Siemens, manufacturer and city representative (died 1905); Johann Entz, businessman and city representative (died 1903); Wilhelm Sudermann, businessman and city representative (died 1902); August Zimmermann, engineer and city councilman; Max Loewens, businessman.

In 1907 it turned out that the old hymnal, which had been in use for over fifty years, was out of print. A new edition was decided upon and after six months of preparation the book that is now in use was introduced on April 5, 1908.

General Assembly of the Alliance of German Mennonite Congregations, Danzig, April 28-30, 1908
It was an important event for our congregation when the *eighth General Assembly* of the Alliance of Mennonite Congregations in the German Empire was held here in Danzig April 28-30, 1908. Detailed descriptions of this conference may be found in our *Book of Minutes*, 208-10, and also in the *Mennonite Journal*, No. 5,[7] and especially detailed in the *Monthly Journal of the Mennonite Congregation of Krefeld (Monatsblättern der Mennonitengemeinde Krefeld)* No. 6 and 7, written by Pastor G. Kraemer.

The conference was begun with a service in our church, on which occasion for the first time in a hundred years a Dutch Mennonite, Pastor Dr. Appeldoorn[8] preached the sermon on Matthew 3:2: "the kingdom of heaven has come near." It has been published in the *Mennonite Journal* of 1908, and in the Krefeld *Monthly Journal* mentioned above.

The guests from elsewhere, some of whom had brought their wives, gathered in the preacher's house after the service for an open discussion with our leadership. There was representation from congregations in Bavaria, Hesse, the Rhineland, East Frisia, Westphalia, Hamburg, Berlin, and East and West Prussia.

In the sessions on April 29 and 30, which took place in our sanctuary, the agenda, which consisted of a budget for three years, support for the smaller congregations, prize competitions,[9] publications, itinerant ministry, widows' fund,

---

[7] Hinrich van der Smissen, "Generalversammlung der zur V. d. M. G. i. D. R. gehörenden Gemeinden in Danzig," *Mennonitische Blätter* 55, no. 5 (May 1908): 39-41.

[8] At that time he was the preacher of our German Mennonite congregation in Emden; now he is professor of theology at Amsterdam University. [Jan Gerrit Appeldoorn (1861-1945); see Nanne van der Zijpp, "Appeldoorn, Jan Gerrit," *Mennonite Encyclopedia* 1:143. Ed.]

[9] [In 1902 the Alliance announced a prize competition for a short volume on Mennonite history that would be suitable for use at home in families and with youth who were being prepared for baptism. The winner was to receive

grants, and elections was gone through and dealt with in brotherly discussion and decision-making.

Taking up the beautiful words of the previous day's sermon by Dr. Appeldoorn, the chair of the General Assembly (Mannhardt of Danzig) stated the task of the Alliance and this conference: "We want to *gather* not everything that *calls* itself Mennonite, just for the sake of the name, but rather everything that is of the Mennonite spirit and wishes to represent it: a personal piety of action, free of literal constraint, with the absolute right of personal conviction and thus also with the duty of broad toleration for the principles of others. The Alliance should be a core around which those may gather who want to work with it."

On April 30, after the completion of the sessions, a fellowship luncheon was held at three o'clock in the Lodge "Unity"[10] and at 7:30 a congregational evening meeting took place at which the members of the congregation appeared in great numbers and related to the guests who had come from elsewhere. Two talks, by Mannhardt (Danzig) and Neff (Weierhof/Pfalz)[11] alternated with songs by a women's choir and single numbers. Mannhardt spoke about the history of the Mennonites and the Danzig congregation. Neff offered a comprehensive outline of "Our History in the Light of German Historical Scholarship in the last 50 Years." This weighty and important address, which assembled the wealth of scholarly literature about the Anabaptist movement, concluded with the sentences:

---

500 marks and have the manuscript published. *Mennonitische Blätter* 49, no. 9 (Sept. 1902), 80. Christine Fellmann Hege in 1908 finally won the prize and her work was published as *Kurze Geschichte der Mennoniten* (Frankfurt a. M., 1909). Ed.]

[10][A Masonic lodge. Ed.]

[11][Christian Neff (1863-1946) was pastor of the Weierhof congregation in the Palatinate. In addition he was a scholar and church statesman, helping to found both Mennonite World Conference and the *Mennonitisches Lexikon*, which formed the core of the *Mennonite Encyclopedia*. Henry DeWind, "Neff, Christian," *ME* 3:820. Ed.]

One thing has been achieved today about which we may rejoice. When Prof. Dr. Troeltsch, in a talk about the meaning of Protestantism for the rise of the modern world, praises the Anabaptists as the actual and main bearers and pioneers for the most important achievements of Protestantism, *religious freedom, freedom of conscience, and religious toleration*, and when Professor Dr. W. Köhler in a special lecture deals with our fellowship and gets his material from our circles, when he, as I have heard, sees the beginnings of the history of religions school, the most prominent school today, focusing on the Anabaptists, then we are confronted with facts which go beyond the hopes of our fathers and the dreams of our young people.[12] When outsiders acknowledge the importance of the Anabaptists, it is disgraceful for us to see and experience how in our own circles there is so often a sad lack of interest. This is unfortunately due to ignorance of our rich tradition, and it shows itself in small-minded pessimism about the future of our fellowship. May the fresh spirit which has animated historical research in the last 50 years also create new life in our congregations!

The days from April 28 to 30 contributed to an acquaintance of our congregation with this new life, but the guests also gained the impression from the Danzig congregation that a healthy branch of Mennonitism was growing here. One of the guests, a sharp critic who had only with difficulty decided to make the long journey and had come with few expectations, later wrote:

---

[12][The history of religions school saw religion as embedded in its historical context and focused less on dogma and more on religious experience and practice. Ernst Troeltsch (1865-1923) was one of the most prominent proponents of this approach to studying religion. Jung, *Protestantismus in Deutschland*, 54-7. Ed.]

The Danzig General Assembly is among the most beautiful events of that sort that I have experienced. Not that there was no opposition. It cannot be absent when the principle of free convictions is present. But the common conviction that went through all the sessions was: 'German Mennonitism is not limited to tending graves and preserving a little longer what is dying. Instead, it has great tasks for the present which are worthy of our dedication, and in that it may claim a right to life and growth. And to serve these goals in all personal freedom and patience with every honest conviction is the strong bond of the Alliance.' It shall and will *be a fellowship, not in name but in spirit and in deed.*

In 1909 Professor Albert Momber died, honored by us all; he had been elected with all 87 votes cast to replace his deceased brother, Julius Momber. He had reached the age of 72 years, and was respected in the city as the senior teacher of the college preparatory high school and especially as director of the "Society for the Study of Nature" (*Naturforschenden Gesellschaft*). His successor was the businessman Johannes Foth, who likewise was elected unanimously by the 97 votes of the brotherhood meeting for twelve years as deacon.

Connections to Holland via Celebrations in Krefeld and Amsterdam
This new relationship with the Dutch brethren was revitalized in 1911. The ninth general assembly of our Alliance took place in Krefeld on May 3 and 4, where the 25th anniversary was celebrated.[13] From Danzig the leaders Claassen and Penner had been delegated, and preacher Mannhardt took

---

[13]A description of this momentous conference may be found in Pastor Kraemer's *Zur Erinnerung an die 25jährige Jubelfeier der Vereinigung der Mennoniten-Gemeinden im Deutschen Reich* (Krefeld: Krefeld Mennonite Congregation, 1911).

part as secretary of the Alliance, and also gave the celebratory sermon in the Krefeld Mennonite church on May 3, at 7 pm.[14] There we met a large number of Dutch Mennonites who were present as guests. One of them, Pastor Binnerts[15] from Haarlem, in August of the same year made a sea trip to Danzig, Elbing, and Königsberg, in order to expand his knowledge of the German Mennonites, and was our guest in the preacher's house for some days. He has described this journey very attractively in his *Yearbook of the Baptism-Minded* 1913.[16]

In the fall of 1911 there was an opportunity to have close fellowship with our Dutch fellow believers. On September 28 the *Algemeene Doopsgezinde Societeit*[17] celebrated the centenary of its founding in Amsterdam. Preacher Mannhardt was invited along with four other representatives of the German Mennonites, and he participated in the edifying celebrations in the church and in the large hall "Artis" in the afternoon. He also on this occasion visited Pastor Binnerts and his congregation in Haarlem, as well as that in Rotterdam, where in the beautiful Mennonite church he gave an evening address about the old relationships between the Danzig and Dutch Mennonites.

In Amsterdam he was able to return the visit of Professor Dr. Samuel Cramer, who had been in Danzig in 1884.[18] Cramer was at the center of the Amsterdam celebration, gave a wonderful address in the old Singelkerk and invited his German friends to his welcoming house on September 29, where they could renew old memories and discuss new hopes.

---

[14]H. G. Mannhardt, *Predigten und Reden*, 2nd ed., 179-87.

[15][Arjen Binnerts, Szn. (1865-1932); see Nanne van der Zijpp, "Binnerts, Arjen, Szn.," *Mennonite Encyclopedia* 1:344. Ed.]

[16][*Doopsgezind Jaarboekje*, the annual journal of the Mennonites of the Netherlands. Ed.]

[17][The General Mennonite Association, the conference of Mennonite congregations in the Netherlands, was organized in 1811. By 1870 all the congregations in the country had joined. The initial main task of the association was supporting the Mennonite seminary in Amsterdam. N. van der Zijpp, "Algemene Doopsgezinde Societeit," *ME* 1:52-3. Ed.]

[18]The highly respected man died on January 30, 1913. A collection of Cramer's letters may be found in our archive.

In this context it is important to note that the relationship with our brothers in Holland had been in place and remained vibrant since the fifties of the nineteenth century through the "Mission Society for the Propagation of the Gospel in the Dutch Colonies" which was located in Amsterdam. The West Prussian Mennonite congregations collected about 6,000 marks annually for this cause.

Organ Renovation

Our church organ, a large instrument with thirty-one stops, had been constructed that way so that its sounds would carry to the nearby old Salvator cemetery, where the deceased of our congregation found their last rest. Since this cemetery had been closed, the full organ was no longer used, and when a thorough inspection showed that a rebuilding of the organ was necessary, the congregation in 1913 approved the sum of 5,500 marks for that purpose. The organ builder Heinrichsdorff of Danzig took on the project and carried it out in the winter of 1913/14. The rebuilt organ, fitted with an electric bellows and equipped with nineteen speaking stops, was put into use on Judica Sunday, March 29, 1914, and demonstrated for the members in an evening service on Good Friday.[19] It found unanimous approval from the congregation.

In connection with the rebuilding of the organ, electric power was introduced to our church and lights were acquired for evening services, so that now since 1913 New Year's Eve services could again be held.

The World War and Its Victims

The *World War* naturally did not pass without leaving deep marks on our congregation. When it began, 138 men ranging from sixteen-year-old volunteers to forty-four-year-old reservists took up arms. In the course of the four years, the

---

[19][*Judica* in the Protestant liturgical year is the name of the fifth Sunday after Lent, which is also the Sunday before Palm Sunday. The name is derived from the first Latin word recited by the congregation in the liturgy after the opening hymn and means "Judge me." Bieritz, *Das Kirchenjahr*, 99. Ed.]

number of draftees rose to 250, or almost half the baptized male church members. Among them were sixty-two officers, four medical doctors, sixty-five non-commissioned officers of all sorts, and over 100 soldiers of all troop types. Twenty fell in the War, eight in field hospitals from wounds or illness. Eighteen soldiers returned home badly wounded. Nine still languish in captivity, whose return home is longingly awaited by their loved ones.

During the hard wartime the congregation related to their fighting brothers not only through their relatives at home, but also through the fact that the leadership from time to time sent them special letters which were to tell them that we were thinking of them with loyalty and gratitude.

Of those taken by the war, seven were buried in their homeland, and the others are sleeping in foreign lands, where they have given their lives for their homeland. But their memory lives on in the hearts of their loved ones and in the congregation, which will memorialize their names on simple tablets in the church.[20]

The war took its toll in the homeland as well. The number of deaths rose substantially. In the first year of the war we lost, among others, our veteran building trustee, city councilman Adolph Claassen, a man who had not only done much for the congregation, but also had been active in many community projects. He died on May 2, 1915, at the age of 77 years after a short illness. Unfortunately, his successor Max Loewens was also taken from us in April 1916, although he was only 54 years old. Then the congregation elected the church council member, businessman Franz Entz, unanimously as deacon. Finally, we must lament the death of one of our most influential and active members, a church council member, city councilman August Zimmermann, who died on March 29, 1919, at the age of 63.

---

[20][Engraved tablets bearing the names of soldiers from the parish who were killed in action appeared in some Protestant churches already at the time of the Napoleonic wars but were something new for Mennonites in World War I. H. G. Mannhardt, *Zwei Gedenktage*, 10-16. Ed.]

Board of the Danzig Mennonite Church 1919. Standing: Johannes Foth, businessman and head of the businessmen's society (*Ältester der Kaufmannschaft*). Seated: 1. Eduard Kepp, businessman, city councilor (*Stadtverordneter*) and commercial arbitrator (*Handelsrichter*); 2. Wilhelm Penner, honorary city elder (*Stadtältester*); 3. H. G. Mannhardt, pastor; 4. Franz Entz, businessman. [Scanned from 1919 German edition. Ed.]

Our Principles Then and Now

Our nation is standing on the divide between past and future, and we stand with it in the turmoil of an unsettled present.

What will become of us? The question is on everyone's lips. And the answer can only be: "We do not know." We do not want to be and cannot be prophets. We can only resolutely do our duty. "Work and do not despair!" That is the best solution now for all those who have still preserved their sense of responsibility.

One of the duties that awaits us is the preservation and further development of our congregational life. The fact that our membership has grown year by year for the past four decades, so that in 1905 we exceeded one thousand and in 1911 twelve hundred members, is mainly due to the arrivals from other Mennonite congregations, which the war had now brought to a standstill. But it is not the number that will decide our future, but rather the spirit that fills us. This spirit must be one of faithfulness to our past and at the same time a spirit of deliberate and steady progress. Our church constitution of 1887 says in its last article: "Since this congregational statute cannot claim to be infallible or to remain forever valid, the congregation retains the right to examine it from time to time and, when required, to make changes."

The time is ripe for such changes and they will come. But they will not touch our Christian religious principles but only give them a more contemporary form. The principles of our forefathers regarding *freedom of the will and the moral responsibility of the individual Christian* remain. Our view of *baptism and communion* are unchanged, namely, that they are no sacraments but rather symbolic acts of worship in the Christian congregation, whose outer use is of no benefit for the human soul if the inner baptism with the fire of Christ's spirit is not part of the water baptism. Enjoying the bread and wine only bind us closer to God and one another if the reconciling love coming from the Cross of Christ is present. Our belief remains that the *congregation* is the bearer of the spiritual gifts and goods, which Christ has brought to humanity, and that one does not require the mediation of the church or priests to attain to them. Now as then it will be a *matter for the congregation* to administer all these matters itself as the highest authority, and to bestow the offices of *preachers* and *deacons* on those *it chooses*. For now and the future we affirm *the refusal of the oath*, which is self-explanatory from Christian truthfulness as well as being an explicit commandment of Christ.[21]

---

[21]Until now we have the following provision in Prussia in the Law of March 11, 1827 as follows:

§1 If a Mennonite is to swear an oath or be heard as a witness or called to an office that requires a swearing-in process, he must produce an affidavit from an elder, preacher, or deacon of his congregation that certifies that he was born into the Mennonite sect or has been a member for at least a year before the start of the court process or appointment to office and has hitherto led a moral life.

§2 This affidavit must include the formulation of the

Finally, as has always been the case in our congregation as a sign of our Christian commitments, we will continue to stand by one another as brothers. The principle will continue in force that the congregation, insofar as it is possible, will seek to prevent the impoverishment of its members and look after those who are truly poor and weak through well-structured programs.

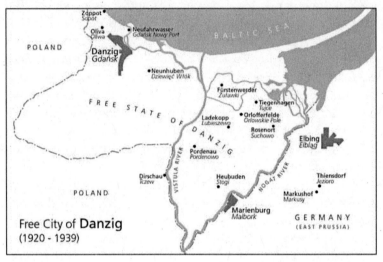

Free City of **Danzig**
(1920 - 1939)

The Mennonites in the Future Free State of Danzig
The Danzig Mennonite congregation for three hundred fifty years has preserved these principles. But it did not remain the same in all respects. It underwent development and has its history like all human institutions. The changing fortunes of

---

affirmation that is usually used by the Mennonites.

§3 This affirmation, which is to be confirmed by handshake, is as legally binding as an oath.

§4 Anyone who abuses this procedure to lie will be charged with perjury.

Our affirmation is formulated as "I affirm (witness, pledge) through my 'Yes' with handshake that ..." Our task now is to secure the legal use of this form in the future. We cannot agree to swear a legal oath by raising our hand and using the expression "I swear."

Danzig's public life are also mirrored in the history of our congregation.

Today the old, storied city again stands at an historical crossroads. It is being torn out of the Prussian state body, in which it was a valuable member for one and a quarter centuries. Foreign despotism is separating it from the German Empire, whose founding it cheered as did all German provinces. It is to become a new Free State. What was called the Free State of Danzig more than a hundred years ago was a dependent construction full of need and suffering. Let us hope that this time it will not be as terrible, even if the separation from the old fatherland is bitter and painful enough.

The new Free State of Danzig will include, apart from our Danzig congregation, the Mennonite congregations of Neunhuben in the Danzig Delta, Fürstenwerder, Ladekopp-Orlofferfelde, Tiegenhagen, Rosenort, and a large part of the Heubuden congregation in the Greater Delta. All together 5,000 — thus half of the Mennonites living in the erstwhile province of West Prussia — will be in the Free State. The others will live partly in the Polish state and partly in Prussia.

For the future much will depend on our staying in touch with each other in spite of the tearing apart of our previous association, just as our predecessors stayed in communion with each other across political boundaries. Especially, though, we Mennonites living in the Free State of Danzig must stay together, not in order to separate ourselves but in order to represent our common interests without limiting the freedom and autonomy of the individual congregation.

In keeping with their principle of the separation of church and state, the Mennonites have never claimed any financial support from the state, but instead they had to pay many taxes for the preservation of the state churches. Since there is not to be an established church in the Free State of Danzig, freedom of conscience will be guaranteed, and we may assume that in matters like the oath, incorporation rights, and autonomy we will not be in a worse position than is the case in Prussia today.

Whatever form the future constitution and government in Danzig may take, we want to take an active part in all the cultural endeavors of the new state and participate in the common good, according to the text: "But seek the welfare of the city where I have sent you into exile, and pray to the Lord on its behalf, for in its welfare you will find your welfare." (Jeremiah 29:7)

Epilogue
The History of the Church Building after World War II[1]
by Tomasz Ropiejko

With the end of World War II a new chapter unfolded for the city of Gdańsk and for Poland. The German inhabitants of Gdańsk, including the Mennonites, fled the Soviet Army or were expelled in the subsequent months. Polish people suffered greatly as well from the fighting and the Soviet occupation. Gdańsk is located in the region that was then called the Regained Territories in which all large land holdings became state property. This was also true for the church building raised by the master bricklayer Bretschneider and master carpenter Fuchs between 1818 and 1819. The building was devastated during World War II as was the entire city of Gdańsk. One wing of the alms house was totally destroyed. The remaining wing, however, and the parsonage were in good enough shape that some people occupied them. Unfortunately the people living there did not have any connection to the church. They were, in fact, reserved at times toward those who would later try to restore dignity to the church building.

Danzig Mennonite church building in ruins, Dec. 11, 1946

---

[1]This article has been based in large part on the thesis written by Sławomir Wanionek, "Dzieje kaplicy Kościoła Zielonoświątkowego – sanktuarium pomenonickiego w Gdańsku" (*Pentecostal Church Building History - the former Mennonite Sanctuary in Gdańsk*), Warsaw Theological Seminary, 1999.

Interior of Danzig Mennonite church in 1946

In 1947 the local government officially granted permission to use the church building for religious purposes at the request of Paweł Bajeński who was the minister for the Church of Christ.[2] Along with the church building, the state also gave the right to use the parsonage with a promise that the people who had already managed to settle there would be relocated to another place. However it took over ten years for the government to fulfill this promise. This started a long and difficult process in the rebuilding of this house of prayer.

Sergiusz Waszkiewicz was another church leader who played an important role in the life of the church as well as in the reconstructing of the church building. He was an experienced minister for the Christian Church of Evangelical Faith.[3] Even though these two ministers represented different churches, they partnered together.

Necessary permits were obtained and, despite the uncooperative surroundings and financial difficulties, work

---

[2]Zjednoczenie Kościołów Chrystusowych w Polsce.
[3]Kościół Chrześcijan Wiary Ewangelicznej. This church was Pentecostal in character.

toward rebuilding the sanctuary started in 1948. Lots of hard work and 1.5 million zlotys (in the old currency) were invested in the rebuilding of the damaged walls, replacing the roof and plastering the building both inside and outside. The annexes at the front and side entrances were also rebuilt and electrical fixtures were added. Inside the sanctuary a new balcony was built.[4]

Unfortunately the functioning of the Church of Christ was disrupted in 1950 due to worsening relations between state and church. Thus the work started on the building was brought to a halt. September 1950 brought major challenges with the arrests of church leaders throughout Poland. They were kept in prison without a trial or sentence. The state confiscated church property and closed meeting places.[5] Paweł Bajeński and Sergiusz Waszkiewicz were arrested as well. This repression, of course, had a negative bearing on the life of the two Gdańsk congregations led by them as well as the restoration of the church building.

Due to a lack of supervision, as none of the church members could live in the parsonage, the sanctuary that had been partially rebuilt was once again plundered and destroyed. The doors along with their frames were stolen, part of the roof was stripped of its tiles and part was smashed. The drainage pipes were pulled out from the walls along with the electrical fixtures. Since the new roof was pulled off, further damage was done due to rain and snow.[6] People living nearby gradually were taking various wooden parts of the building for heating purposes. This state of affairs lasted until 1957.

After an unexpectedly swift release from prison, Paweł Bajeński continued his ministry but soon left Gdańsk, eventually settling in Warsaw. Sergiusz Waszkiewicz, who returned home

---

[4]Paweł Bajeński, "Odbudowa świątyni w Gdańsku" (Reconstruction of the Church Building in Gdańsk), *Chrześcijanin* (*Christian Magazine*) No.1-2 (November 1957), 38-39.

[5]Ryszard Michalak, *Kościoły Protestanckie i władze partyjno-państwowe w Polsce (1945-1956)* (*Protestant Churches and Ruling Party Authorities in Poland (1945-1956)*) (Warsaw:Wydawnictwo Naukowe Semper, 2002), 107-110.

[6]Bajeński, "Odbudowa świątyni w Gdańsku," 38-39.

from prison in mid-1952, resumed leadership of the Gdańsk congregation.

In 1953 the Church of Christ, the Christian Church of Evangelical Faith and three other evangelical groupings, pressured by the communist government, joined together to form the United Evangelical Church (UEC).[7] The state wanted all minority church groups to be under one umbrella in order to control them. As a result of this denominational merger, the two congregations in Gdańsk joined together under the leadership of Sergiusz Waszkiewicz.

Believers continued meeting in private apartments, then later in a photo workshop owned by a Christian couple, places that in reality were unsuitable for such gatherings. However, thanks to God's grace and favorable circumstances, once again they started thinking about rebuilding the house of prayer. It is necessary to add that, in the interim, there had been many efforts by various parties to gain control of this building for use for different purposes.[8] When these cases were brought to government officials, they were rejected.

The small congregation was unable to take on the difficult task of rebuilding the house of prayer alone. However, thanks to the assistance given through the World Council of Churches (WCC), the state, and the National Board of the UEC, it was possible to organize the initial work necessary to secure the building in 1957.

In 1958 the rebuilding of the sanctuary went forward further. The main difficulty that the congregation had to deal with in the upcoming building season was the lack of space in the parsonage for any church members to move into in order to insure the security of the church building. At this time the parsonage was still occupied by people unrelated to the church who were not always favorable to church members. However the National Board of the UEC continued to work hard in order to reclaim the parsonage. They were motivated by the desire to rebuild the sanctuary, keeping it as a house of prayer

---

[7]Zjednoczony Kościół Ewangeliczny.
[8]One of the institutions trying to obtain the church building was a local theater that wanted to turn the building into a storage place.

for the church family as well as a rare architectural historical heritage.[9] Once again the city government promised that the occupants, who were not part of the church, would be evicted from the parsonage by the end of June. The first church members to move into the parsonage were the family of Sergiusz Waszkiewicz, but this did not happen until the end of 1958.

In the second quarter of that same year the work in connection with the rebuilding came close to completion thanks to the great financial sacrifices and hard work of the Gdańsk church members. The rebuilding committee was directed by Sergiusz Waszkiewicz, church overseer, Ferdynand Ruchaj, church secretary, and Paweł Bajeński on behalf of the National Board of UEC. After the flooring was put down and the carpentry work was done, finding the appropriate pews for such a historical building remained a major challenge.

On June 29, 1958, the congregation held a ceremonial opening for the Gdańsk church building, located at Mennonite Street 2, along with its consecration by the Word of God and prayer. It was rebuilt thanks to the financial assistance of the WCC, the state and the National Council of UEC.[10] This ceremony was the coronation of the church members' hard and persistent work - those who sacrificed their strength, time and skills in order to gather in this spacious church building, instead of in the previous dark, confined rooms. Since then, the church building has once again been serving as a house of prayer, as was originally intended when it was raised and dedicated to God by the Mennonites in 1819.

As has been stated the WCC played an important role in funding the reconstruction. The Geneva office donated more than half of the needed funds. Pastors Dr. Howard Schomer (USA) and Daniel Cederberg (Sweden) were the representatives of the WCC to oversee this project. They spoke highly of the

---

[9] *Chrześcijanin*, No.1-2 (January-February 1958), 25.
[10] *Kalendarz Jubileuszowy (Jubilee Calendar)*, 1963, Zjednoczony Kościół Ewangeliczny, 106-107.

way the money had been handled and praised the work done by the congregation in Gdańsk.[11]

Since its official reopening in 1958, the Gdańsk sanctuary has been renovated many times in order to improve the state of this historical building.[12] In 1966 two main beams that had been destroyed and one ceiling beam were replaced under the direction of engineer Olgierd Sankowski. Ceiling insulation was put into place then as well. Unfortunately the lack of resources forced further work on the building to be postponed. In 1974 a thorough technical inspection was completed under the direction of engineer Bogusław Hanuszkiewicz. At this time the roof tiles, drainage pipes and sheeting were all refurbished. Furthermore the necessary building structure elements were replaced, some new wiring was done, the ceiling was reinsulated, the interior of the building was painted and the outer walls were repaired and painted. In June of 1989 the main sanctuary was repainted. In 1991 the roof underwent necessary repairs and a new radiator heating system was installed. The next year extensive rewiring was done under the direction of engineer Z. Drywa. The last major work on the church building was done in 2003. At this time the southern annex was reconstructed and the outer walls of the entire building were completely replastered and painted.

In order to better understand the history of the church building after WWII it is important to see how ownership rights developed. Since 1946 the congregation had the right to use the church building, but it was not until 1972 that they actually obtained full ownership of this property. This was possible due to a decision handed down by the Religious Department of the Regional Government[13] on July 19, 1972. The following year brought another important development with the official

---

[11]Anonymous, "Nieoczekiwane odwiedziny" (An Unexpected Visit), *Chrześcijanin*, No. 1-3 (1959), 21-22.

[12]The following data regarding the renovation work is based on the documentation found in the church office. The list contains only major projects.

[13]Wojewódzka Rada Narodowa, Wydział do Spraw Wyznań.

The parsonage in 2001. [Photo by John D. Thiesen. Ed.]

registration of the church building in the registry of historical buildings protected by law.[14]

In the meantime an important change took place in the organizational structure of the church body. In 1987 all the churches forming the United Evangelical Church decided to reestablish their independence, which previously had not been possible under communist rule. This marked the beginning of the current organizational form of the Pentecostal Church of Poland. On February 1, 1988, the Pentecostal Church of Poland became officially registered as a separate church entity. Throughout the years the leadership as well as most of the church members in the Gdańsk congregation had been Pentecostal so it was natural for the church building to remain in the hands of the Pentecostal Church of Poland.[15]

The next step, in order to put the legal issues right, was to secure for the church the rights to the parsonage. This was possible in the year 1989 when ownership was transferred from the state to the church. The year 2001 brought an unexpected opportunity. Due to the law it was possible for the Pentecostal congregation to apply for ownership of the red brick building

---

[14]Dated October 15, 1973.
[15]Kościół Zielonoświątkowy.

near the church. This building, originally part of the entire church complex, served the Mennonite congregation as an alms house. The ownership was obtained after a complicated process and with the help of Mennonite representatives from USA and Germany who supported this cause.[16] The official decision was dated May 19, 2003. This completed the process of restoring ownership of the entire property to the church.

In reviewing the history of the church building it is important to mention the various leaders of the Gdańsk congregation over the years. The first leader of the church, Sergiusz Waszkiewicz, retired in November 1981. On November 15, 1981 Anatol Matiaszuk, who came from Zielona Góra, became the new overseer of the congregation[17] continuing his ministry for seven years. From May 8, 1988, to October 23, 1988, Jan Krauze served as assistant pastor and fulfilled the responsibilities of the senior pastor due to the post being left vacant. Józef Suski, from Łódź, was chosen to be the new pastor from that time on. The year 2005 brought yet another change in leadership. Long-time pastor Józef Suski retired and in his place Tomasz Ropiejko, who was his assistant for the previous eleven years, assumed the position of senior pastor.

Another important factor to keep in mind when looking at the history of this church building, originally erected by Mennonites, is the good contact that has been kept with Mennonites from different parts of the globe throughout the years. Particularly it is worthwhile to mention here Prof. Dr. Peter J. Klassen, president of the Mennonite-Polish Friendship Association, and Peter J. Foth,[18] a prominent leader of German Mennonites. The various groups that have come to visit this historical church site have generally emphasized two aspects for

---

[16]Two letters were written to the Polish authorities recommending the transfer of the title deed to the Pentecostal Church of Poland. The first one came from the Mennonite-Polish Friendship Association and the second from representatives of the German Mennonites.

[17]In 1983 he was given the title of Pastor. This term became official for the leaders of this church from this time on.

[18]Peter J. Foth of the Hamburg Mennonite Church died suddenly on April 1, 2004.

which they are grateful. First is the gratitude that the building has been restored to an acceptable condition after having been largely destroyed in the past. Secondly they have expressed their appreciation for this building being put to use in accordance with its original purpose. A visible sign of this relationship is the bronze plaque that is located just inside the main entrance to the church building.[19] The inscription on it is written in four languages. In English it reads, "With thanks to God and in grateful memory of our friends in this area for providing a homeland for Mennonites for more than four centuries; for granting religious toleration when religious persecution was common; for restoring this church, built in 1819, but badly damaged in World War II; for seeking to overcome the tragedies of war, flight and expulsion with love and reconciliation."

The former Mennonite church building in Gdańsk in 1998. [Photo by Mark Jantzen. Ed.]

---

[19]The plaque was unveiled on June 25, 1991. It contains inscriptions in Polish, Dutch, German and English.

Bibliography

Works cited by H. G. Mannhardt

Braght, Thieleman J. van. *The Bloody Theatre or Martyrs Mirror.* Amsterdam, 1660.

Brons, Anna. *Ursprung, Entwickelung und Schicksale der altevangelischen Taufgesinnten oder Mennoniten.* Norden: Diedr. Soltau, 1884.

Cramer, S. "Menno Simons." In *Realencyklopädie für protestantische Theologie und Kirche*, ed. D. Albert Hauck, 12: 586-94. 3rd ed. Leipzig: J. C. Hinrichs'sche Buchhandlung, 1903.

Cramer, S. "Mennoniten." In In *Realencyklopädie für protestantische Theologie und Kirche*, ed. D. Albert Hauck, 12: 594-616. 3rd ed. Leipzig: J. C. Hinrichs'sche Buchhandlung, 1903.

Crichton, Wilhelm. *Zur Geschichte der Mennoniten.* Königsberg: Bey Gottlieb Lebrecht Hartung, 1786.

Goldmann, Salka. *Danziger Verfassungskämpfe unter Polnischer Herrschaft.* Leipzig: B.G. Teubner, 1901.

Harder, Carl. *Kurzgefasste Geschichte der Elbinger Mennonitengemeinde.* Elbing, 1884.

Hoop Scheffer, J. G. de. "Menno Simons in seinem Leben und Wirken." In *Jahrbuch der Mennoniten-Gemeinden in West- und Ostpreußen*, ed. H. G. Mannhardt, 74-88. Danzig: Mannhardt, 1883.

Katechismus, oder Kurze und einfältige Unterweisung aus der heiligen Schrift in Frage und Antwort, für die Kinder zum Gebrauch in den Schulen. Elbing, 1778.

Keller, Ludwig. *Ein Apostel der Wiedertäufer.* Leipzig: Verlag von G. Hirzel, 1882.

Kraemer, Gustav. *Zur Erinnerung an die 25jährige Jubelfeier der Vereinigung der Mennoniten-Gemeinden im Deutschen Reich.* Krefeld: Krefeld Mennonite Congregation, 1911.

Lengnich, Gottfried. *Jus publicum civitatis gedanensis oder Der Stadt Danzig Verfassung und Rechte*, edited by Otto Günther. Danzig: T. Bertling 1900.

_____. *Geschichte der Preussischen Lande.* 9 vols. Danzig, 1722-1755.

Mannhardt, H. G. *Festschrift zu Menno Simons' 400jähriger Geburtstagsfeier den 6. November 1892.* Danzig: Selbstverlag der westpreussischen Mennoniten-Gemeinden, 1892.

_____. "Jakob Mannhardt." *Christlicher Gemeindekalender* 1 (1893): 80-91.

_____. *Jahrbuch der Mennoniten-Gemeinden in West- und Ostpreussen.* Danzig, 1883.

_____. *Jahrbuch der altevangelischen Taufgesinnten oder Mennonitengemeinden.* Danzig, 1888.

_____. "Die Mennoniten unter den preußischen Königen." *Christlicher Gemeindekalender* 11 (1902): 98-117.

_____. *Predigten und Reden.* 2nd ed. Danzig: Verlag von John & Rosenberg, 1913.

_____. "Rede am Grabe von Jakob Mannhardt," *Mennonitische Blätter* 32, no. 9 (August 1885): 75-7.

_____. "Zur Entstehung und Geschichte der Koniglichen Kabinettsordre vom 3. Marz 1868." *Christlicher Gemeindekalender* 28 (1919): 97-107.

Mannhardt, Wilhelm. *Gedichte.* Danzig, 1881.

_____. "Der Reichstagbeschluß vom 9. Nov. 1867." *Mennonitische Blätter Beilage* 15, no. 7 (August 1868): 58-60.

_____. *Unser Kirchenbau vor 50 Jahren: Gedenkblatt für die Danziger Mennonitengemeinde.* Danzig, 1869. Also reprinted in *Mennonitische Blätter* 16, No. 7 (September 1869), 51-7.

_____. *Die Wehrfreiheit der altpreußischen Mennoniten.* Marienburg: Selbstverlag der westpreussischen Mennoniten-Gemeinden, 1863.

_____. "Noch einmal der 'Menonit:' Correspondenz zwischen dem Vorstand der Gemeinde zu Danzig und Ernst von Wildenbruch." *Mennonitische Blätter* 35, no. 11 (June 1, 1888): 61-4.

Preussische Gesetzsammlung. Berlin, 1874.

Protokolbuch. 1897.

Rues, Simeon Friderich. *Aufrichtige Nachrichten von dem gegenwärtigen Zustande der Mennoniten oder Taufgesinnten: wie auch der Collegianten oder Reinsburger, beyderseits ansehnlicher kirchlicher Gesellschaften in den vereinigten Niderlanden: samt einer Erzehlung von den Streitigkeiten, in welche dermahlen einige der zuerst benennten verwikelt sind: nebst verschiedenen andern dienlichen Zusäzen.* Jena: Joh. Rudolph Crökers seel. Wittwe, 1743.

Schnaase, Eduard. *Geschichte der evangelischen Kirche Danzigs actenmässig dargestellt.* Danzig: Theodor Bertling, 1863.

Schumacher, Bruno. *Niederländische Ansiedlungen im Herzogtum Preußen zur Zeit Herzog Albrechts 1525-1568.* Leipzig: Duncker & Humblot, 1903.

Simson, Paul. *Geschichte der Stadt Danzig.* Danzig: L. Sauniers Buchhandlung, 1903.

_____. *Geschichte der Stadt Danzig bis 1626.* 3 vols. Danzig: A.W. Kafermann, 1913-18.

Szper, Felicia. *Nederlandsche Nederzettingen in Westpruisen, gedurende den Poolschen tijd.* Enkhuizen: P. Bais, 1913.

van der Smissen, Hinrich. "Generalversammlung der zur V. d. M. G. i. D. R. gehörenden Gemeinden in Danzig." *Mennonitische Blätter* 55, no. 5 (May 1908): 39-41.

van der Smissen, Johannes. "Zur Geschichte der ersten Gemeindebildung in den Mennoniten-Colonien Sud-Rußlands." *Mennonitische Blätter* 3, no. 2 (March 1856):18-21, 3, no. 3 (May 1856):34-37, 3, no. 4 (July 1856):19-51.

Walrave, Simon. *Svccessio Anabaptistica, dat is Babel der vvederdopers: eensdeels in Duytsland maer principael in Nederlandt, in vvelcke de opgevvorpen oorsprong de rasende voortganck, ende bittere verstrouinge in t'cort verhaelt vvort.* Coloniae: Sumptibus Bernardi Gualtheri, 1603.

Zimmermann, C.H. *Gedenkbuch der Danziger Mennoniten-Gemeinde,* Volume 3 (n.p., n.d.).

Works cited by Editors

Geheimes Staatsarchiv Preußischer Kulturbesitz (GStA), Berlin Hauptabteilung (HA) I, Repositur (Rep.) 76 (Kulturministerium), III (Evangelisch-Geistliche Angelegenheiten), Sektion (Sekt.) 1 (Generalia), Abteilung (Abt.) XIIIa (Sekten- und Judensachen), no. 2 (Die Angelegenheiten der Mennoniten).

HA I, Rep. 77 (Innenministerium), Tit. 332t (Militärpflicht), no. 5 (Militarpflichtigkeit der Mennoniten), vol. 1, (1819-1868).

Baecher, Claude, Neal Blough, James Jakob Fehr, Alle G. Hoekema, Hanspeter Jecker, John N. Klassen, Diether Götz Lichdi, Ed van Straten, Annelies Verbeek. *Global Mennonite History Series*. Vol. 2, *Europe: Testing Faith and Tradition*. Intercourse, PA: Good Books, 2006.

Bär, Max. *Die Behördenverfassung in Westpreußen seit der Ordenszeit*. Danzig, 1912. A facsimile of the first edition. Hamburg: Selbstverlag Verein für Familienforschung in Ost- und Westpreußen, 1989.

Bauman, Clarence, ed. and trans. *The Spiritual Legacy of Hans Denck*. New York: E. J. Brill, 1991.

Bender, Harold S., C. Henry Smith, Cornelius Krahn and Melvin Gingerich, eds. *Mennonite Encyclopedia*. Scottdale, PA: Herald Press, 1955-1959.

Bieritz, Karl-Heinrich. *Das Kirchenjahr. Feste, Gedenk- und Feiertage in Geschichte und Gegenwart*. Berlin: Union Verlag, 1986.

Biernat, Czesław. *Staatsarchiv Danzig — Wegweiser durch die Bestände bis zum Jahr 1945*. München: R. Oldenbourg Verlag, 2000.

Blind, August. *Maß-, Münz-, und Gewichtswesen*. Leipzig: G. J. Göschen'sche Verlagshandlung, 1906.

Bogucka, Maria. *Das alte Danzig*. Leipzig: Verlag Koehler & Amelang, 1980.

Bömelburg, Hans-Jürgen. *Zwischen Polnischer Ständesgesellshaft und Preussischem Obrigkeitsstaat: Vom Königlichen Preussen zu Westpreussen (1756-1806)*. Munich: R. Oldenbourg Verlag, 1995.

Brock, Peter. *Freedom from Violence: Sectarian Nonresistance from the Middle Ages to the Great War.* Toronto: University of Toronto Press, 1991.

Brons, Bernhard. *Frau Antje Brons, geb. Cremer ten Doornkat zu Emden, geb. 23. November 1810, gest. 2. April 1902: aus ihrem Leben.* Kaiserslautern: Buchdruckerei Heinr. Köhl, 1904.

Burleigh, Michael. *Germany Turns Eastwards: A Study of Ostforschung in the Third Reich.* New York: Cambridge University Press, 1988.

Cieślak, Edmund and Czesław Biernat. *History of Gdańsk.* Translated by Bożenna Blaim and George M. Hyde. Gdańsk: Fundacji Biblioteki Gdańskiej, 1995.

Davies, Norman. *God's Playground: A History of Poland.* 2 vols. New York: Columbia University Press, 1981-1982.

Doornkaat Koolman, Jacobus ten. *Dirk Philips: Friend and Colleague of Menno Simons, 1504-1568,* translated by William E. Keeney, edited by C. Arnold Snyder. Kitchener, Ontario: Pandora Press, 1998.

Driedger, Michael D. *Obedient Heretics: Mennonite Identities in Lutheran Hamburg and Altona during the Confessional Age.* Burlington, VT: Ashgate, 2002.

Dyck, Cornelius J. *An Introduction to Mennonite History,* 3rd ed. Scottdale, PA: Herald Press, 1993.

Echt, Samuel. *Die Geschichte der Juden in Danzig.* Leer: Verlag Gerhard Rautenberg, 1972.

Friedrich, Karin. *The Other Prussia: Royal Prussia, Poland and Liberty, 1569-1772.* New York: Cambridge University Press, 2000.

Friesen, Abraham. *History and Renewal in the Anabaptist/Mennonite Tradition.* North Newton, KS: Bethel College, 1994.

Friesen, John. "Theological Developments among Mennonites in Poland in the Sixteenth and Seventeenth Centuries." In *Anabaptism Revisited: Essays on Anabaptist/Mennonite Studies in Honor of C. J. Dyck,* edited by Walter Klaassen, 115-22. Scottdale, PA: Herald Press, 1992.

Froese, Wolfgang, ed. *Sie kamen als Fremde: Die Mennoniten in Krefeld von den Anfängen bis zur Gegenwart.* Krefeld: Stadt Krefeld, 1995.

Geistreiches Gesangbuch, zur öffentlichen und besondern Erbauung der mennonitischen Gemeine in und vor der Stadt Danzig Marienwerder: Johann Jacob Kanter, 1780.

Göttner, Erich "Hermann Gottlieb Mannhardt." *Christlicher Gemeinde-Kalendar* 38 (1929): 36-47

Great Chronicle: The Chronicle of the Hutterian Brethren. Rifton, NY: Plough Publishing House, 1987.

Harder, Carl. *Kurzgefaßte Geschichte der Elbinger Mennonitengemeinde.* Elbing: Vorstand der Elbinger Mennonitengemeinde, 1883.

Hildebrand, Peter. *From Danzig to Russia: The First Emigration of Mennonites from the Danzig Region to Southern Russia.* Winnipeg: CMBC Publications, 2000.

Hildebrandt, Julia. "Antje Brons als Mennonitin." *Mennonitische Geschichtsblätter* 23 (1966): 41-58.

Historisches Ortschaftsverzeichnis Danzig-Westpreussen. Bd. 7, *Reihe historischer Ortschaftsverzeichnisse für ehemals zu Deutschland gehörige Gebiete — Zeitraum 1914 bis 1945.* Frankfurt: Institut für Angewandte Geodäsie, 1997.

"Jahrhundertfeier in Danzig am 14. September." *Mennonitische Blätter* 66, no. 10 (Oct. 1919): 74-5.

Janson, H. W. *19th-Century Sculpture.* New York: Harry N. Abrams, Inc., 1985.

Jantzen, Mark. "At Home in Germany? The Mennonites of the Vistula Delta and the Construction of a German National Identity, 1772-1880." Ph. D. diss., University of Notre Dame, 2002.

_____. "Mennonites in Poland – Mennonites in Prussia: A Look at Recent Mennonite Scholarship." *Mennonite Life* 47, no. 2 (June 1992): 11-14.

Jost, Walter. "The Hymn Tune Tradition of the General Conference Mennonite Church." Ph. D. diss., University of Southern California, 1966.

Jung, Martin. *Der Protestantismus in Deutschland vom 1815 bis 1870.* Leipzig: Evangelische Verlagsanstalt, 2000.

Kaemmerer, M., ed. *Ortsnamenverzeichnis der Ortschaften jenseits von Oder und Neiße.* Leer: Verlag Gerhard Rautenberg, 1988.

Katalog der Danziger Stadtbibliothek. 6 vols. Danzig: Stadtbibliothek, 1892-1921.

Kauffman, J. Howard and Leo Driedger. *Mennonite Mosaic: Identity and Modernization.* Scottdale, PA: Herald Press, 1991.

Keim, Albert N. *Harold S. Bender, 1897-1962.* Scottdale, PA: Herald Press, 1998.

Kellermann, Ludwig. *Schillers Werke.* Leipzig: Bibliographisches Institut, 1895.

Klaassen, Walter. "Menno Simons Research 1837-1937, 1986-1990." Chap. 9 in *Menno Simons: A Reappraisal,* edited by Gerald R. Brunk. Harrisonburg, VA: Eastern Mennonite College, 1992.

Klassen, Peter J. *A Homeland for Strangers: An Introduction to Mennonites in Poland and Prussia.* Fresno, CA: Center for Mennonite Brethren Studies, 1989.

Klippenstein, Lawrence. "The Mennonite Migration to Russia, 1786-1806." In *Mennonites in Russia, 1788-1988: Essays in Honor of Gerhard Lohrenz,* edited by John Friesen. Winnipeg: CMBC Publications, 1989.

Koch, H. W. *A History of Prussia.* New York: Barnes and Noble Books, 1993.

Langewiesche, Dieter. *Nation, Nationalismus, Nationalstaat in Deutschland und Europa.* Munich: Verlag C. H. Beck, 2000.

Lichdi, Diether Götz. *Die Mennoniten in Geschichte und Gegenwart: Von der Täuferbewegung zur weltweiten Freikirchen.* Weisenheim am Sand: AGAPE-Verlag im Zusammenarbeit mit dem Mennonitischen Geschichtsverein, 2004.

Loewen, Harry, and Steven Nolt. *Through Fire and Water: An Overview of Mennonite History* Scottdale, PA: Herald Press, 1996.

Luther, Martin, *On Christian Liberty,* trans. W. A. Lambert. Philadelphia: Fortress Press, 1957.

Mannhardt, H. G. *Bericht über die in Berlin am 2. und 3. October 1884 stattgehabte Conferenz deutscher Mennoniten erstattet in einer Ansprache an die Brüder-Versammlung der Danziger Mennoniten-Gemeinde am 19. October 1884.* Danzig: Self-published, 1884.

_____. "Der Bischof Eylert und die Mennoniten: Zur Abwehr falscher Urtheile." *Mennonitische Blätter* 31, no. 3 (March 1884): 17-20.

_____. "Die Danziger Gem. an ihre Männer im Felde." *Mennonitische Blätter* 65, no. 9 (September 1918): 66-8.

"Innere Mission." 49, no 7 (July 1, 1902): 54-55; "Innere Mission II." no. 8 (August 1, 1902): 67-69; "Innere Mission III." no. 9 (September 1, 1902): 74-75.

_____. "Jahresbericht der Vereinigung der Mennoniten-Gemeinden im Deutschen Reich über ihre Tätigkeit in den Jahren 1918 und 1919." *Mennonitische Blätter* 67, no. 11 (November 1920): 84-5.

_____. "Mennoniten-Gemeinden und Diakonissenhäuser." *Mennonitische Blätter* 40, no. 8 (August 1894): 60-1.

_____. *Predigten und Reden.* Danzig: John & Rosenberg, 1905.

_____. "Was predigen wir in der Kriegszeit?" *Mennonitische Blätter* 64, no. 1 (January 1916): 2-4.

_____. "Zur Abwehr." *Mennonitische Blätter* 35, no. 14 (July 2, 1888): 82-3.

_____. "Zur Entstehung und Geschichte der Königliche Kabinettsordre vom 3. März 1868, betreffend den Heeresdienst der Mennoniten." *Christlicher Gemeinde-Kalender* 28 (1919): 97-107.

_____. *Zwei Gedenktage der Danziger Mennonitengemeinde im Herbst 1919.* Danzig, 1919.

Mannhardt, Heinz-Jürgen, ed. *Die Mennonitenfamilie van der Smissen und Ihre Nachkommen.* 2nd ed. Darmstadt: Mannhardt, 1999.

Neff, Christian. "H. G. Mannhardt." *Mennonitische Blätter* 74, no. 9 (Sept. 1927): 75-80.

Penner, Horst, Horst Gerlach and Horst Quiring. *Weltweite Bruderschaft: Ein mennonitisches Geschichtsbuch,* 5th ed. Weierhof: Selbstverlag Horst Gerlach, 1995.

Penner, Horst. *Die Ost- und Westpreußischen Mennoniten,* 2 vols. Weierhof: Mennonitischer Geschichtsverein, 1978 and Kirchheimbolanden: Selbstverlag, 1987.

_____. "West Prussia," *Mennonite Encyclopedia,* 4:920-6.

Plett, Harvey. "Georg Hansen and the Danzig Flemish Mennonite Church: a Study in Continuity." Ph.D. diss., University of Manitoba, 1991.

Rauert, Matthias H., and Annelie Kümpers-Greve. *van der Smissen: Eine mennonitische Familie vor dem Hintergrund der Geschichte Altonas und Schleswig-Holstein.* Hamburg: Nord Magazin, 1992.

Regier, James. "Where the Two Kingdoms Merge: The Struggle for Balance Between National and Religious Identity among Mennonites in Wilhelmine Germany." Master's thesis, Wichita State University, 2006.

Reiswitz, Georg Leopold von, and Friedrich Wadzeck. *Beiträge zur Kenntniß der Mennoniten-Gemeinden in Europa und America, statistischen, historischen und religiösen Inhalts*. Berlin: by the authors, 1821.

Reiswitz, Georg Leopold von. *Beiträge zur Kenntniß der taufgesinnten Gemeinden oder der Mennoniten, statistischen, historischen und religiösen, auch juristischen Inhalts. Zweiter Theil*. Breslau: Carl Friedrich Fritsch, 1829.

Roosen, Berend Carl. *Geschichte der Mennoniten-Gemeinde zu Hamburg und Altona*. Hamburg: H.O. Versiehl, 1886-1887.

See, Klaus von. *Die Ideen von 1789 und die Ideen von 1914: völkisch Denken in Deutschland zwischen Französischer Revolution und Erstem Weltkrieg*. Frankfurt a. M.: Athenaion, 1975.

Smith, C. Henry. *Smith's Story of the Mennonites*, 5th ed., edited by Cornelius Krahn. Newton, KS: Faith and Life Press, 1981.

Sprunger, Mary. "Anna Brons and Ludwig Keller: Partners for Historical Renewal." BA thesis, Bethel College, North Newton, Kansas, 1984.

Snyder, C. Arnold. *Anabaptist History and Theology: An Introduction*. Kitchner, Ontario: Pandora Press, 1995.

Thiesen, John D. "First Duty of the Citizen: Mennonite Identity and Military Exemption in Prussia, 1848-1877." *Mennonite Quarterly Review* 72 (April 1998): 161-187.

Verduin, Leonard, trans. *The Complete Works of Menno Simons*. Edited by J. C. Wenger. Scottdale, PA: Herald Press, 1956.

Visser, Piet, and Mary Sprunger. *Menno Simons: Places, Portraits and Progeny*. Altona, Manitoba: Friesens; Morgantown, PA: Masthof Press, 1996.

Works by H.G. Mannhardt
Compiled by Eric Stucky & Braden Hiebner

This bibliography covers the known books, pamphlets and journal articles written by H. G. Mannhardt. We omitted encyclopedia articles he wrote for *Mennonitisches Lexikon* (some of which were later translated for *Mennonite Encyclopedia*) and *Altpreußische Biographie* because these works do not include author indexes and we were thus unable to locate easily Mannhardt's entries. Articles *about* Mannhardt rather than *by* him are listed separately at the end.

Books and Pamphlets

Bericht über die in Berlin am 2. und 3. October 1884 stattgehabte Conferenz Deutscher Mennoniten: erstattet in einer Ansprache an die Brüder–Versammlung der Danziger Mennoniten Gemeinde am 19. October 1884. Danzig: Druck von Edwin Goering, 1884.

Die Danziger Mennonitengemeinde: ihre Entstehung und ihre Geschichte von 1569-1919. Danzig: Danziger Mennonitengemeinde, 1919.

Festpredigt bei der Lob- und Dankfeier der westpreussischen Mennoniten Gemeinden zur Erinnerung an das 400–jährige Bestehen unserer Glaubensgemeinschaft: gehalten am 4. Juni 1925 in der Mennonitenkirche zu Heubuden. Marienburg: Willy Korsch, 1925.

Festschrift zu Menno Simons' 400-jähriger Geburtstagsfeier, den 6. November 1892. Danzig: Selbstverlag der westpreussischen Mennoniten-Gemeinden, 1892.

Jahrbuch der Altevangelischen. Danzig: Selbstverlag, 1888.

Jahrbuch der Mennoniten-Gemeinden in West- und Ostpreussen. Danzig: Selbstverlag, 1883.

Predigten und Reden aus fünfundzwanzigjähriger Amtszeit. Danzig: Verlag von John & Rosenberg, 1905.

Zwei Gedenktage der Danziger Mennonitengemeinde im Herbst 1919. Danzig, 1919.

Articles published in *Mennonitische Blätter* (in chronological order)

"Aus vergangen Tagen: Rückblicke in die Geschichte unserer Gemeinschaft." 30, no. 6 (June 1883): 46-47; no. 8 (August 1883): 62-63; no. 9 (September 1883): 66-67; no. 11 (November 1883): 82-83; no. 12 (December 1883): 90-91; 31, no. 1 (January 1884): 4-5; no. 2 (February 1884): 10.

"Etwas über den Oelbaum." 30, no. 8 (August 1883): 58-60.

"Druckfehler-Berichtigung." 30, no. 9 (September 1883): 72.

"Anzeige." 30, no. 12 (December 1883): 98; 31, no. 1 (January 1884): 8.

"Der Bischof Eylert und die Mennoniten." 31, no. 3 (March 1884): 17-20.

"Wie viele Traufragen sollen wir den Verlobten Vorlegen." 31, no. 6 (June 1884): 44-46.

"Aus Westpreussen." 31, no. 9 (September 1884): 66-69.

"Bericht eines deutschen Reisenden über die Mennoniten-Ansiedelungen in Kansas." 31, no. 10 (October 1884): 75-77.

"Bericht über die in Berlin am 2. und 3. Oktober 1884 stattgehabte Conferenz deutscher Mennoniten." 31, no. 12 (December 1884): 90-93.

"Endlich haben wir eine 'Geschichte der Mennoniten.'" 32, no. 1 (January 1885): 4.

"Freundliche Bitte an die lieben Amtsbrüder." 32, no. 1 (January 1885): 8.

"Nachrichten aus Berlin." 32, no. 3 (March 1885): 22-23.

"Vorläufige Anzeige." 32, no. 3 (March 1885): 24.

"Ein zeitgemässer Vorschlag." 32, no. 4 (April 1885): 26-27.

"Wie steht es gegenwärtig mit der Ausführung unserer Berliner Beschlusse?" 32, no. 5 (May 1885): 43-44.

"Anzeige." 32, no. 5 (May 1885): 46; 32, no. 6 (June 1885): 54.

"Erfreulicher Anwachs der Zeichnungen für die Vereinigung deutscher Mennoniten-Gemeinden." 32, no. 10 (September 1885): 81-82.

"Die nothwendigen Ziele der Vereinigung deutscher Mennoniten." 32, no. 12 (November 1885): 98-101.

"Die Lehre der zwölf Apostel: Ein wiedergefundenes Werk aus urchristlicher Zeit." 33, no. 1 (January 1886): 2-3.

"Ein bruderliches Antwortschreiben." 33, no. 3 (March 1886): 18-20.

"Constituierende Generalversammlung der Vereinigung der Mennoniten–Gemeinden im Deutschen Reich." *Extra - Nummer* (June 1886): n.p. (with other authors)

"Die Reisepredigt in unseren Gemeinden." 33, no. 9 (September 1886): 70-71; 33, no. 10 (December 1886): 75-76.

"Die Erwerbung von Korporationsrechten durch die Mennoniten-Gemeinden in Preussen." 34, no. 1 (January 1887): 4-6.

"Eine wichtige Entscheidung des Reichsgerichts." 34, no. 2 (February 1887): 10-11.

"Die Bedeutung der Sekten für Kirche und religiöses Leben." 34, no. 3 (March 1887): 17-18.

"Eine neue Ausgabe der 'Deutschen Theologie.'" 34, no. 3 (March 1887): 21-22.

"Quittung." 34, no. 3 (March 1887): 23.

"Eine Familienbibel." 34, no. 4 (April 1887): 26-27.

"Nachrichten aus unserer Gemeinschaft." 34, no. 4 (April 1887): 31-32.

"Corpus Schwenckfeldianorum." 34, no. 6 (June 1887): 44-45.

"Statistisches aus der Danziger Mennoniten-Gemeinde." 34, no. 7 (July 1887): 49-50.

"Quittung." 34, no. 7 (July 1887): 56.

"Kleinere Mittheilungen." 34, no. 8 (August 1887): 62-63.

"Bitte." 34, no. 8 (August 1887): 64.

"Verschiedenes." 34, no. 10 (October 1887): 77.

"Verschiedenes." 34, no. 11 (November 1887): 84-85.

H. G. Mannhardt and H.V.D. Smissen. "Zur freundlichen Beachtung." 34, no. 11 (November 1887): 86.

"Emil Eglis neues Buch über die 'St. Galler Täufer.'" 34, no. 12 (December 1887): 89-91.

"Das Jahrbuch der Mennoniten-Gemeinden." 34, no. 12 (December 1887): 93.

"Der Weheruf der verstockenen Liebe." *Beilage zu No. 3,* 34 (March 1887): 9-12.

"Der Weckruf des Advents." *Beilage zu No. 12,* 34 (December 1887): 47-49.

"Armenpflege und Diakonie in der apostolischen Gemeinde."
35, no. 1 (January 1, 1888): 4-5; no. 3 (February 1, 1888): 16-
17

"Jahrbuch der Altevangelischen Taufgesinnten oder
Mennoniten-Gemeinden." 35, no. 3 (February 1, 1888): 18-
19; no. 4 (February 15, 1888): 21-23.

"Notwendige Erklärung." 35, no. 5 (March 1, 1888): 25-26.

"Nachrichten aus den Gemeinden." 35, no. 5 (March 1, 1888):
30-31.

"Kaiser Wilhelm heimgegangen." 35, no. 6 (March 15, 1888):
33.

"Eine mennonitische Bibliothek." 35, no. 8 (April 15, 1888): 47-
48.

"Verschiedenes." 35, no. 10 (May 15, 1888): 59-60.

"Zur Abwehr." 35, no. 14 (July 2, 1888): 82-83.

"Quittung." 35, no. 14 (July 2, 1888): 84.

"Die Einweihung der Kirche auf dem Kohlhof bei Spener in
der Pfalz." 35, no. 17 (September 1, 1888): 101-102.

"Thäter des Worts und nicht Hörer allein." 35, no. 17
(September 1, 1888): 100-101; 35, no. 18 (September 15,
1888): 105-106.

"Nachrichten aus den Gemeinden." 35, no. 21 (November 1,
1888): 127-128.

"Priester und Laien: Zeitgemässe Beobachtungen." 35, no. 23
(December 1, 1888): 134-135.

"Eine Wächterstimme." 35, no. 23 (December 1, 1888): 136-
137.

"Eine bescheidene Empfehlung." 35, no. 24 (December 17,
1888): 146.

"Eine für Mennoniten wichtige Rechtsbestimmung." 36, no. 3
(February 1, 1889): 15-16.

"Die Sklaverei in Afrika und die Nothwendigkeit ihrer
Beseitigung." 36, no. 5 (March 1, 1889): 27-29.

"Aus Westpreussen." 36, no. 7 (April 1, 1889): 42-43; 36, no. 8
(April 15, 1889): 47-48.

"Nachrichten aus den Gemeinden." 36, no. 16 (August 15,
1889): 95-96.

"Quittung." 37, no. 7 (April 1, 1890): 44.

"Versuch einer harmonischen Weltanschauung." 37, no. 14 (July 15, 1890): 81-82; no. 15 (August 1, 1890): 89-90.

"Das Beste in der Welt." 37, no. 18 (September 15, 1890): 106-108.

"Gesang und Musik in den Gottesdiensten unserer Gemeinden." 37, no. 19 (October 1, 1890): 111-113.

"Zweite Auflage des Buches von Frau Brons." 37, no. 23 (December 1, 1890): 137.

"Der Mattenbauer." 37, no. 23 (December 1, 1890): 137-138.

"Geschichte der Predigt in den deutschen Mennoniten Gemeinden." 38, no. 3 (February 1, 1891): 18-19; no.4 (February 16, 1891): 22-23; no. 5 (March 1, 1891): 28-29; no. 7 (April 1, 1891): 37-38.

"Verschiedenes." 38, no. 10 (May 16, 1891): 58-60.

"Etwas über Kirchengesang: aus den russischen Kolonien." 38, no. 11 (June 1, 1891): 63-65.

"Empfangsbescheinigung." 38, no. 23 (December 1, 1891): 139.

"Ein gutes Buch." 39, no. 5 (March 1, 1892): 38-39.

"Anzeigen. Stimmen aus der Reformationszeit." 39, no. 6 (March 16, 1892): 48; no. 8 (April 13, 1892): 64; no. 9 (May 2, 1892): 72; no. 10 (May 16, 1892): 80; no. 11, (June 1, 1892): 88; no. 12 (June 16, 1892): 96; no. 13 (July 1, 1892): 104; no. 14 (July 16, 1892): 112; no. 17 (September 1, 1892): 136; no. 18, (September 16, 1892): 144; no. 19 (October 1, 1892): 152.

"Anzeigen. Zur freundlichen Beachtung." 39, no. 22 (November 16, 1892): 176.

"Das Gedächtnis der Entschlafenen." 39, no. 23 (December 1, 1892): 177-180.

"Anzeigen. Festschrift zur vierhundertjährigen Gedächtnisfeier Mennos." 40, no. 2 (January 16, 1893): 16.

"Die Monatshefte der Comenius-Gesellschaft." 40, no. 3 (February 1, 1893): 22.

"Anzeigen." 40, no. 3 (February 1, 1893): 24.

"Bernardino Ochino von Siena." 40, no. 4 (February 16, 1893): 27-28; no. 7 (April 1, 1893): 49-51; no. 8 (April 16, 1893): 58-60.

"Ein wichtiger Hinweis für unsere jungeren Landwirthe." 40, no. 4 (April 1, 1894): 31.

"Empfangsbescheinigung." 40, no. 9 (May 1, 1893): 72.

"Mennoniten-Gemeinden und Diakonissenhäuser." 41, no. 8 (August 1, 1894): 60-61.

"Verscheidenes." 42, no. 3 (March 1, 1895): 21-22.

"Zum Fall Throner." 42, no. 5 (May 1, 1895): 33-34.

"Neue Schriften." 43, no. 2 (February 1, 1896): 13-14.

"Empfangsbescheinigung." 44, no. 12 (December 1, 1897): 102.

"Carl Julius Momber." 48, no. 1 (January 1, 1901): 5-6.

"Anzeigen." 48, no. 2 (February 1, 1901): 16; no. 3 (March 1, 1901): 24.

"Das alte Hospital oder Armenhaus der Danziger Mennoniten-Gemeinde." 49, no. 2 (February 1, 1902): 12-13.

"Innere Mission." 49, no 7 (July 1, 1902): 54-55; "Innere Mission II." no. 8 (August 1, 1902): 67-69; "Innere Mission III." no. 9 (September 1, 1902): 74-75.

"Berichtigung und Ergänzung." 49, no. 9 (September 1, 1902): 75-76.

"Preisausschreiben." 49, no. 11 (November 1, 1902): 100; 50, no. 3 (March 1, 1903): 26; no. 6 (June 1, 1903): 50; no. 7 (July 1, 1903): 62.

"Unser Preisausschreiben." 51, no. 5 (May 1904): 36.

"Noch Einmal 'Die unterdruckte Uebersetzung von Mennos Schriften.'" 51, no. 6 (June 1, 1904): 48-49; no. 7 (July 1, 1904): 54-55; no. 8 (August 1, 1904): 60-61.

"Ein Urteil über die Mennoniten des Marienburger Werders." 52, no. 5 (May 1, 1905): 42-43.

"Preisausschreiben." 52, no. 10 (October 1, 1905): 88; no. 11 (November 1, 1905): 96; no. 12 (December 1, 1905): 107.

"Adventsgedanken." 52, no. 12 (December 1, 1905): 97-98.

"Anzeigen." 52, no. 12 (December 1, 1905): 106.

"Einige Ergänzungen zu den Artikeln über Abraham Nickel." 54, no. 3 (March 1, 1907): 18-20.

"Bescheid des preussischen Kultusministers in Sachen des Religionsunterrichts durch mennonitische Lehrer und Lehrerinnen." 57, no. 9 (September 1, 1910): 66.

"Statistisches." 60, no. 4 (April 1, 1913): 26.

"Eine Nationalspende für die Mission in den Deutschen Kolonien." 60, no. 5 (May 1, 1913): 34-35.

"Konferenz der Westpreussischen Mennoniten-Gemeinden zu Dragass, Gemeinde Gruppe, am 21. Mai." 60, no. 7 (July 1, 1913): 50-52.

"Aus dem Jahresbericht der Danziger Mennonitengemeinde." 61, no. 4 (April 1, 1914): 30-31.

"Der Krieg und wir." 61, no. 10 (October 1, 1914): 74-75; no. 11 (November 1, 1914): 82-83.

"Der Krieg und die Mission." 61, no. 11 (November 1, 1914): 85.

"Stadtrat Adolph Claassen - Danzig." 62, no. 6 (June 1, 1915): 44-45.

"Abrechnung." 62, no. 7 (July 1, 1915): 54-55.

"Was predigen wir in der Kriegszeit?" 63, no. 1 (January 1916): 2-4; no. 2 (February 1916): 10-11; no. 3 (March 1916): 20-21; no. 4 (April 1916): 28-31; no. 6 (June 1916): 44-47.

"Adressen." 64, no. 1 (January 1, 1917): 8.

"Protokoll der 11. Ordentl. Generalversammlung der Vereinigung der Mennoniten-Gem. im D.R." 64, no. 9 (September 1, 1917): 68-69.

"Die Danziger Gem. an ihre Männer im Felde." 65, no. 9 (September 1, 1918): 66-68.

"Empfangsbescheinigungen." 65, no. 10 (October 1, 1918): 80.

"Die einstigen Menn. Gemeinden bei Schwetz." 66, no. 2 (February 1, 1919): 10-11.

"Verhandlungen der 'Freistaatgemeinden' zu Eichwalde." 67, no. 4 (April 1, 1920): 27-28.

"Jahresbericht der Vereinigung der Mennoniten-Gemeinden im Deutschen Reich über ihre Tätigkeit in den Jahren 1918 und 1919." 67, no. 11 (November 1, 1920): 84-85.

"Aus dem Jahresbericht für 1920 der Danziger Mennonitengemeinde." 68, no. 7 (July 1921): 53-54.

"Verhandlungen des westpreussischen Lehrdienstes zu Marienburg am 25. Mai 1921." 68, no. 10 (October 1921): 74-75.

"Adressen." 69, no. 1 (January 1922): 8; 70, no.2 (January 1923): 8.

"Zum Geleit." 74, no. 1 (January 1, 1927): 1-2.

"Wo bleiben unsere Täuflinge?" 74, no. 6 (June 1927): 44-45.

"Die Mennoniten im Danziger Gebiet." 74, no. 9 (September 1927): 84.

Articles published in *Christlicher Gemeinde-Kalendar* (in chronological order)

"Johann Amos Comenius." 1 (1892): 113-116.
"Jakob Mannhardt, weiland Prediger der Danziger Mennoniten-Gemeinden." 2 (1893): 80-91.
Gerhard Mondberg [H. G. Mannhardt]. "Als die Sterbenden und siehe, wir leben." 3 (1894): 65-102.
"Die Mennoniten unter den preussischen Königen." 11 (1902): 98-117.
"Unsere Familiennamen." 12 (1903): 76-83.
"Die Statistik in den Mennoniten Gemeinden." 19 (1910): 66-72.
"Zur Jubelfeier der 'Algemeene Doopsgezinde Societeit' in Amsterdam am 23. September 1911." 22 (1913): 109-121.
"Die preussischen Mennoniten zur Zeit der Befreiungskriege." 23 (1914): 103-109.
"Das Predigtamt im ersten Kriegsjahre." 25 (1916): 101-112.
"Das Predigtamt im zweiten und dritten Kriegsjahr." 27 (1918): 63-79.
"Zur Entstehung und Geschichte der Konigl. Kabinettsordre vom 3. Marz 1868." 28 (1919): 97-107.
Gerhard Mondberg [H. G. Mannhardt]. "Ein Mann am rechten Platze. Erzählung aus dem Leben und Wirken Hans von Steens zu Danzig, 1705-1781." 36 (1927): 58-75.

Articles about Hermann Gottlieb Mannhardt

"Am Sarge von Prediger H.G. Mannhardt." *Mennonitische Blätter* 74, no. 8 (August 1927): 65.
Kraemer, Gustav. "H.G. Mannhardt. Predigten und Reden aus fünfundzwanzigerjähriger Amtszeit." *Mennonitische Blätter* 52, no. 2 (February 1905): 14; 52, no. 3 (March 1905): 25-27.
Göttner, E. "Hermann Gottlieb Mannhardt." *Christlicher Gemeinde-Kalendar* 38 (1929): 36-47.

_____. "Ansprache am Sarge bei der Trauerfeier für Herrn Prediger H.G. Mannhardt." *Mennonitische Blätter* 74, no. 9 (September 1927): 73-75.

Händiges, Emil. "Prediger H.G. Mannhardt." *Mennonitische Blätter* 74, no. 8 (August 1927): 66-67.

Neff, D. Chr. "H.G. Mannhardt." *Mennonitische Blätter* 74, no. 9 (September 1927): 75-80.

Place Names — German and Polish

In cases where we were unable to determine a modern Polish
equivalent for an older German place name, the German is
not included in the tables below.

German	Polish
Bischofsberg	Biskupia Górka
Dirschau	Tczew
Einlage	Przegalina
Elbing	Elbląg
Ermland	Warmia
Fürstenwerder	Żuławki
Graudenz	Grudziądz
Heiligenbrunn	Studzienka
Holm	Ostrów
Königsberg	Królewiec (Kaliningrad)
Krampitz	Krępiec
Ladekopp	Lubieszewo
Landau	Lędowo
Langfuhr	Wrzeszcz
Marienburg	Malbork
Markushof	Markusy
Montau	Mątawy
Neufahrwasser	Gdańsk Nowy Port
Neugarten	Nowe Ogordy
Neu Schottland	Nowe Szkoty
Neunhuben	Dziewięc Włók
Nobel	Niegowo
Ohra	Orunia
Oliva	Oliwa
Orloff	Orłowo
Orlofferfelde	Orłowskie Pole

German	Polish
Petershagen	Zaroślak
Preussisch Holland	Pasłęk
Reichenberg	Bogatka
Rosenort	Suchowo
Scharffenberg	Bystra
Schidlitz	Siedlce
Schmerblock	Błotnik
Schönfeld	Łostowice
Schottland	Stare Skoty
St. Albrecht	Św. Wojciech
Stolzenberg	Chełm
Stüblau	Steblewo
Thiensdorf	Jezioro
Thorn	Toruń
Tiegenhagen	Tujce
Tiegenhof	Nowy Dwór Gdański
Warnau	Kościeleczki
Wesslinken	Wiślinka
Wotzlaff	Wocławy
Zoppot	Sopot

Street names

Heilige Geistgasse	Św. Ducha
Heumarkt	Targ Sienny
Schüsseldamm	Łagiewniki
Sandgrube	Rogaczewskiego

Polish	German
Biskupia Górka	Bischofsberg
Błotnik	Schmerblock

Polish	German
Bogatka	Reichenberg
Bystra	Scharffenberg
Chełm	Stolzenberg
Dziewięc Włók	Neunhuben
Elbląg	Elbing
Gdańsk Nowy Port	Neufahrwasser
Grudziądz	Graudenz
Jezioro	Thiensdorf
Kościeleckzi	Warnau
Krępiec	Krampitz
Królewiec (Kaliningrad)	Königsberg
Lędowo	Landau
Lubieszewo	Ladekopp
Łostowice	Schönfeld
Malbork	Marienburg
Markusy	Markushof
Mątawy	Montau
Niegowo	Nobel
Nowe Ogordy	Neugarten
Nowe Skoty	Neu Schottland
Nowy Dwór Gdański	Tiegenhof
Oliwa	Oliva
Orłowo	Orloff
Orłowskie Pole	Orlofferfelde
Orunia	Ohra
Ostrów	Holm
Pasłęk	Preussisch Holland
Przegalina	Einlage
Siedlce	Schidlitz
Sopot	Zoppot

Polish	German
Stare Skoty	(Alt) Schottland
Steblewo	Stüblau
Studzienka	Heiligenbrunn
Suchowo	Rosenort
Św. Wojciech	St. Albrecht
Tczew	Dirschau
Toruń	Thorn
Tujce	Tiegenhagen
Warmia	Ermland
Wiślinka	Wesslinken
Wocławy	Wotzlaff
Wrzeszcz	Langfuhr
Zaroślak	Petershagen
Żuławaki	Fürstenwerder

Street names

Łagiewniki	Schüsseldamm
Rogaczewskiego	Sandgrube
Św. Ducha	Heilige Geistgasse
Targ Sienny	Heumarkt

Index

Joris, David, 15

K

Kahle (Protestant district pastor), 221

Kaminczynski (Vice-Woywode of Pomerania), 89

Kamke, von (commander), 171

Kämmerer, David, 68

Kampen, Heinrich van, 196

Kampen, Jakob van, 196, 198

Kampen, Johann Jacob van, 189, 189, 194-196, 209

Kampen, Jost van, 53

Kauenhowen, Arend, 110-111

Kauenhowen, Johann, 131, 137, 152, 155, 159, 183

Keller, Ludwig, xxi, 230

Kherson, 144

Klassen, Peter J., 252

Kliewer, Friedrich Gustav, 189, 195, 200

Kliewer, Jacob, 154, 156, 157, 159, 159, 178-179, 182

Kliewer II, Jakob, 159

Köhler, W., 235

Königsberg, 108, 138, 141, 167, 180

Kraemer, G., 233

Krampitz, 45

Krauze, Jan, 252

Krefeld Mennonite Church, 237

Krüger (construction supervisor), 216

Kühnel (junior police official), 168, 171

Kujavia, Bishop of, 44

L

Lambertz, Jan, 128

Lambertz, Johann, 129

Landau, 38

Langfuhr, 44, 92, 104, 137

Langgarten, 143

Lasco, John á, 23, 31

Lascy (General), 100

Laws and edicts

Charters of Privilege, 67, 71-73, 84, 115, 140

Lace Trim Manufacturer's Privilege (October 30, 1623), 66

Mennonite Edict (1789), 141-142, 155, 206

Mennonite Edict of King Wladislaw (June 10, 1647), 73-74

Mennonite Law (June 12, 1874), 207-208, 223

Non-combatant Royal Cabinet Order (March 3, 1868), 198, 204

Revised Defence Order of the City of Danzig (1733), 127

Royal Privilege of King Wladislaw IV (December 22, 1642), 72

Lepp, Eduard, 226, 232

Leszczynski, Stanislaw, 99

Leubnitz, von (Saxon court counselor), 105

Library

Danzig Church, xxxii, 189, 198, 231

Danzig City, xxviii, xxxiii, 81

Mennonite Historical Library, Goshen, xxix

Mennonite Library and Archives at Bethel College, xxvii

see also Archives, and Records

Liechtenstein, Leonhard von, 9

Linde, Adrian von der, 77

Loewen, Christina, 113

Loewens, 211

Loewens, Eduard, 212, 225

Loewens, Max, 232, 239

Löschin, G., 171, 196

Low Countries, *see* Netherlands

Löwens, Anna, 196

Loysen, Hans von, 49

Loysen, Simon von, 49

Lübeck, 24

Ludwichsen, Gerhard, 166

Lüneburg, 24

Luther, Martin, xxii, 1-5, 7, 11, 20, 27
Lutherans, xxii, 9, 11, 14, 24, 34, 44, 54, 56, 71, 98, 141, 142, 155, 159, 171
see also Protestants

M
Mahl, 47
Mahl, Gerd, 60
Mahl, Isaac, 189
Mahl, Jakob, 155, 159
Mannhardt, Hermann Gottlieb, xviii, xix, 210, 214, 217, 221, 229, 232, 234, 237
Mannhardt, Jacob, xviii, xxxiv, 185-185, 193, 194, 193, 199, 209, 212, 213, 216, 219, 221
Mannhardt, Wilhelm, xviii, xxxii, xxxiv, 161, 193-198, 210, 214, 221
Mannhardt, Luise, xix
Mannhardt, Margot, xix
Mannstein, von (Governor), 157
Manz, Felix, 8
Marienburg, 49, 72-74, 83, 89, 98-99, 139
 Provincial Parliament, 89
 Prussian Parliament, 83
Marriage customs, 48, 91, 123-124, 129, 159, 193, 205, 208, 215
Martyrdom, *see* Persecution
Matiaszuk, Anatol, 252
Maximilian (Holy Roman Emperor), 1
Menno Simons, xvi, xxii, 16, 19-35, 41, 42, 44-46, 229
Mennonite Central Committee, xxvi-xxvii
Mennonite identity, xvii, xxiii, 27-31, 63, 83, 93, 98, 115, 116, 130, 141-142, 153-154, 183, 191, 198, 204-206, 234, 241
 Mennonites as nation, 81
 see also Confessions of faith
Mennonite Journal, 193
 see also Mennonitische Blätter

Mennonite Library and Archives at Bethel College, xxvii
Mennonitische Blätter, xix, 192
 see also Mennonite Journal
Merschoot, Jost, 58
Michael Korybut Wisniowiecki, King of Poland, 77-81
Micron, Martin (de Cleyne), 31
Military service, xix, xxiii, 124, 139-140, 142, 143, 159, 190, 191, 195, 198, 198, 205, 238
 see also Conscription and Non-resistance
Ministry of War, 169-170
Molen, Jacob van der, 48
Momber, 211
Momber, Albert, 232, 236
Momber, August, 200, 214
Momber, Berend, 163
Momber, Carl Heinrich, 213
Momber, Carl Julius, 214, 226-227, 236
Momber, Hans, 119, 128, 149, 151, 155, 157, 159, 183
Momber, Jacob, 100
Montau, 47
Moor, Carl, 122
Moor, Cornelius, 112, 118
Moravia, 8, 13, 24, 32
Mottlau, 45
Münnich (Field Marshall), 100
Münster, 4, 15-16, 21, 22
Müntzer, Thomas, 3
Myllen, Paul von, 47

N
Napoleon, xx, 156-157, 163, 191
Napoleonic Wars (1800-1815), xiv, 156-157
Nationalism, xvii, xxiii, xxiv, 198-204
 see also Germany
Neff, Christian, 234
Netherlands 37-38, 41, 42, 47, 55, 56
 Low Countries, 7, 13, 24, 37, 38, 47

Contributors

Victor G. Doerksen was born in Winnipeg, Manitoba, Canada, and educated at the University of Manitoba (M. A.) and Zürich University (Dr. phil.). He was professor and head of the Department of German and Slavic Studies at the University of Manitoba, and Professor Emeritus since 1996, when he retired to British Columbia.

Mark Jantzen is associate professor of history at Bethel College where he teaches courses in European and Mennonite history. He has degrees from Bethel College, Associated Mennonite Biblical Seminary, and the University of Notre Dame and has studied in Germany at the Bergische University Wuppertal and Humboldt University in Berlin. His main area of research is on the impact of German nationalism on Prussian Mennonites in the nineteenth century.

Tomasz Ropiejko was born and raised in Gdańsk. He graduated from Warsaw Theological Seminary (BA) and is now studying for the M. Th. degree at the University of Wales at Bangor/Mattersey Hall. Since 2000 he has served on the National Leadership Team for the Pentecostal Church of Poland. In 1994 he was appointed associate pastor of the Pentecostal Church of Poland, Assembly in Gdańsk (Kościół Zielonoświątkowy Zbór w Gdańsku) and in 2005 pastor.

John D. Thiesen, a native of Newton, Kansas, graduated from Bethel College and Wichita State University (M. A.) He is co-director of libraries at Bethel College and archivist for Mennonite Church USA.